Confucianism, Chinese History and Society

CONFUCIANISM, CHINESE HISTORY AND SOCIETY

Edited by

Wong Sin Kiong
National University of Singapore

NEW JERSEY · LONDON · SINGAPORE · BEIJING · SHANGHAI · HONG KONG · TAIPEI · CHENNAI

Published by
World Scientific Publishing Co. Pte. Ltd.
5 Toh Tuck Link, Singapore 596224
USA office: 27 Warren Street, Suite 401-402, Hackensack, NJ 07601
UK office: 57 Shelton Street, Covent Garden, London WC2H 9HE

Library of Congress Cataloging-in-Publication Data
Wong, Sin Kiong.
　Confucianism, Chinese history, and society / Sin Kiong Wong.
　　p. cm.
　ISBN-13: 978-9814374477
　ISBN-10: 9814374474
　1. Confucianism--China--History. 2. Religion and science--China--History. I. Title.
　BL1840.W66 2012
　181'.112--dc23
　　　　　　　　　　　　2012005129

British Library Cataloguing-in-Publication Data
A catalogue record for this book is available from the British Library.

Copyright © 2012 by World Scientific Publishing Co. Pte. Ltd.
All rights reserved. This book, or parts thereof, may not be reproduced in any form or by any means, electronic or mechanical, including photocopying, recording or any information storage and retrieval system now known or to be invented, without written permission from the Publisher.

For photocopying of material in this volume, please pay a copying fee through the Copyright Clearance Center, Inc., 222 Rosewood Drive, Danvers, MA 01923, USA. In this case permission to photocopy is not required from the publisher.

In-house Editor: Lum Pui Yee

Typeset by Stallion Press
Email: enquiries@stallionpress.com

Printed in Singapore.

FOREWORD

Confucianism, Chinese History and Society is a collection of Wu Teh Yao Memorial Lectures. The authors of the book are world renowned scholars and Sinologists who have delivered their speeches at the Wu Teh Yao Memorial Lecture Series.

Wu Teh Yao (吴德耀) was born in Wenchang, Hainan province, China in 1917. He came to Penang, Malaya for family reunion at the age of nine. After he graduated from Chung Ling High School in 1936, he returned to China and studied Arts, majoring in English and History, at Nanking University (now known as Nanjing University). He received postgraduate training in the USA, obtained a Master of Arts degree from Fletcher School of Law and Diplomacy, Tufts University, following by a doctoral degree in Political Science from Harvard University in 1946.

Wu's exciting life and achievements began with his career at the United Nations where he participated in the drafting of the Universal Declaration of Human Rights. In 1951, he co-authored the Fenn-Wu Report on Chinese Education in Malaya after he was invited to conduct a survey of the educational system of the British colony. Wu was appointed President of Tunghai University, Taiwan in 1957 and held the post until 1971. From then until 1976 he was Head of Department of Political Science of University of Singapore.[1] He was later invited to Nanyang University and served as Dean of the College of Graduate studies, and Acting

---

[1] Many accounts indicate that Wu's service at the Political Science Department was from 1971 to 1975. Based on the department record provided by Professor Terry Nardin, Head of Department of Political Science of the National University of Singapore, Wu's tenure as Head of Department was from 1971 to 1976. Thanks Professor Nardin for the information provided.

Vice-Chancellor in 1976–77. Wu was appointed Director of Institute of East Asian Philosophies, which has evolved into East Asian Institute of The National University of Singapore, from 1986–1988.

Soon after Professor Wu Teh Yao died in April 1994, a group of friends and well-wishers formed a committee and established a special Fund called the Wu Teh Yao Memorial Fund to commemorate him. The main objective of the Fund is to hold an annual lecture to be delivered by an outstanding scholar. Professor Tu Wei-ming (杜维明) of Harvard University was invited to deliver the first lecture in 1995. Subsequently, 14 more distinguished scholars were invited to deliver their lectures from 1996 to 2011.

The first eleven distinguished scholars gave two lectures each in the Memorial Lecture series, one in English and another Chinese. This book is the collection of the first ten English lectures. In addition to Professor Tu Wei-ming, the other nine distinguished lecturers are Professor Wang Gungwu (王赓武) of East Asian Institute in Singapore, Professor Ho Peng Yoke (何炳郁) of Needham Research Institute of Cambridge University, Late Professor Liu Ts'un-yan (柳存仁) of Australia National University, Professor Leo Ou-fan Lee (李欧梵) of Harvard University, Professor Chiu Ling-yeong (赵令扬) of University of Hong Kong, Professor Yue Daiyun (乐黛云) of Peking University, Professor Cho-yee To (杜祖贻) of University of Michigan, Professor Hsiung Ping-chen (熊秉真) of Academia Sinica of Taiwan and Professor Philip Y.S. Leung (梁元生) of Chinese University of Hong Kong. The themes of their lectures include Confucianism, nationalism, Chinese history and culture, literature and philosophy, science and education.

As the authors are authoritative scholars in their respective fields, each of them has their own distinguished perspective as well as unique style of writing and presentation. Little editorial changes have been made for the sake of uniformity of style among the various essays.

Last but not least, it is acknowledged that the publication of this book has been made possible by the generous support of the Wu Teh Yao Memorial Fund.

Wong Sin Kiong
National University of Singapore

CONTENTS

Foreword   v
by Wong Sin Kiong

1   A Confucian Perspective on Human Rights   1
      Tu Wei-ming

2   Nationalism and Confucianism   23
      Wang Gungwu

3   Did Confucianism Hinder the Development of Science in China?   49
      Ho Peng Yoke

4   East Meets West: The Impact on China and Her Response   67
      Liu Ts'un-Yan

5   Across Translingual Landscape: Crisis and Innovation in Contemporary Chinese Cultures   89
      Leo Ou-Fan Lee

6   Zheng He: Navigator, Discoverer, and Diplomat   111
      Chin Ling-Yeong

7   Plurality of Cultures in the Context of Globalization and a New Perspective of Comparative Literature   127
      Yue Daiyun

8   The Scientific Merit of Educational Studies   145
      Cho-Yee To

| 9 | In the Beginning: Searching for Childhood in Chinese History and Philosophy
Hsiung Ping-Chen | 171 |
| 10 | The Walls and Waters: A Comparative Study of the City Cultures in Modern China — Beijing, Shanghai, and Hong Kong
Philip Y.S. Leung | 221 |

| Index | 247 |
| Editor | 253 |

❧ 1 ☙
A CONFUCIAN PERSPECTIVE ON HUMAN RIGHTS*

TU WEI-MING

Harvard University, USA

Professor Wu Teh Yao was an original drafter of the United Nation's Universal Declaration of Human Rights in 1948.[1] I learnt from him that the idea of human rights is predicated on the respect for the dignity of the person[2] and that Confucian Humanism, with belief in and commitment to the intrinsic worth of being human "among the lives of myriad things between heaven and earth, human beings are the most precious" (*tiandi zhixing renweigui*)[3] is profoundly meaningful for rights-consciousness as well as the sense of duty. I share his belief that the Confucian tradition offers rich spiritual resources for human rights discourse.

The original conception of human rights under Eleanor Roosevelt's leadership included economic, social, and cultural rights as well as political rights. This is compatible with group rights as well as individual rights. Human rights are inseparable from human responsibilities.[4] Although

---

*I am grateful to Nancy Hodes and Rosanne Hall-Tu for their thoughtful critique and editorial help. In preparing for this lecture, I have used material from two unpublished essays of mine — a statement prepared for the Panel on Human Rights at the annual meeting of the Committee of 100 (Los Angeles, February 25, 1994) and a paper entitled "Beyond the Enlightenment Mentality — Humanity and Rightness: Exploring Confucian Democracy," submitted to the Seventh East–West Philosophers' Conference, East–West Center, Honolulu, January 13, 1995. This chapter is a reproduction of the Wu Teh Yao memorial lecture given by the author in 1995.

in the Confucian tradition, duty-consciousness is more pronounced than rights-consciousness — to the extent that the Confucian tradition underscores self-cultivation, family cohesiveness, economic well-being, social order, political justice and cultural flourishing — it is a valuable spring of wisdom for an understanding of human rights. The argument that Confucian humanism is incompatible with human rights needs to be carefully examined. Human rights as "the common language of humanity," to borrow from United Nations Secretary-General Boutros-Ghali, is a defining characteristic of the spirit of our time.[5] The foundation of the Universal Declaration of Human Rights has been broadened and strengthened by governments, nongovernmental organizations, and conscientious citizens throughout the world for almost half a century since 1948 when Professor Wu Teh Yao took part in an unprecedented effort to inscribe not only on paper but also on human conscience the bold vision of a new world order rooted in respect for human dignity as the central value for political action.

In an historical and comparative cultural perspective, this vision emerged through a long and arduous process beginning with the Enlightenment movement in the modern West in the 18th century. The Enlightenment mentality underlies the rise of the modern West as the most dynamic and transformative ideology in human history. Virtually all major spheres of interests characteristic of the modern age are indebted to this mentality: science and technology, industrial capitalism, market economy, democratic polity, mass communication, research universities, and professional organizations. So are the values we cherish as definitions of modern consciousness, including: liberty, equality, progress, the dignity of the individual, respect for privacy, government for, by and of the people, and due process of law. We are so seasoned in the Enlightenment mentality that we assume the reasonableness of its general spiritual thrust. We find the values it embodies self-evident. The Enlightenment faith in progress, reason, and individualism may have lost some of its persuasive power in New York, London, and Paris but it has remained a standard of inspiration for intellectual leaders throughout the world. Beijing, Hong Kong, Taipei, and Singapore are no exception. A fair understanding of the Enlightenment mentality requires frank discussion of its negative consequences and destructive power as well.

The runaway technology of development may have been a spectacular achievement of human ingenuity in the early phases of the Industrial Revolution, but the Faustian drive to explore, to know, to conquer, and to subdue has been the most destabilizing ideology the world has ever witnessed. As the Western nations assumed the role of innovators, executors, and judges of the international rules of the game defined in terms of competition for wealth and power, the stage was set for growth, development, and unfortunately, exploitation. The unleashed juggernaut blatantly exhibited unbridled aggressiveness toward humanity, nature, and itself. This unprecedented destructive engine has for the first time in human history made it problematic for the viability of the human species. We have been worrying about all kinds of endangered species without knowing that we human beings, mainly due to our own *avidya* (the Buddhist concept of ignorance), have joined the list of endangered species.

With this cultural background in mind, we must heed the advice of Mr Boutros-Ghali that our human rights discourse averts a dual danger:

> The danger of a cynical approach, according to which the international dimension of human rights is nothing more than an ideological cover for the *realpolitik* of States; and the danger of a naive approach, according to which human rights would be the expression of universally-shared values toward which all the members of the international community would naturally aspire.[6]

We, as citizens of the global community, maintain the universality of human rights broadly conceived in the 1948 declaration as a source of inspiration for the human community; we defend the moral and legal imperative that any civilized state treat its citizens in accordance with the political rights guaranteed by its own constitution; and we profess the desirability of democracy as providing to this day the most effective framework in which human rights are safeguarded. However, we must acknowledge that the human rights movement is a dynamic process rather than a static structure and that the human rights discourse ought to be dialogical, communicative, and hopefully, mutually beneficial.

The gradual evolution of the human rights agenda in the United States — a country blessed with a very strong tradition of civil society which immensely impressed the sagely French aristocrat Alexis de Tocqueville in the middle of the 19th century — illustrates the dynamism of the process. While the framers of the American Constitution were profoundly serious about political rights, they were not particularly concerned about either civil or economic rights. It was not until the late 19th century that Socialists, indeed Communist thinkers, addressed the maldistribution of wealth and income, the concentration of capital, and the exploitation of labor as central political issues. The perception of justice as fairness is as much a Socialist as a Liberal contribution. It was in the late 1960s that the civil rights movement made substantial progress in solving the American dilemma of racism, which to this day remains a serious threat to the vitality of the American body politic. We should also remind ourselves, especially those in the United States, that the whole issue of immigration rights, particularly in reference to the Jewish population in the former Soviet Union, was an important aspect of US official human rights agenda in the 1970s. This clearly indicates that a sophisticated understanding of human rights as evolving enterprise in the West itself requires historical consciousness, geopolitical analysis, and most of all, self-reflexivity. The assumption that some of us are champions of human rights because our exemplary teaching gives us the authority to be considered so is either cynical or naive, or perhaps both.

The Vienna Declaration and program of action resulting from the World Conference on Human Rights in June 1993 directs our attention to women, children, minorities, disabled persons, and indigenous people, groups not included in the original conceptions of human rights. The three key regional meetings in Tunis, San Jose, and Bangkok were an integral part of the preparatory process for the Vienna Conference in which several human rights declarations outlining particular concerns and perspectives of the African, Latin American and the Caribbean, and Asia-Pacific regions were produced.[7] The recognition of interdependence between democracy, development and human rights led to the cooperation of international organizations and national agencies in broadening the concept of human rights to include the right to development.[8] While this confluence of social and economic concerns may have undermined the effectiveness of some national and international instruments focusing on well-defined political rights, it has engendered new mechanisms for the promotion of human rights.

The Social Summit convened in Copenhagen in January 1995 which focused on the critical issues confronting the global community (poverty, unemployment, and social disintegration) is indicative of a new awareness that human rights ought to be broadly defined to include economic, social, and cultural dimensions of the human experience. The idea of human dignity features prominently in the preparatory documents for the Summit. Indeed, the participants of the Seminar on the Ethical and Spiritual Dimensions of Social Development organized by the preparatory committee strongly endorsed the view that human rights which have more to do with ethics, law, and politics and whose respect can be verified and measured constitute preferred means of putting into practice the concept of human dignity. They also underscored the inseparability of human rights as a political agenda and human dignity as an ethical-religious concern.[9]

Implicit in this new awareness is a critique of the claim that since human rights are understood differently according to culture, history, stage of economic development, and concrete political situation, they cannot be universally appreciated as values and aspirations for the global community. However, this does not call into question the underlying assumptions of Asian "core values": the perception of the person as a center of relationship rather than simply as an isolated individual, the idea of society as a community of trust rather than merely a system of adversarial relationships, and the belief that human beings are duty-bound to respect their family, society, and nation. Indeed, it may not be far-fetched to insist that these values are not only compatible with the implementation of human rights but also, in a sophisticated way, can enhance the universal appeal of human rights.

Actually there is virtual consensus that since respect for rights and exercise of responsibility are evidence of human nature, individual rights and responsibility are inseparable in all domains of human flourishing: self-cultivation, regulation of family, order in society, governance of state, peace throughout the world, and harmony with nature. In any concrete experience of human encounter, rights and responsibility form an interactive mutual relationship signifying a necessary continuum for human well-being.[10] The Asian values discussion which emerged in the regional meeting in Bangkok in 1993 provides us with an opportunity to develop a truly ecumenical agenda allowing the human rights discourse to become a continuously evolving and edifying conversation.[11] The danger (I must underscore this) of using Asian values as a cover for authoritarian practices, notwithstanding the authentic possibility of dialogue, communication, and mutually beneficial exchange, must be fully explored. The perceived Asian preference for duty, harmony, consensus, network, ritual, trust, and sympathy need not be a threat to rights-consciousness.

The critique of acquisitive individualism, vicious competitiveness, pernicious relativism, and excessive litigiousness help us to understand that Enlightenment values do not necessarily cohere into an integrated guide for action. The conflict between liberty and equality and the lack of concern for community have significantly undermined the persuasive power of human rights based exclusively on the self-interests of isolated individuals. Asian values, which are richly textured with ideas of human flourishing, can serve as a source of inspiration for representing human rights as the common language of humanity.

Under the leadership of Theodore de Bary of Columbia University, a colleague and friend, students of Chinese Studies in North America and Mainland China are in the process of organizing a conference on Confucianism and Human Rights jointly sponsored by the East–West Center in Honolulu and the Confucius Foundation in Beijing.[12] Our purpose is to ascertain the common ground between Confucianism, the ethical underpinning of China and other East Asian societies, and Western conceptions of human rights, and to explore the possibilities for the enlargement and deepening of human rights concepts and practices through intercultural exchange. Some of the topics to be addressed include:

i. Confucian conceptions of self, person, and individual in relation to state and society;
ii. Confucian conceptions of self-cultivation, self-control, and mutual respect as the key to governance;
iii. Rights protected in Confucian ritual and Chinese law;
iv. The relation between rights, responsibilities, and duties; and
v. Human rights in the perspective of Confucian and Western conceptions of social and economic justice.

We hope that a communal critical self-awareness will emerge so that instruments for promoting human rights, while universally connected, are firmly grounded in indigenous Asian conditions as well. We hope that through intercultural dialogue, communication in person, and mutually beneficial exchange, the conceptualization of human rights will overcome its narrowly defined instrumental rationality, intellectual naiveté, and self-imposed parochialism. We hope that this is not only a moral basis for the new discourse on world order but also a spiritual joint venture for human coexistence and mutual flourishing.

A key to the success of this spiritual joint venture is to recognize the conspicuous absence of the idea of community, let alone the global community, in the Enlightenment project. Fraternity (remember in the French revolution, the three cardinal virtues of liberty, equality, and fraternity), the functional equivalent of community has received scant attention in modern Western economic, political, and social thought. I am told that some theory-minded political scientists, including Professor Samuel Huntington of Harvard University, have lamented the fact that the category of family, which features so prominently in political order, is absent in virtually all the major classics in modern Western political thought. It seems that Western political theoreticians, either by choice or by default, have abdicated their responsibility to consider family as a critical issue in adjudicating the relationship between the individual and the state, allowing the sociologists and anthropologists to worry about the political implications of the family.

The willingness to tolerate inequality, faith in the salvific power of self-interest, and the unbridled affirmation of aggressive egoism have greatly poisoned the goodwill of progress, reason, and individualism. The need to express a universal ethic for the formation of a global village and to articulate a possible link between the fragmented world we experience in our ordinary daily existence and the imagined community for the human species as a whole is deeply felt by an increasing number of concerned intellectuals. This requires, at the minimum, the replacement of the principle of self-interest no matter how broadly defined, with a new golden rule: "Do not do to others what we would not want others to do to us."[13] Since the new golden rule is stated in the negative, it will have to be augmented by a positive principle:

> In order to establish ourselves, we must help others to establish themselves; in order to enlarge ourselves; we must help others to enlarge themselves.[14]

A comprehensive sense of community based on the communal critical self-consciousness of the reflective minds is an ethico-religious goal as well as a philosophical ideal. The mobilization of three kinds of spiritual resources is necessary to ensure that this simple vision be grounded in the historicity of the cultural complexes guiding our way of life today.

The first kind involves the ethico-religious traditions of the modern West, notably Greek philosophy, Judaism, and Christianity. The very fact that they have been instrumental in giving birth to the Enlightenment mentality makes a compelling case that they re-examine their relationships to the rise of the modern West in order to create the new public sphere for the transvaluation of typical Western values. The exclusive dichotomy of matter/spirit, body/mind, sacred/profane, man/nature, or even creator/creature, must be transcended to allow supreme values such as the sanctity of the earth, the continuity of being, the beneficiary interaction between the human community and nature, and the mutuality between humankind and heaven to receive the saliency they deserve in both philosophy and ideology. The Greek philosophical emphasis on rationality, the biblical image of "man having dominion over the fish of the sea, and over the fowl of the air, and every living thing that moveth around earth,"[15] and the so-called Protestant work ethic provide the necessary, if not sufficient, sources for the Enlightenment mentality. However, the unintended negative consequences of the rise of the modern West have so undermined the sense of community implicit in the Greek, specifically the Hellenistic idea of the citizen, the Judaic idea of covenant, and the Christian idea of fellowship or universal love that it is morally imperative for these great traditions which have maintained highly complex and tension-ridden relationships with the Enlightenment mentality to formulate their critique of the blatant anthropocentrism inherent in the Enlightenment project.

The second kind of spiritual resources are derived from non-Western historical civilizations which include Hinduism, Jainism, Sikhism, and Buddhism in South and Southeast Asia; Confucianism and Taoism in East Asia; and Islam. It is both intriguing and significant to note that Islam ought to have been considered an integral part of Western civilization because Islam in fact contributed to the emergence of the Renaissance and therefore, by implication, the advent of the Enlightenment mentality. Yet in North American and Western European societies, Islam has in recent years often been stigmatized by the academic community as well as the mass media as radical otherness. These ethico-religious traditions provide very sophisticated and practicable resources in world views, rituals, institutions, styles of education, and patterns of human relatedness. Moreover, they can help to develop new ways of understanding the world and styles of life both as continuation of and as alternative to the Western European and North American exemplification of the Enlightenment mentality.

Having presented a synopsis of the non-Western axial-age civilizations, let us turn our attention to industrial East Asia, which, under the influence of Confucian culture among other traditions, has already developed a less adversarial, less individualistic, and less self-interested modern civilization. The co-existence of market economy with government leadership, democratic polity with meritocracy, and individual initiatives with group orientation has made this region economically and politically the most dynamic area of the world since the Second World War. The cultural implications of the contribution of Confucian ethics to the rise of industrial East Asia for the possible emergence of Hindu, Jain, Buddhist, and Islamic forms of modernity are far-reaching. The Westernization of Confucian Asia including Japan, the North and South Korea, Mainland China, Hong Kong, Taiwan, Singapore, and Vietnam may have forever altered the spiritual landscape, but its indigenous resources, including Mahayana Buddhism, Taoism, Shamanism, Shintoism, and other folk traditions, have the resilience to resurface and make their presence known in the new synthesis.

The caveat, of course, is that having been humiliated and frustrated by the imperialist and colonial domination of the modern West for more than a century, the rise of industrial East Asia symbolizes the instrumental rationality of the Enlightenment heritage with a vengeance. Indeed, the mentality of Japan and the Four Mini-Dragons is today characterized by mercantilism, commercialism, and international competitiveness. Surely the possibility of their developing a more humane and sustainable community should not be exaggerated nor should it be undermined. My recent experience in Malaysia taught me that Islamic–Confucian dialogue can offer practicable measures as well as theoretical guidance for the realization of this possibility.[16]

The third kind of spiritual resources involve the "primal" or the indigenous traditions such as native American, Hawaiian, Maori, Malaysian, Taiwanese, and numerous other nativistic tribal traditions. They have demonstrated with physical strength and aesthetic elegance that a sustainable human form of life has been possible since the Neolithic age. The ecological implications for our practical living are far-reaching. Their style of human flourishing is not a figment of the mind but an experienced reality in our modern age.

A distinctive feature of primal traditions is a profound sense and experience of rootedness. Each indigenous religious tradition is embedded in a concrete place symbolizing a way of perceiving, a mode of thinking, a form of living, an attitude, and a world view. Can we learn from native Americans, Hawaiians, and others to whom we often refer as "primal" peoples? Can they help us solve our ecological crisis?

Given the unintended disastrous consequences of the Enlightenment mentality, there are obvious lessons that the modern mindset can learn from indigenous religious traditions of primal peoples. A natural outcome of primal peoples' embeddedness in concrete locality is their intimate and detailed knowledge of their environment; indeed demarcations between their human habitat and nature are often muted. Implicit in this model of existence is the realization that mutuality and reciprocity between the anthropological world and the cosmos at large are both necessary and desirable. We can learn a new way of perceiving, a new mode of thinking, a new form of living, a new attitude, and a new world view from indigenous peoples. A critique of the Enlightenment mentality and its derivative modern mindset from primal consciousness as interpreted by the concerned and reflective citizens of the world could be thought-provoking.

An equally significant aspect of the primal way of living is the ritual of bonding in ordinary daily human interaction. The density of kinship relations, the rich texture of interpersonal communication, the detailed and nuanced appreciation of the surrounding natural and cultural world, and the experienced connectedness with ancestors point to communities grounded in ethnicity, gender, language, land, and faith. The primordial ties are constitutive parts of their being and activity. In Huston Smith's characterization, what they exemplify is participation rather than control in motivation, empathic understanding rather than empiricist apprehension in epistemology, respect for the transcendent rather than domination over nature in world view, and fulfilment rather than alienation in human experience.[17] As we begin to question the soundness or even sanity of some of our most cherished ways of thinking such as regarding knowledge rather than wisdom as power, asserting the desirability of material progress despite its corrosive influence on our soul and justifying the anthropocentric manipulation of nature even at the cost of destroying the life-support system, primal consciousness emerges as a source of inspiration.

A scholar of world spirituality, Ewert Cousins, in response to the ecological crisis, poignantly remarks that, as we look toward the 21st century with all the ambiguities and perplexities we experience, earth is our prophet and the indigenous peoples are our teachers.[18] Realistically, however, those of us who are seasoned in the Enlightenment mentality cannot abdicate the hermeneutic responsibility to interpret the meaning of the earth's prophecy and to bring understanding to the primal peoples' message. The challenge is immense. For the prophecy and the message to be truly heard in the modern West, we may have to voice them through active and transformative dialogue with non-Western axial-age civilizations. Such a collaborative effort across cultural and other boundaries is necessary to enable primal consciousness to be fully present in our self-reflexivity as we address the issues of globalization.

I, of course, am not proposing any romantic attachment to or nostalgic sentiments for primal consciousness, and I am critically aware that claims of primordiality are often modernist cultural constructions dictated by the politics of recognition. Rather, I suggest that, as both beneficiaries and victims of the Enlightenment mentality, we show our fidelity to our common heritage by enriching, transforming, and restructuring it by using all three kinds of spiritual resources to help us develop a truly ecumenical sense of global community. As previously discussed, "fraternity" seems to have attracted least attention of the three great Enlightenment values in the French Revolution in the subsequent two centuries. The re-presentation of the *Problematik* of community in recent years is symptomatic of the confluence of two apparently contradictory forces in the late 20th century: the global village as both a virtual reality and an imagined community in our information age and the disintegration and restructuring of human togetherness at all levels, from family to nation.

A critique of the Enlightenment mentality and its derivative modern mindset from primal consciousness as interpreted by the concerned and reflective citizens of the world could be thought-provoking, heuristic, and educational. It may be modest to say that we are beginning to develop a fourth kind of spiritual resource from the core of the Enlightenment project itself: our disciplined reflection, a communal rather than an isolated individual act, is a first step toward a new kind of thinking envisioned by religious leaders and ethical teachers. The feminist critique of tradition (especially the broadly conceived and yet, at the same time, historically and culturally grounded humanistic feminism), the environmental concerns (notably the spiritually informed project of deep ecology) and the persuasion of religious pluralism are obvious examples of this new communal critical self-awareness. These need to go beyond the Enlightenment mentality without either deconstructing or abandoning its commitment to rationality, liberty, equality, human rights, and distributive justice requires a thorough re-examination of modernity as "layered" concept and modernization as a complex process.

Asian intellectuals have been devoted students of Western learning for more than a century. They have been students of Dutch (*Rangaku*, to use the Japanese expression), British, French, German, and more recently, American learning for industrial East Asia and Westernized Soviet learning for socialist East Asia. Now that Asian intellectuals are well informed by the Enlightenment project of the West without losing sight of their own indigenous resources, the time seems ripe for European and American intellectuals in academia, government, business and the mass media to appreciate what Confucian humanism, among other rich spiritual resources in Asia, has to offer toward the cultivation of a global ethic.

The central *Problematik* in the Confucian discourse consists of four issues as exemplified in the *Book of Mencius*. The first one is *renqinzhibian* — the essential difference between man (humanity) and beast (other members of the animal kingdom). The second one is *yixiazhibian* — the essential difference between civilization and barbarism. The third one is *yilizhibian* — the essential difference between rightness and profit. The fourth one is *wangbazhibian* — the essential difference between kingship (benevolent government) and hegemony (politically powerful and economically efficient but morally inadequate polity).[19]

In the Confucian perspective, human beings are not merely rational beings but political animals, tool-users, or language-manipulators. The Confucians seem to have deliberately rejected simplistic reductionist models. They define human beings in terms of five integrated visions:

- Human beings are a sentient being, capable of internal resonance not only among themselves but also with other animals, plants, trees, mountains, and rivers, indeed nature as a whole.
- Human beings are social beings. As isolated individuals, human beings are weak by comparison with other members of the animal kingdom but if they are organized to form a society, they have inner strength not only for survival but also for flourishing. Human-relatedness as exemplified in a variety of networks of interaction is necessary for human survival and human flourishing. Our sociality defines who we are.
- Human beings are political beings in the sense that human-relatedness is, by biological nature and social necessity, differentiated in terms of hierarchy, status, and authority. While Confucians insist upon the fluidity of these artificially constructed boundaries, they recognize the significance of "difference" in an "organic" as opposed to "mechanic" solidarity. Therefore the centrality of the principle of fairness and the primacy of the practice of distributive justice in a humane society.
- Human beings are also historical beings sharing collective memories, cultural traditions, ritual praxis, and "habits of the heart."
- Human beings are metaphysical beings with the highest aspirations not simply defined in terms of anthropocentric ideas but characterized by the ultimate concern to be constantly inspired by and continuously responsive to the Mandate of Heaven.

The Confucian way is a way of learning to be human. Learning to be human in the Confucian spirit is to engage oneself in a ceaseless, unending process of creative self-transformation, both as a communal act and as a dialogical response to Heaven. This involves four inseparable dimensions — self, community, nature, and the transcendent. The purpose of learning is always understood as for the sake of the self, but the self is never an isolated individual (an island) but a center of relationships (a flowing stream). The self as a center of relationships is a dynamic open system rather than a closed static structure. Therefore mutuality between self and community, harmony between human species and nature, and continuous communication with Heaven are defining characteristics and supreme values in the human project.[20]

Since the Confucians take the concrete living human being at present as their point of departure in the development of their philosophical anthropology, they recognize the embeddedness and rootedness of the human condition. Therefore, the profound significance of what we call primordial ties — ethnicity, gender, language, land, class, and basic spiritual orientation — intrinsic in the Confucian project is a celebration of cultural diversity (this is not to be confused with any form of pernicious relativism). Often, the Confucians understand their own path as learning of the body and mind (*shenxinzhixue*) or learning of nature and destiny (*xingmingzhixue*). There is a recognition that each one of us is fated to be a unique person embedded in a particular condition. By definition, we are unique human beings, but at the same time each individual has the intrinsic possibility for self-cultivation, self-development, and self-realization. Despite fatedness and embeddedness as necessary structural limitations in our conditionality, we are endowed with infinite possibilities for self-transformation in our process of learning to be human. We are, therefore, intrinsically free. Our freedom, embodied in our responsibility for ourselves as center of relationships, creates our worth. That alone deserves and demands respect.

The Confucian way for human survival and human flourishing, then, is predicated on the two basic ethical principles already mentioned: "Do not do unto others what we would not want others to do unto us." This is a principle of considerateness, a principle of reciprocity. The reason that it is stated in the negative is based on the belief that what is best for me may not be best for my neighbor. I like spicy food (Thai or Szechuanese), but I should not impose that taste upon my children because they may not be ready to appreciate it. So that which is good for me may not be good for my children. This, on the surface, seems to violate the basic requirement of universality in ethical thinking. Yet, the need for this critical self-awareness is not only the recognition of the integrity of the other but also the practical value of "analogical imagination."[21] The practice of sympathetic understanding (a form of "embodied knowing") enhances one's self-knowledge, as Confucius notes, "the ability to take that which is near at hand as an analogy is indeed the method of humanity!"[22]

The second principle is duty-consciousness; it is a manifestation of the ethic of responsibility: "In order to establish ourselves, we must help others to establish themselves; in order to enlarge ourselves; we must help others to enlarge themselves." This is not simply altruism; it is not that because I have a great deal of surplus energy or extra resources available, I might as well share with others. Rather, as I am a center of relationships, my own human flourishing necessitates that I involve myself, in the spirit of empathy to be sure, in the affairs of others. The word "help," added in the English translation, directs toward not only the others but ourselves as well for, in the literal sense, the Chinese text simply notes "desiring to establish ourselves (myself), we (I) establish others."

In this process of learning to be human, five basic virtues are to be embodied: humanity, perhaps more appropriately rendered as co-humanity, which entails a feeling of sympathy; uprightness, which is often understood in a nuanced way. For example, when a student presented the Taoist argument: "How nice would it be if we can repay malice with kindness." Confucius retorted, "How are you going to repay kindness?" His recommendation was then: "repay malice with rightness (uprightness); repay kindness with kindness."[23] Aside from humanity (co-humanity) and uprightness, there are also the virtues of civility, wisdom, and trust. Civility, an idea that the recently deceased American sociologist, Edward Shils, considered essential for the development of any "civil society." The Confucian notion of ritual (*li*), as a civilized mode of conduct, has much richer and complex connotation than civility entails, but, in the present context, it can serve as a functional equivalent of civility. Impressed by the sophisticated discourse on civility in the *Analects*, Shils, partly in jest, honored Confucius as a forefather of "civil society."[24] Wisdom, then, is not insights derived from contemplation as the Greeks would have it. Rather, it is closely associated with knowing persons and doing things. Confucian wisdom is the cumulative result of "embodied thinking"[25] on daily practical living. Wisdom grows from conscientious engagement in social praxis instead of speculative meditation on abstract ideas.

So far as trust is concerned, I am reminded of a rather intriguing phenomenon in the vocabulary of modern English: some of the very elegant traditional words with a kind of "gravity of spirit," such as trust, fidelity, community, cooperation, and company, have now all become financial institutions. Whether politics should be understood as moral leadership, or is just the distribution or the arrangement of power; whether economics is simply enhancement of profit, or is the management of wealth and resources and, therefore, implicit in it is the idea of justice and fairness; whether we cherish religious pluralism or submit ourselves to religious exclusivism; whether we consider multiculturalism as a value or simply accept our own language and our own way of life as the most and even the only authentic expression of modernity. These are not simply Confucian issues; these are issues we need to address as reflective modern persons, if we are serious in transforming "human rights" into a universal language of humanity.

To return to the Confucian project, we can actually envision the Confucian perception of human self-development, based upon the dignity of the person, in terms of a series of concentric circles: self, family, community, society, nation, world, and cosmos. We begin with a quest for true personal identity, an open and creative self-transformation which, paradoxically, must be predicated on our ability to overcome selfishness and egoism. We cherish family cohesiveness. In order to do that, we have to go beyond nepotism. We embrace communal solidarity, but we have to go beyond parochialism to fully realize its true value. We can be enriched by social integration, provided that we overcome ethnocentrism and chauvinistic culturalism. We are committed to national unity, but we ought to transcend aggressive nationalism so that we can be genuinely patriotic. We are inspired by human flourishing but we must endeavor not to be confined by anthropocentrism, the full meaning of humanity is anthropocosmic rather than anthropocentric. On the occasion of the International Symposium on Islamic–Confucian dialogue organized by the University of Malaya (March, 1995), the Deputy Prime Minister of Malaysia, Anwar Ibrahim, quoted a statement from Huston Smith's *The World's Religions*. It truly captures the Confucian spirit of self-transcendence:

> In shifting the center of one's empathic concern from oneself to one's family one transcends selfishness. The move from family to community transcends nepotism. The move from community to nation transcends

parochialism and the move to all humanity counters chauvinistic nationalism.²⁶

We can even include the move toward the unity of Heaven and humanity (*tianrenheyi*) transcends secular humanism, a blatant form of anthropocentrism characteristic of the intellectual ethos of the modern West. Indeed, it is in the anthropocosmic spirit that we find communication between self and community, harmony between human species and nature, and mutuality between humanity and Heaven. This integrated comprehensive vision of learning to be human can very well serve as the core of the so-called Asian values.

The page constraint does not allow me to further explore how the discourse on Asian values can contribute to the international human rights discussion. I am convinced that such a discourse can broaden and deepen the conceptual and practical resources of human rights, both as a culturally and historically embedded modern Western concept and as a potentially universalizable praxis. However, the art of having such a discourse conducted in a sophisticated comparative civilizational context devoid of highly charged political passions is a daunting task. We are not opting for an ideal speech situation. Nor are we ready to defend a new "communicative rationality"²⁷ based upon abstract principles. In our limited attempt to keep human rights a live issue from a Confucian point of view, we want to make sure that our initial interpretive stance is properly understood. Needless to say, Asian values, as informed by Confucian humanism, have a significant role to play for a sophisticated understanding of human rights in a comparative cultural perspective. Should we understand the self as an isolated individual or as a center of relationships? Should we approach our society as a community based upon trust or simply the result of contractual arrangements of conflicting forces? As we begin to appreciate that we are so much embedded in our linguistic universe, not to mention our historicity, that we cannot escape a de facto parochialism, no matter how open-minded we intend to be and how liberated we think we are, we must respect alternative intelligence and radical otherness.

This is particularly pertinent to the English-speaking community whether it is in London, Sydney, Madras, Kuala Lumpur, or Singapore. As a Chinese-American, I am, of course, most sensitive to the situation in the United States. Again this strikes home: when you know a few languages you may be considered as multilingual. If you know two languages, you are bilingual. If you know only one language, you are most likely an American. This is not a strength but a limitation, even if the myth that English is the universal language was partially true. I think that the time is ripe for the American general public as well as the academic community to come to the realization that bilingual and multilingual competence is a social capital and cultural asset that a modern civilization cannot afford to lose. Surely, for a number of reasons, Malaysians and Singaporeans are multilingual. However, a full recognition of the value of such social capital and cultural asset requires the active participation of the English-speaking political elites in Asian countries to nurture and cultivate it. After all, languages are not merely tools for communication, they are also depositories of knowledge, wisdom, and values necessary for personal self-understanding and communal solidarity.

East Asian intellectuals are earnestly engaged in probing the Confucian tradition(s) as a spiritual resource for economic development, nation building, social stability, and cultural identity. While they cherish the hope that their appreciation of their own cultural values will provide ethical moorings as they try to locate their niche in the turbulent currents of the modern world, they remain active participants in the Enlightenment project. The revived Confucian values are no longer fundamentalist representation of nativistic ideas; they are, in general, transvaluated traditional values compatible with and commensurate to the main thrust of modern ideology defined in term of Enlightenment ideas. Actually, since East Asian intellectuals have been devoted students of the modern West for several generations, the Enlightenment values, including human rights, have become an integral part of their own cultural heritage. To reiterate an earlier point, East Asian intellectuals in general, not to mention the English-speaking political elite, are more familiar with the life-orientation of the modern West than with any traditional Asian way of living. The recent revival of interest in Confucian ethics in East Asia, whether or not it presages a cultural renaissance, does not indicate an outright rejection of the Enlightenment mentality. On the contrary, as I have already alluded to, the Enlightenment belief in instrumental rationality, material progress, social engineering, empiricism, pragmatism, scientism, and competitiveness seems to have more persuasive power in Hong Kong, Taipei, and Singapore than in Paris, London, New York, or Cambridge, Massachusetts.

The critical issue, then, is not only Asian values versus modern Western values, but how East Asian intellectuals can be enriched and empowered by their own cultural roots in their critical response to already partially domesticated Enlightenment heritage. The full development of human rights requires their ability to creatively transform the Enlightenment mentality of the modern West into a thoroughly digested cultural tradition of their own; this, in turn, is predicated on their capacity to creatively mobilize indigenous social capital and cultural asset for the task. They must be willing to ask difficult fundamental questions, identify complex real options, and make painful practicable decisions. The conflicts between liberty and equality, economic efficiency and social justice, development and stability, individual interests and the public good, not to mention rights and duty, are harsh realities in practical living. The enhancement of liberty, economic efficiency, development, individual interests, and rights are highly desirable, but to pursue these values exclusively at the expense of equality, social justice, stability, the public good, and duty is ill-advised. As the supposedly exemplification of modernity, North America and Western Europe continues to show ignorance of the cultures of the rest of the world and insouciance about the people who do not speak their languages, East Asia cannot but choose its own way. It is in this sense that a Confucian perspective on human rights is worth exploring.

Paradoxically, the Confucian personality ideals — the authentic person (*junzi*), the worthy (*xianren*), or the sage (*shengren*) — can be realized more fully in the liberal democratic society than either in the traditional imperial dictatorship or a modern authoritarian regime. East Asian Confucian ethics must creatively transform itself in light of Enlightenment values before it can serve as effective critique of the excessive individualism, pernicious competitiveness, and vicious litigiousness of the modern West.[28]

Notes

1. See his "Biography" in *Hainan Yidai Zheren*, commemorative publication in memory of Professor Wu Teh Yao. Singapore: Hainan Huiguan, 1940, p. 13.

2. Professor Wu notes:

> Man, in the traditional Confucian concept, is born conscience free with self-respect and in human dignity. He is not born to a social class from which he cannot divest himself: nor is he born to a family of position and wealth so that he can enjoy life forever. A man is judged by his moral character and not by his social position or wealth.

Wu Teh Yao (1988). "The Confucian concept and attributes of man and the modernization of industrial East Asia". In *The Triadic Accord: Confucian Ethics, Industrial East Asia and Max Weber*, Tu Wei-ming (ed.), p. 403. Singapore: Institute of East Asian Philosophies.

3. The statement is attributed to Confucius in a dialogue between the Master and his disciple, Zheng Zi. See *Xiaojing* (*The Classic of Filial Piety*), in the "Shengzhi" (Sagely governance) chapter (reprint of the original Song edition, 1815), 5: 1a.

4. See not only the *Universal Declaration on Human Rights*, G.A. Res. 217A, U.N. Doc. A/810 (1948) but also *Declaration of Delhi*, January 5–10, 1959, and *The Rule of Law in a Free Society*. Geneva: International Commission of Jurists, 1959.

5. Boutros Boutros-Ghali, "Human Rights: The Common Language of Humanity," statement made in Vienna at the opening of the World Conference on Human Rights on June 14, 1993. *World Conference on Human Rights: The Vienna Declaration and Programme of Action*, June 1993 (New York: the United Nation's Department of Public Information), p. 5.

6. *Ibid.*, p. 9.

7. *Ibid.*, p. 3.

8. See (1995) "The human rights to development". In *United Nations World Summit for Social Development*, pp. 11–14. New York: American Association for the International Commission of Jurists, Inc.

9. *Ethical and Spiritual Dimensions of Social Progress*. New York, United Nations Publication, 1995, pp. 25–34.

10. Based on the Confucian insight originally presented in the *Great Learning*, see Gardner, Daniel K. (1986). *Chu Hsi and the Ta-hsueh*: *Neo-Confucian Reflection on the Confucian Cannon*. Cambridge, MA: Council on East Asian Studies, Harvard University.

11. In addition to the famous Bangkok Governmental declaration endorsed by all the Asian governments at the April 1993 Asian regional preparatory meeting for the Vienna World Conference on Human rights, there is also the statement of Asian NGOs (nongovernmental organizations) issued on March 27, 1993. For an informative account of the vital issues involved, see Ghai, Yash (1994), "Human rights and governance: The Asian debate," Occasional Paper No. 4, The Asia Foundation: Center for Asian Pacific Affairs. For a thought-provoking account of a new vision on human rights from an Islamic perspective, see Muzaffar, Chandra (1993). *Human Rights and the New World Order*. Penang: Just World Trust.

12. The meeting, scheduled for August 1995, expects to have attendance from Cultural China (Mainland, Taiwan, Hong Kong, and overseas Chinese communities) and North America.
13. *Analects*, V: 11, XII: 2.
14. *Ibid.*, VI: 28.
15. *Genesis*, 1: 24.
16. The occasion was an international seminar on Islam and Confucianism: A Civilizational dialogue, sponsored by University of Malaya, March 12–14, 1995.
17. Huston Smith's unpublished paper presented to the International Conference on An Exploration of Contemporary Spirituality: Axial-Age Civilizations and Primal Traditions sponsored by the Institute of Culture and Communication, East–West Center, June 10–14, 1991.
18. Ewert Cousins, an oral statement made at the Conference mentioned above, which was subsequently published in a pamphlet entitled *Local Knowledge, Ancient Wisdom*, Steve Friesen (ed.). Honolulu: East West Center, 1991. For a more elaborated theological exposition of this idea, see Cousins, Ewert (1992). *Christ of the 21st Century*. Rockport, MA: Element, pp. 7–10.
19. For a general discussion on the Mencian humanist perception, see Tu Wei-ming (1984), "The idea of the human in Mencian thought: An approach to Chinese aesthetices". In *Theories of the Arts in China*, Susan Bush and Christian Murck (eds.), pp. 57–73. Princeton: Princeton University Press. The essay is also anthologized in Tu Wei-ming (1986). *Confucian Thought: Selfhood as Creative Transformation*. Albany, NY: State University of New York Press.
20. See Tu Wei-ming (1993), "Confucianism". In *Our Religions*, Arvind Sharma, pp. 195–197. San Francisco: Harper San Francisco.
21. The expression is based on Tracy, David (1991). *The Analogical Imagination: Christian Theology and the Culture of Pluralism*. New York: Crossroad.
22. *Analects*, XIX: 6.
23. *Ibid.*, XIV: 34.
24. Shils, Edward (1996), "Reflections on civil society and civility in the Chinese intellectual tradition". In *Confucian Traditions in East Asian Modernity: Exploring Moral Education and Economic Culture in Japan and the Four Mini-Dragons*, Tu Wei-ming (ed.), Chapter 2. Cambridge, MA: Harvard University Press.
25. For a preliminary exploration of this idea, see Tu Wei-ming (1971), "Lun Jujia de 'tizhi' dexing zhizhi de hanyi" (On "embodied knowing" — the implications of moral knowledge in the Confucian tradition). In *Jujia lunli yentaohui wenji* (*Essays from The Seminar on Confucian Ethics*), Liu Shu-hsien, (ed.) Singapore: Institute of East Asian Philosophy.
26. Quoted in the address by Anwar Ibrahim at the opening of the International Seminar on Islam and Confucianism: A Civilizational Dialogue, sponsored by University of Malaya, March 13, 1995. It should be noted that Huston Smith, in this particular reference to the Confucian Project, is based on my discussion on the meaning of

self-transcendence in Confucian humanism. If we follow my "anthropocosmic" argument through, we need to transcend "anthropocentrism" as well. See Smith, Huston (1991). *The World's Religions*. San Francisco: Harper San Francisco, pp. 182, 193, and 195 (notes 28 and 29).
27. Habermas, Jurgen (1984). *The Theory of Communicative Action* (transl. Thomas McCarthy), vol. 1. Boston: Beacon Press.
28. This idea was first presented in Chinese at the conclusion of the international conference celebrating the 2545th anniversary of Confucius' birth and the formation of the International Association of Confucian Studies, sponsored by the Confucius Foundation, Beijing, October 5, 1994.

☙ 2 ❧

NATIONALISM AND CONFUCIANISM*

WANG GUNGWU

National University of Singapore

This chapter is in memory of Professor Wu Teh Yao, educator, political scientist, and scholar of Confucianism. He was also an inspiration to the Institute of East Asian Philosophies (the predecessor of the present East Asian Institute), especially in the Institute's efforts to study Confucianism in Eastern Asia. My subject today would have interested him. As a political scientist, who lived through a period when many varieties of nationalism could be found throughout the region, he understood the phenomenon professionally and personally. As a Chinese scholar, he knew the Confucian classics well and appreciated the extent to which the life of the Chinese people was permeated by Confucian ideas.

My subject today, nationalism and Confucianism, is a complicated one. The two words are commonly used and we feel we know what they denote. But, though common, they have become difficult words because of the many meanings that have accrued to each of them. Most people interpret these words according to their own history and background. My interest in nationalism is largely historical, for example, the origins of nationalism in China and the region, its development in this century under different conditions; what forms it has taken and why; its contributions to modernization; and the difference it has made to the culture and society of each country that has followed the course of nation-building, and so on.

---

* This chapter is a reproduction of the Wu Teh Yao memorial lecture given by the author in 1996.

There are thus many ways of understanding nationalism and many efforts at arriving at a definition. Perhaps it is enough to distinguish its meaning among the following three: the nation, the state, and the ethnic group (Connor, 1978; Smith, 1971). All three can be linked with nationalism although, strictly speaking, the word is derived from nation and is closest to that in usage, particularly in Europe, where the nation-state was first evolved (Hayes, 1949; Kamenka, 1973; Kedourie, 1960; Tilly, 1975). The state at various stages of its formation could easily use nationalism, which has strong emotional appeal, when needed and, if a unified nation was not yet in existence, could even determine the kind of nationalism that it wants. And many ethnic groups, if large enough, are potential nations if the conditions for their independence and separate existence are right (Connor, 1987). This is not the place to engage ourselves in all aspects of the subject, but the following account is relevant to the connection between Chinese nationalism and Confucianism.

Nationalism normally occurs among people who have lived together in a territory with a shared history and a common culture long enough to see themselves as a nation as well as want to continue being one. There are many words in different languages to express this sense of identity, but the key ingredients are place and territory, a long duration together, and the bonds of culture and community (Kohn, 1955; Snyder, 1954). In due course, nations needed stronger organizations to defend themselves or help them achieve more ambitious goals. The most successful are these nations, notably nation-states, that is, states that are dominated by a single nation or national group, in order to enable them to change, respond, adapt, and modernize more quickly (Breuilly, 1982; Guibernau, 1996). The sentiments generated to give the nation-states direction and purposefulness produced modern nationalism (Gellner, 1964; Greenfeld, 1992; Smith, 1995). The best example of such nationalism in Asia is that of Japan. It had all the ingredients of a nation before there was nationalism. But when the concept was introduced, the nation responded with a full-blown nationalism with little difficulty or delay (Hardacre, 1989).

A strong state can also use nationalism to build a new nation out of communities each of which, under different circumstances, might have claimed to be nations. In fact, most nation-states are more or less multi-national (McNeill, 1986). The Soviet Union before its breakup consisted of many different groups of people who had many ingredients needed to form a nation. In Asia, multinational states like the Union of India and the People's Republic of China are clear examples (Chatterjee, 1986 and 1993; Dreyer, 1976; Heberer, 1989); so are most of the states that were once colonies of European empires (Emerson, 1960). Although there is an ongoing debate about the nature of the pre-modern Chinese political community, Chinese nationalism is a relatively new phenomenon (Duara, 1993; Townsend, 1996). China was an empire and certainly not a nation state until the 20th century. Its unifying force was its culture and civilization. Hence some historians have called China a civilization state rather than a nation before the 20th century (Smith, 1971; Thierry, 1989).

Nationalism in its modern form is found in all member-states of the United Nations Organisation (Rustow, 1967; Seton-Watson, 1977). In common speech, all the nations or states are also called countries. This can be confusing because some of them consist of a single dominant nation, such as Turkey, the Koreas, and Germany, while others are constituted by a number of nations: [I have mentioned the former Soviet Union, but even Russia today still has many nations] Myanmar, Vietnam, and Sri Lanka are smaller examples of the same phenomenon (Beling and Totten, 1970; Connor, 1972). But all of them, whether called nation-states or countries, appeal to patriotism. This patriotism stresses loyalty to the state or country to the legal or constitutional entity, rather than to a specific national or ethnic group.

Confucianism is also a word with many meanings. Most commonly, it is used to refer to the body of ideas and institutions that have shaped Chinese civilization and served to support and perpetuate an empire-state for 20 centuries (Ch'ien, 1979). It is this public face of a once successful, much respected, and powerful tradition that I shall concentrate on. This tradition included, among other things, state sponsorship of Confucian learning and selection of public officials, the use of Confucian criteria to determine all matters of public morality, and broad categories of duties and relationships which provide powerful support for an authoritarian system. From that point of view, Confucianism is strongly linked to the formation of China and can be said to be one of the foundations of Chinese national identity and consciousness, and, therefore, closely related to the roots of nationalism. I will also refer to the personal commitments to Confucian ideals, and the social and family attachments to the ethical values associated with Confucius, because these ideals and values continue and will always play an important role in the lives of ordinary Chinese (Ch'ien, 1979). However, I shall not discuss here the nature of Confucian philosophy, or what Confucius and his followers said and meant. But we should note that Confucianism is not exclusive to the Chinese. It has been shared by other ethnic groups in Eastern Asia, notably the Koreans, the Vietnamese, and the Japanese (de Bary, 1988).

Why choose to talk about nationalism and Confucianism today? The main reason is that, since the early 1980s and more particularly after the Tiananmen tragedy, there had been a revival of some forms of Chinese nationalism in the People's Republic of China at the same time as there were moves to reassess the contributions of "new Confucians." These new Confucians range from philosophers like Liang Souming and Feng Youlan, to others who had read widely in modern Western philosophy like Xiong Shiyi, Tang Junyi, and Mou Zongsan (Fang, 1989; Metzger, 1977), to a new generation of Marxist theorists like Li Zehou and his students and critics, and also to intellectual historians like Qian Mu (Ch'ien, Mu), Yu Ying-shih, and Tu Wei-Ming.

That there is such a reassessment is in itself interesting, but the more important question is, to what extent are the two, that is, nationalism and Confucianism, compatible and complementary? This question arises because most Chinese are aware that, earlier this century, China had been through a stage when a heightened nationalism led Chinese youth to reject Confucianism in no uncertain terms. This happened after the May Fourth Movement of 1919 and had ramifications for decades afterward (Chow, 1963; Lin, 1979). In a more destructive form, the Cultural Revolution period of 1966–1976 sought to uproot all vestiges of traditional values, among which the most prominent was Confucianism. Although this was done in the name of a communist revolution, there were also strong nationalist impulses behind the rejection of what was considered the major cause of China's backwardness in modern times.

The following short summary of the relationship between nationalism and Confucianism during the last hundred years of Chinese history would be useful to remind us of the background:

- From 1890s to 1925, many Confucians were prepared to accept the new forces of nationalism, with the young nationalists being

also well-schooled in the Confucian classics (Chan and Etzold, 1976; Chang, 1987). Not many people at that time doubted that the two would support each other effectively to revive Chinese power against the external enemy, the expansionist empires of the West and Japan.
- From 1925 until the mid-1950s, a new national school system had been introduced successfully, but Confucianism was marginalised by the rapid acceptance of modern Western ideas, not only about science and technology but also about political ideologies and economic modernisation (Chuang, 1929; *Report*, 1928; Tsang, 1967). Nationalism was universally accepted: the intense disagreements that led to civil war were whether China should seek transformation and renewal through national capitalism or revolutionary socialism. Confucianism was all but irrelevant during this period (Eastman, 1974; Tien, 1972).
- From the mid-1950s to the end of the Cultural Revolution period in 1976, when the Cultural Revolution became an extreme form of nationalism, there was an all-out attack on all vestiges of Confucianism, including the teachings of Confucius, Mencius, and their followers throughout Chinese history. In some cases, other traditions were drawn upon to denigrate the central tenets of the official Confucianism that had provided the pillars of the Chinese traditional state (Elvin, 1990; for a history written from within China, see Yan Jiaqi and Gao Gao (1986 and 1996)).
- I come to the fourth period, our own period. Since the death of Mao Zedong and the return of Deng Xiaoping, we come to the latest period, when economic reforms proposed and supported in the name of national interests have been its most important feature. As the people struggle with revisionist ideas about Marxist–Leninist doctrines and the mistakes of Mao, there have been increasing appeals to patriotism. These appeals have referred to the national spirit, national unity, and national prosperity. They include the new importance given to the position of Sun Yat-sen as the man who inspired China's battle for national rejuvenation. Seen from outside the People's Republic of China, by Chinese and non-Chinese alike, the patriotic calls seem indistinguishable from earlier forms

of nationalism (a representative collection of papers are in *Zhanlue yu guanli* [*Strategy and Management*] 15, by Pi Mingyong, Xiao Gongqin, and Chen Mingming).

Many questions are raised by the latest development in the context of the previous decades of history. They follow from the extensive debates in recent decades about the contribution of Confucianism toward the dramatic economic successes in Eastern Asia, especially in Japan and the so-called Four Tigers which had little but Confucian traditions in common among them (Tu, 1991; Wang, 1991a, pp. 181–197; Wang, 1992, pp. 301–313).

Let me mention some of the questions being asked. Does it mean that the long period (half-century) of contradiction between nationalism and Confucianism is over? Do the Chinese leaders now believe that nationalism cannot be separated from the Confucian structure of ideas that had been the bulwark of Chinese nation-building since the Han dynasty? Or, does it mean that nationalism is the message, and Confucianism is only one of the means to give nationalism the moral weight and make it respectable? Is this no more than a small retreat to the position of 1895–1925, when Confucianism had a chance to prove itself as adaptable to modernity but failed to impress the impatient youth of the time?

Or, are we facing a new Confucianism altogether? Is this new manifestation so modernized, so different from its traditional form, that it now knows how to support modern nationalism? Has it rid itself of its "feudal residues" and taken its place among the major alternatives to the "Enlightenment Project" which has enabled the West to dominate the world for the past two centuries? Can Confucianism now offer itself once again as the nation-building ideology it had been for centuries, one that is not only morally uplifting but also politically unifying?

The questions show varying degrees of confidence in the future of Confucianism. Some come from the premise that Confucianism was found lacking earlier this century. There is certainly no agreement as to how vital Confucianism still is and how durable it will be. That the questions are asked at all illustrates the profound doubt that has grown about the relevance of Confucianism to modern urban life. Thus one of the most interesting features of the current debate is the way it now assumes that

Confucianism is much more resilient than people realized. Is Confucianism so innately strong that the revival of nationalism would not be possible without its reassuring presence?

There are at least three ways to deal with the aforementioned questions. We could take a philosophical approach and analyze the key elements in nationalism and Confucianism separately. Then, after comparing each of these elements, we might try to determine whether nationalism is compatible with Confucianism or not. Another way is to follow the subject empirically and look at the present group of nationalists in and outside China and compare what they are doing with what the Confucian revivalists are advocating. This way we could weigh the possibility of the two groups coming together to effectively provide the country with new alternatives and a stronger sense of direction.

Otherwise, we could take an historical approach. There was a time, at the beginning of the 20th century, when nationalism and Confucianism were not in contradiction and seemed even mutually supportive. It would be instructive to begin with that period and examine how the two co-existed and supported each other. During most of the 30 years from 1895 to 1925, the nationalists had Confucian backgrounds and the surviving Confucian literati, the products of the Qing Empire, were prepared to stand equally with the nationalists to defend first the empire and later the republic against foreign dominance. For example, although the spectrum of views from loyal Qing officials to the anti-Qing triad leaders and their secret societies was very wide, they focused on the ideal of saving China from dismemberment. Many of them certainly would be described as nationalists today.

As an historian, I prefer to take this third approach to try and answer some of the questions being asked. I would start with the overarching question: is the long period of contradiction between nationalism and Confucianism now over?

That long period referred to the half century from the 1920s to the 1970s, when three generations of young Chinese progressively rejected the Confucian past in favor of foreign models such as Western democracy or communism. The question implies that the period before the 1920s was one when the nationalists had no problems with their Confucian heritage and the Confucians were willing to embrace nationalism. If that were so from the end of the 19th century, why did it not continue?

There have been numerous detailed studies about the three decades following China's humiliating defeat by the Japanese in 1895. From these studies, we know that two kinds of nationalist voices called loudly for drastic steps to be taken to save China. The best known were the large groups of supporters of two remarkable men. One was the unorthodox Confucian scholar, Kang Youwei. Kang Youwei would have seen himself as a patriot rather than as a nationalist, but many of his younger followers, including Liang Qichao, would have had no difficulty calling themselves nationalists. The other was the medical graduate from Hong Kong, Sun Yat-sen, whose knowledge of the Confucian classics was basic compared with his familiarity with Western science and political institutions. He was certainly China's first great nationalist and was the voice of the non-elites, pushing for the overthrow of the Manchus. He went further than others and was proud to identify himself as a revolutionary nationalist.

Kang Youwei inspired a vigorous and idealistic, some say utopian, form of Confucianism among younger scholars like Liang Qichao and Tan Sitong (Hsiao, 1975). For them, there was never any doubt that the long line of followers of Confucius for 2,500 years had the answers to China's intellectual and spiritual needs. If Qing China in its last years had lost its way, it had been due either to departures from key Confucian ideas through neglect and misinterpretation, or to the failure to adapt those ideas to changing times (Chang, 1900). Kang Youwei led his disciples to ask themselves, what would Confucius have done had he been alive in the 19th century? The principles Confucius espoused were there and still valid. What was needed was a new understanding of those principles that would make them applicable to the salvation of China.

Kang Youwei did not approve of avowed nationalists like Sun Yat-sen, but that was more because Sun Yat-sen called for *geming*, revolution against the Qing dynasty and the driving out of the Manchus. But Kang Youwei admired the appeal of nationalism from the leaders of the Meiji Restoration that infused the spirit of Japan and enabled the Japanese to make sacrifices for their country in ways unknown to the Chinese of Qing China. And it was, after all, his student, Liang Qichao, who introduced the Japanese word *minzoku* (or *minzu*), which translated the Western concept of nation, into China. The Japanese equated *minzoku* with how they felt about their country and its ambitions (Levenson, 1968).

After Liang Qichao, Sun Yat-sen enthusiastically adopted the word to stimulate something equally inspiring among the patriotic Chinese who were ready to give their lives to revive China. At the same time, Kang Youwei also aroused severe criticisms from other Confucians for his personal and sometimes eccentric interpretations of Confucius' ideas, and some of his greatest Confucian critics like Zhang Binglin were also strong nationalists (Laitinen, 1990; Wong, 1989). For these nationalist critics too, Confucianism was the backbone of the great achievements of Chinese civilization, and therefore the very essence of the national spirit. It would have been inconceivable for them to imagine the Chinese nation without the contributions of Confucian values. Indeed, this was so obvious that some of the best scholars did not think it necessary to defend Confucianism.

But soon after the Republic of China was founded in 1911, there were some pathetic attempts by reactionaries to revive the monarchy in the name of state Confucianism, by Yuan Shikai, the President of the Republic himself in 1915 and by the general Zhang Xun in 1917, which did its credibility immense damage. By the 1920s, Confucian loyalists saw how far the young generation of activists had turned the iconoclastic May Fourth Movement into an effective political weapon against all tradition. By that time, it was too late for state Confucianism in any form. In despair, some Confucian scholars withdrew from public life, a few committed suicide, and many of the remainder retreated to their classrooms and studies to re-examine the roots of Confucian thought in the light of the Western philosophical challenge (Alitto, 1978). Those who adapted their Confucianism to enable them to join the Guomindang as *the* Nationalist Party, and those who set aside their Confucian backgrounds to support various rival parties, including the rising Communist Party, found that the fundamental ideas that had sustained 20 centuries of imperial China had become at best marginal and often totally irrelevant.

But, for almost 30 years, there were many who dreamed of a potential marriage of newfound nationalism with at least one of two kinds of Confucianism. One of them emphasized the return to the purity of the original classics which had demonstrated their universal value by the way they had converted conquerors, neighbors and barbarians alike for over

2,000 years. Kang Youwei and many of his contemporaries had anticipated this to some extent by highlighting the sage–prophet-cum-religious teacher qualities of Confucius. Although the Confucians who held this view did not always agree about the significance and the correct interpretation of the classics, there were echoes among them of something like the Lutheran–Calvinist reaction in Europe against the Catholic Church and the accretions of interpretations through the centuries, which had distorted the original meanings of the surviving texts. This returning to the pristine original texts in order to cleanse the national soul was similar to the Reformation ideal and, in that way, was one of the stronger manifestations of modern nationalism.

The other kind of Confucianism comes closer to the other European phenomenon, the achievements of the Counter-Reformation "defenders of the Faith." The Confucians who supported this approach were those who believed in the continuities of the Great Tradition. Such defenders were not necessarily conservative. Most of them would point to the adaptability of the great Confucians throughout history. These Confucians were great precisely because they were able to revive Confucianism each time after it had been seriously challenged, after its defects and weaknesses had been shown up by new ideas, especially if a new world view had come from outside, like Buddhism, Islam, Christianity, and other religions.

Some nationalists like Zhang Binglin and his friends and students, including the best of those from the National Essence (*Guocui*) School, had ambitions to restore the sense of continuous development that proved the resilience and viability of the Confucian heritage. The young Liang Souming was the most outstanding of those who believed that the best was yet to come when history would show that much Western modernism was really transient and could never compete with the thought formations achieved by later Confucian philosophers (Liang, 1922). More stubborn were those who taught the classics and philosophy in the colleges and universities who not only dug deep within the Tradition but also stretched themselves to master various schools of Western philosophy in order to show that there was much that was perennial and universal in Confucianism. Feng You Ian would represent the first generation of such scholars and was perhaps the most successful in the face of determined attacks on Confucianism by the radical youth in most of the political parties.

Some of the followers of Sun Yat-sen and loyal supporters of the Guomindang had come from strict Confucian backgrounds but were more open to new ideas from the West, notably Cai Yuanpei, Wu Zhihui, and Wu Yuzhang (Cai, 1927 and 1967; Wu, 1949; Wu, 1964) who had direct experience of nationalism in Europe, and Yu Youren, Hu Hanmin, and Zhu Zhixin (Hu, 1959; Yu, 1953; Zhu, 1927) whose introduction to nationalist journalism had come from years in Japan. Their own Confucian credentials were impeccable, but they were aware that young Guomindang party members questioned the value of Confucianism for the future. They rarely spoke publicly on the subject other than to confirm that Confucianism was part of the heritage that nationalists would expect to preserve. Already it was clear by the end of the 1920s that those who openly advocated the return to Confucian values would not have got very far with most of their young followers.

The point is that, up till the establishment of the Guomindang government in Nanjing, nationalists in general were not hostile to Confucianism. They tended to take it for granted that Confucianism was one of the main markers of Chinese-ness, whether asserted as such or not. What then disturbed this passive relationship during the next decade?

Most historical studies show that the rift began with the May Fourth Movement following the calls for democracy and science that were closely linked with the slogan, "Down with the Confucius shop," or "Down with Confucius and Sons" (Chow, 1963). But soon afterward, the Guomindang was reorganized and revived by Sun Yat-sen with the help of Soviet advisers. It reached the peak of its power in 1927 when the party led the Northern Expedition to capture the Yangzi valley and establish the Nanjing government. There was no official break with Confucianism. In fact, all the forms were gradually restored and strictly followed. The Kong family members, the direct descendants of Confucius, were given their respected places in the national hierarchy, proper rituals were observed, the national anthem itself embodied verse in the best classical tradition, and the new education goals included the transmission of Confucian values. By 1934, the government launched the New Life Movement to reaffirm its commitment to the Confucian heritage, and remained true to that even after it moved to Taiwan. The combination of nationalism and Confucianism was actually seen by the Guomindang elders as the great bulwark against communism and this official view of its political and educational value continued to receive international support until well into the 1950s (Eastman, 1974; Shieh, 1970).

The May Fourth Movement brought forth a generation of intellectuals, teachers, and students who challenged that heritage. They combined to undermine what they considered the blind acceptance of the Confucian dominance in Chinese history. The Chinese Communist Party, in the name of progress and national salvation, encouraged the young to reject what they considered to have been the main cause of China's defeats and humiliations by the West. However, the fact remains that these were minority views held mostly in the modern cities, especially Shanghai and other Treaty Ports. Doubting Confucius was not a popular position for anyone to take among the bulk of the population in the countryside (Duara, 1988). I suggest that the failure of Confucianism to make a greater impact on modern nationalist China should be found elsewhere.

Two factors are the most likely in creating the conditions for Confucianism's eclipse. These are, first, the ambiguous use of the idea of *geming* as revolution and, second, the failure of the Nanjing government to deliver its promises to the people. Let me explain.

Geming is an ancient word used in modern times to translate the Western concept of revolution. It really was an ingenious choice for that translation, for it originally conveyed the idea of seizing the Mandate of Heaven from an imperial house that deserved to be replaced (Wang, 1993b). Sun Yat-sen was very pleased to be called such a revolutionary, *geming zhe*, when he became an international figure in 1895. He was the rebel with a price on his head who threatened to bring down the Manchus and the Qing dynasty. Therefore, when *minzu* came into use a few years later, he saw no difficulty in combining it with *geming* to make *minzu geming* or sometimes *guomin geming*, the national revolution. This became significant when he metamorphosed as the major nationalist leader after 1911. He began to see the sorry state of republican China as something that could only be rescued from degeneracy by a real revolution in its economic and political structures.

With the emphasis shifted to revolution as the only way to save China, it opened his Nationalist Party to the communists and other radical allies who supported the cause of social and cultural revolution as well. In this way, the iconoclasts of the May Fourth generation were allowed to seek more radical changes within the Party in the name of saving the country from decline. In this way, *geming* as modeled on the French, American, and Russian revolutions became the driving ideal, something well beyond that of changing a dynasty.

Thus, the historic role of Confucianism as the pillar of imperial China became out of place. The new *geming* as revolution, unlike mere nationalism, was about the processes of transformation. It had little time for the finer points of past glories, even the secret of Confucian successes at all levels of Chinese society. It was quickly accepted that modern alternatives like state capitalism, or national socialism or international (Soviet) communism would have more answers for China. In the service of revolution, Confucianism was at best marginal.

The second factor, the failure to deliver, reinforced the first. The Nationalist government, which still supported the vestiges of Confucianism, failed to unify the country, failed to resist Japan, China's most dangerous enemy, and failed to bring public order and guarantee the basics of the people's livelihood (Bedeski, 1981; Eastman, 1974). There were many reasons for this, and it was certainly not entirely the fault of the nationalist leaders. There were some successes in regaining national prestige and independence; and there were external forces beyond the powers of the Nanjing government to control. Confucianism was not to blame for any of the failures. On the other hand, the advocates of Confucian values could not show what part Confucianism played in the successes and whether it had any part in preventing the failures. From that point, its irrelevance amounted to a declaration that it was of no use to a modernizing state.

There was no time to weigh all the factors and give Confucianism a judicious hearing before the Sino–Japanese War of 1937–1945, even less during the civil war which the Nanjing government lost and its leaders retreated to Taiwan. The detractors of Confucianism had expected its demise and were now confirmed that they had been right all along. They all believed as good nationalists that a revolution was needed to save China, and that a revolution did not need Confucianism. Some would go further and say that Confucianism, by extolling the past and seeking continuity with it, was reactionary and actually an obstacle to revolutionary change. To them, Confucianism represented all that was feudalistic, backward, and unprogressive for the Chinese people. The victory of the

Chinese Communist Party in 1949 endorsed the supremacy of revolution as the most effective way to defeat imperialism and achieve national unity, to restore independence and national pride, and to reconstruct all that the earlier nationalists had promised but failed to do. As a result, in their eyes, revolution was the answer to national salvation and, therefore, the truer and greater nationalism. Thus it was never necessary to appeal to nationalism during the years of Mao Zedong, from 1949 to his death in 1976 (Mao, 1977).

Strenuous efforts were made after 1957, when the Great Leap Forward was launched, to eliminate all "feudal" ideas. During the Cultural Revolution decade, 1966–1976, the aim had become to bury Confucianism, and the methods used remind us of Qin Shi Huangdi's decision to bury Confucians more than 2000 years ago (Yan and Gao, 1986).

My next question takes us to the present. Some obvious features of nationalism have now appeared under the name of patriotism and the calls for this are loud and clear (Barme, 1996; Hu, 1995; Whiting, 1995). There is little doubt that this is happening because internationalism and revolutionary ideology no longer appeal to most Chinese. There is at the same time considerable discussion about reviving Confucianism. Does this mean that nationalism is now the message, and Confucianism is being used as one of the means to give that nationalism moral weightage and make it respectable? From what I said earlier on in the talk, it would seem on the surface that the present position is a retreat to the position during the first decades of nationalism, the years 1895–1925. You will recall that this was the time when Confucianism had a chance to prove its adaptability to modernity but had failed to impress the young political activists. If such an analogy could be made, has a second chance come for Confucianism to be a partner of nationalism again?

The fact that the great era of revolution is over is important. Without a revolutionary burden, nationalist appeals to the glorious past become legitimate. The vital role that Confucianism played in the past would mean that it would have a respectable place as long as nationalism roots itself in that past (Chou, 1996). But it is far from clear that this will be so. The main thrust of Deng Xiaoping's economic reforms and the nationalism that has generated is progressive (Shirk, 1993; Tsou, 1986). The models the Chinese have used are mainly modified from those of the developed nations of the

West and of Eastern Asia, notably Japan and the Four Dragons. If continuities are sought, Jiang Zemin appears to be seeking them from the Party's original ideals and practices of Spartan self-sacrifice for a strong China. A concrete example of their new nationalism is the political goal of reunification, the restoration of Taiwan within China's historical borders (*Nineties*, Nov. 1996; Wang, 1996).

The only appeals to Confucianism have come in two ways, both indirect. One comes from the remarkable economic performance of Chinese outside the People's Republic of China, especially those in Taiwan, Hong Kong, and Singapore. Many scholars, both Chinese and non-Chinese, have attributed these successes to the presence of Confucian qualities expressed through kinship structures, educational ideals and practices, and entrepreneurial initiatives (Berger and Hsiao, 1988; Redding, 1990). It is not clear from official pronouncements how much the present Beijing leadership subscribes to this view, although there have been several conferences held in China on Confucius and Confucianism with the government's encouragement. Down in the provinces and townships, however, where reviving traditional practices is less inhibited, there is considerable evidence that local officials give credence to the importance of certain Confucian concepts as spurs to entrepreneurship. The Confucian classics have been reprinted with modern translations and annotations. Lectures, seminars, and symposiums on a whole range of philosophical and historical texts have been organized regularly. Under a strongly utilitarian banner, Confucian values are being sifted for the help they can give to modern needs (Liang, 1995; *Nineties*, Nov. 1996; Xiao, 1996).

At another and deeper level, there are intellectual concerns about the moral supports of the new socialist market economy. Without the revolutionary ideals which guided earlier generations of cadres, what can be done to save China from becoming an increasingly money-grubbing society? After years of Confucius-bashing within the Communist Party, there is little readiness to turn to Confucianism for help. But the growing nationalism that pervades the country rejects the idea of dependence on foreign value-systems (Barme, 1996; Song *et al.*, 1996). And the stronger the nationalism, the greater the urge to look within the Chinese tradition for the new moral order to fill the vacuum the cultural leaders see around them. Thus, the new nationalism leads indirectly back to those forces in history which had moulded the Chinese nation, and nothing qualifies better among those forces for respect and attention than Confucianism. Thus if nationalism is the message, Confucianism can give it moral weightage and make it respectable.

This leads us to the third question. Now that Confucianism has been given a second chance by a revival of nationalism, will it succeed? Is there a new Confucianism that can support modern nationalism?

The debates over the new Confucians during the past decade have been invigorating and have been conducted in Taiwan, the People's Republic of China, and Hong Kong at several levels. At the highest philosophical level, there has been renewed admiration for the early writings of Liang Souming and Feng Youlan, and a reassessment of the achievements of scholars like Xiong Shili, Tang Junyi, Mou Zongsan, and Qian Mu (Lo et al., 1989). There has also been great interest in the Marxist philosopher Li Zehou and his remarkable reinterpretation of Chinese traditional thought. Outside the China region, historians of ideas like Yu Ying-shih and Tu Wei-ming have sought to place these scholars in perspective.

At this level, Confucian philosophy is its own master. It does not and cannot serve as the partner of nationalism. The formula of "Cultural China" proposed by Tu Wei-ming has been particularly effective in drawing attention to the autonomy of Confucian thought, stressing its greater persuasiveness and power when it is not linked with Chinese national needs. They remind us that Chinese individuals who are settled outside China, and who are non-Chinese nationals, can be Confucians without being nationalist patriots. And non-Chinese, who would not be associated in any way with Chinese nationalism, could choose, if they want to, to be Confucians (Tu, 1991).

At the next level, the discussions are more down-to-earth. New Confucianism can help to build a new sense of identity among the Chinese, thus contributing to the reunification not merely of territory, but also of the hearts and souls of the people of Taiwan and Hong Kong with those of their compatriots on the Mainland. There is a likelihood that the slogan of "Cultural China" would separate Confucian values from political issues of nationality and patriotism. This would make it easier for Confucianism to be co-opted to serve a utilitarian purpose and produce, however indirectly, a sense of cultural unity to support nationalist aspirations. And there is also the practical matter of a rejuvenated Confucianism assisting the People's Republic of China in reproducing the qualities of hard work, loyalty, discipline, concern for family, mental toughness, and trustworthiness that the country needs for an orderly and prosperous society.

At yet another level, it is more direct and obvious. I have already mentioned the successes of the Chinese outside the People's Republic of China. The wooing of the Chinese of this "external China," the Chinese of the periphery, whether for their investments, their tourism, or their ultimate ethnic identification, is conducted with much reference to kinship ties, local village loyalties, language and dialect or provincial origins, myths, legends, archaeological and historical sites, and other sentimental appeals. None of these actions could be described as Confucian or peculiarly Chinese, but there is no mistaking the Confucian tone of the many quotes and texts used to support these appeals. Popular writings in magazines and the press; films, plays, operas, and dance performances; talks and panel discussions in the electronic media; new school textbooks, including a host of new versions of the *San Zijing* (Three-Character Classics), all help to convey a growing revivalist spirit. Furthermore, there have been connections made outside China between economic success and Confucian values. These connections have been widely appreciated in China among the small but active middle class in the cities and townships. There will, therefore, be more comparisons with the lifestyles of the Chinese elsewhere and their links, however indirect, with Confucianism.

However, the interactions would also create much ambivalence, for most Chinese now living as nationals of foreign polities are likely to display many contradictory characteristics. These Chinese overseas have absorbed many foreign values, both from their countries of residence and from their contacts with the West (Wang, 1991b). While Confucianism may have some value for them on a personal level, it will be difficult for them to think of it in connection with any kind of nationalism. There will not be any clear examples of Confucianism complementing nationalism out there among the Chinese overseas.

Let us return to the first overarching question: now that nationalism has returned in China and Confucianism has become respectable again, is the contradiction between them over? From the aforementioned, it is believed that it is about to be. The main reason for saying this is that the word revolution has now been displaced by the word patriotism, and here patriotism is a euphemism for nationalism. This is so because the word nationalism still has some negative associations. The excesses of the past, whether during the civil war or the Japanese invasion of China, are still recent enough for many to shy away from the word. It is also a word that could arouse expectations in many of the larger national minorities living on the borders of the People's Republic of China, and therefore a word to be used with great care.

Once patriotism replaces revolution, however, there is no contradiction with Confucianism, which is recognized as the most important body of thought in the formation of the patria (the fatherland). If that remains valid, I can answer the subsidiary question as follows: nationalism can no longer deny its close relationship with the Confucian structure of ideas that had been the bulwark of Chinese nation-building since, at least, the Han dynasty. This may not be enough for the immediate purpose of national modernization which would demand evidence that Confucianism can help the country. The historical record of 20th century China offers no such proof. If the revived nationalism and a new Confucianism are to co-exist and help each other, there would have to be a long view. I shall conclude by offering some thoughts on that long view.

There is no reason to believe that the state Confucianism that supported dozens of dynastic houses will ever be restored to that historical role in a modern state. The needs of an agrarian empire which state Confucianism had served so well for so long are totally incompatible with those of a modern industrial nation. For most Chinese, the distinction is becoming ever clearer: that state or official Confucianism belongs to history, but personal and social Confucianism remains pervasive and deep-rooted among the ordinary people. It is this latter form that is re-emerging as a positive force in efforts to build something akin to a modern civil society after decades of cultural destruction. It is a force that can support patriotic and even national ideals when people are no longer made to feel that the surviving areas of their Confucian heritage are unprogressive, conservative or backward (He, 1995). That role is, in any case, not the future that Confucian thinkers today would want for their ideals. Their claims are that Confucianism contains many ideas and judgments, especially on matters of ethics and social relations, which are universal and not peculiar to China. They could be valid and even useful anywhere else.

Such a position does not contradict nationalism because the Chinese can count themselves lucky to have enjoyed these Confucian values longer than everybody else, and have benefited from the way these ideas had contributed to their distinctive national identity. The future China, therefore, can take advantage of that position to remould a new nationalism with a Confucianism that has been tested by the challenge of Western philosophy and has overcome what has been called its "feudal and mediaeval residues."

The goal of the new Confucians today is to modernize Confucian thought through intensive, comparative, and integrative studies of the secular traditions of the Western Enlightenment. They are confident that, if they can succeed in enhancing Confucian philosophy in this way, it could take its place as one of the major alternatives to the secular humanism of the West. The philosophers earlier this century who tried to show the way, like Feng Youlan and Tang Junyi, have not worked in vain. Younger Confucian scholars today are following them, not only in studying modern Western philosophers like Locke, Descartes, Kant, Mill, Hegel and Marx but also Weber, Durkheim, Popper and Hayek, to name a few (Gu, 1992; Li, 1987; Liu, 1995; Yang, 1994; Yu, 1996). They have brought fresh ideas to enrich their understanding of Confucianism and deepened the hold that Confucian values still have on them. This has nothing to do with nationalism. But should they succeed in breathing yet more new life into the body of ideas that support Chinese civilization, the new Confucianism might well play the role again as a factor in future nation-building for the Chinese people. Once again, it will be morally uplifting and politically unifying and engender the national pride that supports nationalism in a constructive and peaceful way.

In conclusion, it might be said that there is no contradiction between nationalism and Confucianism. For the Chinese, the two have been, and could again be, complementary. But it must be clear, from the outline of this desultory relationship over the past century in China that, while Chinese nationalism could benefit from a deeper understanding of Confucianism, Confucian values do not depend on nationalism or on a nationalist government. In their original form, they have an autonomy which has survived violent attacks by the uncomprehending and also all kinds of governments.

They do not necessarily have to depend on the support of the Chinese. Anyone can become a Confucian by studying the classics. Thus, I would suggest, Confucianism may contribute to nation-formation but it does not need nationalism for its perpetuation.

References

Alitto, Guy (1978). *The Last Confucian: Liang Shu-ming and the Chinese Dilemma of Modernity*. Berkeley: University of California Press.

Anderson, Benedict (1991). *Imagined Communities: Reflections on the Origin and Spread of Nationalism*. Revised edition. London: Verso Editions and New Left Books.

Barme, Geremie R (1996). "To screw foreigners is patriotic: China's Avant-Garde nationalists". In *Chinese Nationalism*, Jonathan Unger (ed.), pp. 1–30. Armonk, NY: M.E.Sharpe.

Barth, Frederick (1969). *Ethnic Groups and Boundaries*. Boston: Little, Brown.

Bedeski, Robert E (1981). *State-Building in Modern China: The Kuomintang in the Prewar Period*. Berkeley: UC Berkeley Center for Chinese Studies.

Beling, Willard A and G.O. Totten (eds.) (1970). *Developing Nations: Quest for a Model*. New York: Van Nostrand Reinhold.

Berger, Peter L. and Michael Hsiao Hsin-huang (eds.), (1988). *In Search of an East Asian Development Model*. New Brunswick, N.J.: Transaction Books.

Breuilly, J. (1982). *Nationalism and the State*. Manchester: Manchester University Press.

Cai, Yuanpei (1927). *Zhongguo lunlixue shi* (*History of Ethical Thought in China*). Shanghai: Commercial Press.

Cai, Yuanpei (1967). *Ts'ai Yuan-p'ei hsuan-chi* (*Selected Works of Cai Yuanpei*). Taipei: Wen-hsing.

Chan, F. Gilbert and T.H. Etzold (1976). *China in the 1920s: Nationalism and Revolution*. New York: New Viewpoints.

Chang, Chih-tung (1900). *China's Only Hope* (*An Exhortation to Learning*) [Transl. by SI Woodbridge] New York: F.H. Revell.

Chang, Hao (1987). *Chinese Intellectuals in Crisis: Search for Order and Meaning, 1890–1911*. Berkeley: University of California Press.

Chatterjee, Partha (1986). *Nationalist Thought and the Colonial World: A Derivative Discourse?* London: Zed Books.

Chatterjee, Partha (1993). *The Nation and its Fragments*. Princeton: Princeton University Press.

Chen, Mingming (1996). "Zhengzhi fazhan shijiao zhongdi Minzu yu Minzu zhuyi". *Zhanlue yu Guanli (Strategy and Management)*, 15, 63–71.

Ch'ien, Mu (1956). *Zhongguo Lidai Zhengzhi Deshi (Political Success and Failure in Chinese History)*. Hong Kong: Hsin-hua.

Ch'ien, Mu (1979). *Cong Zhongguo Lishi Laikan Zhongguo Minzu Jiqi Zhongguo Wenhua. (The Chinese Nation and Chinese Culture as Seen from Chinese History)*. Hong Kong: The Chinese University of Hong Kong Press.

Chou, Yu-Sun (1996). "Nationalism and patriotism in China". *Issues and Studies*, 32(11), November.

Chow, Tse-Tsung (1963). *The May Fourth Movement: Intellectual Revolution in Modern China*. Cambridge, MA: Harvard University Press.

Chuang, Chia-Hsuan (1929). *How to Make Education in China Chinafied*. Shanghai: Min Chi.

Connor, Walker (1972). "Nation-building or nation-destroying?" *World Politics*, XXIV, 319–355.

Connor, Walker (1978). "A nation is a nation, is a state, is an ethnic group, is a ...." *Ethnic and Racial Studies*, 1(4), 378–400.

Connor, Walker (1987). "Ethnonationalism." In *Understanding Political Development*, M Weiner and S Huntington (eds.), pp. 196–220. Boston: Little, Brown.

Connor, Walker (1994). *Ethnonationalism: The Quest for Understanding*. Princeton: Princeton University Press.

De Bary, Wm. Theodore (1988). *East Asian Civilizations: A Dialogue in Five Stages*. Cambridge, MA: Harvard University Press.

Deng, Xiaoping (1983). *Deng Xiaoping Wenxuan (1975–1982). (Selected Works)*. Beijing: Renmin.

Deutsch, Karl W (1953). *Nationalism and Social Communication*. Cambridge, MA: M.I.T. Press.

Dreyer, JT (1976). *China's Forty Millions*. Cambridge, MA: Harvard University Press.

Duara, Prasenjit (1988). *Culture, Power, and the State: Rural North China, 1900–1942*. Stanford: Stanford University Press.

Duara, Prasenjit (1993). "De-constructing the Chinese nation". *Australian Journal of Chinese Affairs*, 30, 1–26.

Eastman, Lloyd E. (1974). *The Abortive Revolution: China under Nationalist Rule, 1927–1937.* Cambridge, MA: Harvard University Press.

Eber, Irene (ed.) (1986). *Confucianism: Dynamics of Tradition.* New York: Macmillan.

Elvin, M (1990). "The collapse of scriptural Confucianism". *Papers on Far Eastern History*, 41, 45–76.

Emerson, Rupert (1960). *From Empire to Nation.* Cambridge, MA: Harvard University Press.

Fang, Keli (ed.) (1989) *Xiandai xinruxue yanju lunji.* Beijing: Chinese Social Science Publishing Co.

Fitzgerald, John (1996). *Awakening China: Politics, Culture, and Class in the Nationalist Revolution.* Stanford: Stanford University Press.

Gellner, Ernest (1964). *Nations and Nationalism.* Oxford: Blackwell.

Greenfeld, Liah (1992). *Nationalism: Five Roads to Modernity.* Cambridge, MA: Harvard University Press.

Gu, Xin (1992). *Zhongguo Qimeng di Lishi Tujing: Wusi Fansi yu Dangdai Zhongguodi Yishixingtai Zhi Zheng* (*The Historical Image and Prospects of the Chinese Enlightenment*). Hong Kong: Oxford University Press.

Guibernau, Montserrat (1996). *Nationalisms: The Nation-State and Nationalism in the Twentieth Century.* Cambridge: Polity Press.

Hardacre, Helen (1989). *Shinto and the State, 1868–1988.* Princeton: Princeton University Press.

Hayes, Carleton JH (1949). *The Historical Evolution of Modern Nationalism.* New York: Macmillan.

He, Baogang (1995). "The ideas of civil society in Mainland China and Taiwan, 1986–1992". *Issues and Studies*, 31(6), 24–64.

Heberer, Thomas (1989). *China and its National Minorities: Autonomy or Assimilation?* Armonk, NY: M.E. Sharpe.

Hobsbawm, E (1990). *Nations and Nationalism since 1870.* Cambridge: Cambridge University Press.

Hobsbawm, E and T Ranger (eds.) (1983). *The Invention of Tradition.* Cambridge: Cambridge University Press.

Hoiton, G. A (1994). *The State, Identity, and the National Question in China and Japan.* Princeton: Princeton University Press.

Hsiao, Kung-Chuan (1975). *A Modern China and a New World: Kang Yu-wei, Reformer and Utopian, 1858–1927.* Seattle: University of Washington Press.

Hu, Guoheng [Henry K.H. Woo] (1995). *Dugong Nanshan Shou Zhongguo*. (*In Defence of China*). Hong Kong: The Chinese University of Hong Kong Press.
Hu, Hanmin. (1959) *Selected Works*. Taipei: Pamir Books.
Kamenka, Eugene (ed.) (1973, 1976). *Nationalism, the Nature and Evolution of an Idea*. London: Arnold.
Kedourie, E (1960). *Nationalism*, 4th expanded Ed. (1993). Oxford: Basil Blackwell.
Kedourie, E (1971). *Nationalism in Asia and Africa*. London: Weidenfeld & Nicolson.
Kohn, Hans (1955). *Nationalism, its Meaning and History*. Princeton: Van Nostrand.
Laitinen, Kauko (1990). *Chinese Nationalism in the Late Qing Dynasty: Zhang Binglin as an Anti-Manchu Propagandist*. London: Curzon Press.
Levenson, Joseph R (1968). *Confucian China and its Modern Fate: A Trilogy*. Berkeley: University of California Press.
Li, Zehou (1987). *Zhongguo Xiandai Sixiang Shi Lun*. (*History of Contemporary Chinese Thought*) Beijing: Dongfang.
Liang, Souming (1922, 1968). *Dongxi Wenhuajiqi Zhexue* (*Eastern and Western Civilizations and their Philosophies*). Taipei: Hung-ch'iao shu-tien.
Liang, Xiaosheng (1995). *Suishi Choulou di Zhongguoren Jiusan Duanxiang* (*Who is the Ugly Chinese?*). Hong Kong: Cosmos Books.
Lin, Yu-Sheng (1979). *The Crisis of Consciousness: Radical Antitraditionalism in the May Fourth Era*. Madison: The University of Wisconsin Press.
Liu, Shuxian (1995). "Duiyu dangdai xinjuxue di chaoyue neisheng" (On the transcendental self of the new Confucians today). *Zhongguo wenhua*, 12, 33–59.
Lo, Yijun *et al.* (1989). *Ping xinrujia*. (*On the New Confucians*). Shanghai: Renmin.
Mackerras, Colin (1994). *China's Minorities: Integration and Modernization in the Twentieth Century*. Hong Kong: Oxford University Press.
MacNair, Harley. F (1925). *The Chinese Abroad*. Shanghai: Commercial Press.
McNeill, William (1986). *Polyethnicity and National Unity in World History*. Toronto: Toronto University Press.
Mao, Zedong (1964). *Mao Zedong Xuanji* (*Heding Yijuanben*) (*Selected Works*). Beijing: Renmin.
Mao, Zedong (1977). *Mao Zedong Xuanji*, Vol. 5 (*Selected Works*). Beijing: Renmin.
Metzger, Thomas A (1996). *"Transcending the West": Mao's Vision of Socialism and the Legitmization of Teng Hsiao-p'ing's Modernization Program*. Hoover Essays No. 15. Stanford: Hoover Institution.

Metzger, Thomas A (1977). *Escape from Predicament: Neo-Confucianism and China's Evolving Political Culture.* New York: Columbia University Press.

Nineties, The (Jiushi niandai) (November 1996) Hong Kong. Essays by He Li, Yu Jiwen, Yu Ying-Shih (Interview); Cheng Ying, Yin Huimin, Zhu Gaozheng. pp. 58–80.

Pi Mingyong (1996). Minzu zhuyi yu Rujia wenhua cong Liang Qichao di minzu zhuyi lilun jiqi kunjing tanqi (Nationalism and Confucian culture). *Zhanlue yu Guanli (Strategy and Management),* 15, 51–57.

Redding, Gordon (1990). *The Spirit of Chinese Capitalism.* Berlin: de Gruyter.

Report of the National Education Congress (1928). Nanking: National Academy (Ta Hsuen Yuan).

Rustow, Dankworth (1967). *A World of Nations.* Washington D.C.: Brookings Institution.

Schwarcz, Vera (1986). *The Chinese Enlightenment: Intellectuals and the Legacy of the May Fourth Movement.* Berkeley, CA: University of California Press.

Seton-Watson, Hugh (1977). *Nations and States: An Inquiry into the Origins of Nations and the Politics of Nationalism.* London: Methuen.

Shafer, Boyd C (1955). *Nationalism: Myth and Reality.* New York: Harcourt, Brace and World.

Shieh, Milton JT (Jan-tze) (1970). *The Kuomintang: Selected Historical Documents,* 1894–1969. New York: St John's University Press.

Shirk, Susan L (1993). *The Political Logic of Economic Reform* in *China.* Berkeley: University of California Press.

Sih, Paul KT (1976, 1970). *The Strenuous Decade: China's Nation-Building, Efforts,* 1927–1937. New York: St John's University Press.

Smith, AD (1971, 1983). *Theories of Nationalism.* London: Duckworth. 1995. *Nations and Nationalism* in *a Global Era.* Cambridge: Polity Press.

Snyder, Louis (1954). *The Meaning of Nationalism.* New Brunswick: Rutgers University Press.

Song, Qiang *et al.* (1996). *Zhongguo Keyi Shuobu Lengzhan Houqidi Zhengzhi Yu Qingganjueze. (China Can Say No!).* Beijing: Zhonghua gonshang lianhe.

Stalin, J.V (1974). *Marxism and the National Question. Works,* Vol. 2. Calcutta: Gana-Sahitya Prakash, pp. 194–215.

Sun, Yat-Sen (1981). *Sun Chung-shan Quanji (Complete Works).* Beijing: Zhonghua.

Sun, Yat-Sen (1927). *San Min Chu I (The Three Principles of the People).* [Transl. by FW Price] Shanghai: Institute of Pacific Relations.

Thierry, Francois (1989). "Empire and minority in China". In *Minority Peoples in the Age of Nation-States*, G Chaliand (ed.). London: Pluto Press.

Tien, Hung-Mao (1972). *Government and Politics in Kuomintang China, 1927–1937*. Stanford: Stanford University Press.

Tilly, Charles (ed.) (1975). *The Formation of National States in Western Europe*. Princeton: Princeton University Press.

Townsend, James (1996). "Chinese nationalism". In *Chinese Nationalism*, Jonathan Unger (ed.). Armonk, NY: M.E. Sharpe.

Tsang, Chiu-Sam (1967, 1933). *Nationalism in School Education in China*. Hong Kong: Progressive Education Publishers.

Tsou, Tang (1986). "Political change and reform: The middle course". In *The Cultural Revolution and Post-Mao Reforms: A Historical Perspective*, Tang Tsou. Chicago: The University of Chicago Press.

Tu, Wei-ming (1991). "Cultural China: The periphery as the center". *Daedalus*, Spring, reprinted in Tu Wei-ming (ed.), *The Living Tree: The Changing Meaning of Being Chinese Today*. Stanford: Stanford University Press, pp. 1–34.

Unger, Jonathan (ed.) (1996). *Chinese Nationalism*. New York: M.E. Sharpe.

Wang, Gungwu (1991a). *China and the Chinese Overseas*. Singapore: Times Academic Press.

Wang, Gungwu (1991b). "Among non-Chinese". *Daedalus*, Spring, reprinted in Tu Wei-ming (ed.), *The Living Tree: The Changing Meaning of Being Chinese Today*. Stanford: Stanford University Press, pp. 127–146.

Wang, Gungwu (1992). *Community and Nation: China, Southeast Asia and Australia*. St. Leonard's, NSW: Allen & Unwin.

Wang, Gungwu (1993a). "Greater China and the Chinese overseas". *The China Quarterly*, London, 136, 44–66.

Wang, Gungwu (1993b). "To reform a revolution: Under the righteous mandate". *Daedalus*, Spring, and in Tu Wei-ming (ed.), *China in Transformation*. Cambridge, MA: Harvard University Press, pp. 71–94.

Wang, Gungwu (1995). *The Chinese Way: China's Position in International Relations* (Nobel Institute Lectures 1995). Oslo: Scandinavian University Press.

Wang, Gungwu (1996). *The Revival of Chinese Nationalism*. (International Institute of Asian Studies Annual Lecture, Amsterdam). Leiden: LIAS.

Whiting, Allen S (1995). Chinese nationalism and foreign policy after Deng. *China Quarterly*, 142, 295–316.

Wong, Young-Tsu (1989). *Search for Modern Nationalism: Zhang Binglin and Revolutionary China*, 1869–1936. Hong Kong: Oxford University Press.

Wu, Yuzhang (1949). *Zhongguo Lishi Jiaocheng Xulun*. (*Introduction to the Teaching of Chinese History*). Beijing: Xinhua.

Wu, Zhihui (1964). *Wu Zhihui Xiansheng Xuanji*. (*Selected Works*). Taipei: Kuomintang chung-yang.

Xiao, Gongqin (1996). "Zhongguo minzu zhuyi di lishi yu qianjing". *Zhanlue yu Guanli* (*Strategy and Management*), 15, 58–62.

Yan, Jiaqi and Gao Gao (1986). *Zhongguo "wenge" shinianshi*. (*A History of the Ten Years of the "Cultural Revolution"*). Two volumes. Hong Kong: Dagong Baoshe.

Yan, Jiaqi and Gao, Gao (1996). *Turbulent Decade: A History of the Cultural Revolution*. DWY Kwok (Transl. and ed.). Honolulu: University of Hawaii Press.

Yang, Guorong (1994). *Shan di licheng: Rujiajiazhitixidi lishi yanhuajiqi xiandai zhuanbian*. (*The Evolution of the Confucian Value System and its Contemporary Transformation*). Shanghai: Renmin.

Yu, Youren. (1953) *Wo de qingnian shiqi* (My Youth Period). Taipei: Zheng Chung Books.

Yu, Ying-Shih (1996). *Xiandai Ruxue Lun*. (*On the New Confucians*). River Edge, NJ: Global Publishing.

Zhu, Zhixin (Chu Chih-hsin) (1927). *Chu Chih-hsin Wen-ch'ao*. Compiled by Yuanzhong Zhao. Shanghai: Min Chih.

DID CONFUCIANISM HINDER THE DEVELOPMENT OF SCIENCE IN CHINA?*

HO PENG YOKE

Needham Research Institute, Cambridge, UK

3.1. Introduction

The two key words in the title of this chapter are "Confucianism" and "science." As their coverage is too wide, I need to set a boundary so as not to lose my way. The word "Confucianism" immediately brings to mind the ancient Chinese philosopher-educator Kong Qiu (孔丘) (551–479 BC), respectfully referred to by the Chinese people as Kong fuzi (孔夫子) and acknowledged by them as their greatest sage. Confucianism means the many schools of teaching based on his philosophical thoughts. I would rather confine to the meaning of the Chinese term "rujia (儒家)" than that of the English term which has some religious nuance. I would also like to take the late 16th century just before the coming of the Jesuit Mitten Ricci (1552–1610) to China and the beginning of the Scientific Revolution in Europe as the lower time limit of the topic of this chapter. Hence by science, it is referred to the science prior to the Scientific Revolution in Europe. In this way I can speak freely about science in traditional China before European influence was felt. Science in Europe ultimately led to the Scientific Revolution in the 17th century, but there never was a Scientific Revolution in traditional China. Was Confucianism the stumbling block? This issue is addressed in this chapter.

---

* This chapter is a reproduction of the Wu Teh Yao memorial lecture given by the author in 1997.

3.2. Confucius versus Science

In the May Fourth Movement in 1919, science and democracy were acclaimed as the two pillars upon which the salvation of China must rest, while Confucius was blamed for most of the things that hindered progress. During the so-called Cultural Revolution in China during the late 1960s to the early 1970s, Confucius came again under attack. He was regarded as the culprit who retarded the development of science in China. Let us examine the criticisms made against him on that score.

It can be demonstrated that some of the criticisms came from those who had little knowledge of the history of science itself. For example, Confucius has been criticized for talking about natural phenomena and politico-ethics at the same time instead of dealing with science for its own sake, thus hindering the progress of science in China. However no account was taken of the fact that Socrates (470–399 BC) and Plato (427–347 BC), who flourished about a century after Confucius also linked natural philosophy with ethics and education, had not prevented the development of science in Europe into modern science.

Other charges against Confucius have been shown to be either misinterpretation of the text or quotations out of context from the *Lunyu* (论语), hereafter known by its English title *Confucian Analects* after James Legge.[1] Some examples are given below.

Some accused Confucius for being anti-science and anti-agriculture, if not ignorant of these subjects, while citing the following quotation from the *Confucian Analects* as supporting evidence:

> Fan Chi 樊迟 requested to be taught the art of farming. The Master said, "I am not as good as an old farmer." When requested to be taught the art of gardening, he said, "I am not as good as an old gardener". After Fan Chi left the Master said, "What a person of the common-herd (Fan) Xu 须 (i.e., Fan Chi) (intends) to be!" When the ruler loves propriety, his people will not dare to be irreverent. If he loves righteousness, his people will not dare to disobey. If he loves to be trustworthy, his people will not dare to be insincere. This being so people from the four quarters will flock to him bearing their children on their backs. What need is there for him to be learning the art of farming?
>
> *Confucian Analects*, XIII Zi Lu (子路)[2]

A recent study by Bo Shuren (薄树人) suggests that if Confucius had been unaware of the art of farming and horticulture, his disciple Fan Chi would not have asked him about these techniques and that the important objective of Confucius was to teach his disciples to be good civil servants and to assist the ruler to govern with propriety, righteousness, and trustworthiness. Confucius would rather leave the teaching of farming and gardening to the more experienced professionals. To substantiate his statement that Confucius was knowledgeable in many techniques of the common people, Fin Shuren quotes the following passage from the *Confucian Analects*[3]:

> A high-ranking officer questioned Zi Gong 子贡 saying, "Isn't your master a sage? How rich and various is his ability!" Zi Gong replied, "Heaven has boundlessly endowed him to become a sage, and moreover, he also possesses a range of abilities". When the Master heard about the conversation he remarked, "Did that high-ranking officer know about me? When I was young I was of humble social status and I have acquired a range of abilities from the common folk. Does a junzi 君子 need to have such a range of abilities? No, a range of abilities is not a requirement for him. "According to Lao 牢 (i.e., the disciple Zi Zhang 子张 the Master said, "Having no official appointment (when I was young) I therefore acquired a range of various abilities."
>
> *Confucian Analects* Zi ban (子罕)[4]

Besides showing the wide range of knowledge Confucius possessed, the above passage also indicates that Confucius never showed any disdain for the arts of the common people. In fact, Confucius did attach importance to agriculture as illustrated by the following two passages:

> The Master said, "To rule a country of a thousand chariots, matters should be reverently attended to with trust, economy should be exercised in expenditure, love should be extended to all subjects, who must not be called from their husbandry at improper seasons (for military service and public works)." (*Confucian Analects* I, Xue er 学而)[5] and Nangong Kuo 南宫适 asked (the Master's comments) saying, "Yi 羿 was skilful in archery while Ao, could drag a boat ashore, but neither of them died a natural death. Yu 禹 and Ji 稷 engaged themselves in the toils of husbandry and (eventually) possessed a kingdom." The Master made no

reply, but after Nangong Kuo left he said, "A junzi indeed is such a person! An esteemer of virtue indeed is such a person."

Confucian Analects XIV, Xian Wen (宪问)

One of the sentences in the *Confucian Analects* that had been misinterpreted consists of only the four characters "jun zi bu qi (君子不器)" (II, Wei zheng 为政). Read as "The junzi does not use instrument," it was quoted by some to criticize Confucius for looking down upon the artisan. James Legge renders this sentence more correctly as "An accomplished scholar is not a utensil," meaning that he is not to be used as a tool. We can find many examples to support this interpretation, such as the following two quotations showing that Confucius was aware of the importance of the artisan and his tools.

The first quotation comes from the *Confucian Analects* (XV, Wei 卫灵公): "The Master said, 'An artisan wishing to do his work well must first sharpen his tools'."[8] The second comes from the Zhongyong 中庸 (*Doctrine of the Mean* Doctrine of the Mean XX, Aigong Wenzheng 哀公问政. It quotes Confucius: "By encouraging all classes of artisans to come, his (i.e. the king's) resources for expenditure are rendered ample." According to Confucius this was one of the nine standard rules to be followed for good government, namely to give encouragement to all classes of artisans in order to bring about a healthy state of economy.[9]

Even the great Joseph Needham (1900–1995) has made a rather unfavorable comment on Confucius. In his monumental work *Science and Civilisation in China*, Vol. 2, he picks up a sentence consisting of only seven characters — Zi bu yu guai li luan shen, 子不语怪力乱神 — from the *Confucian Analects* (II, Shuer 述而), which James Legge renders as, "The subjects which the Master did not talk were — extraordinary things, feats of strength, disorder and spiritual things." Needham interprets the word "li, 力" as "phenomena of extraordinary force in nature."[10] Pointing out the importance of extraordinary phenomena in the understanding of nature, he says that Confucius did not wish to discuss those natural phenomena in nature which seemingly had no connection with social problems, and Confucian scholars in the next 2000 years followed his example to the disappointment of the Taoists and the technicians. It has been shown recently by Xi Zezong (席泽宗) that interpreting "li" as extraordinary phenomena in nature is incorrect, because Confucius himself did have an interest in natural phenomena.[11] This can be proved by *the Spring-and-Autumn Annals* (Chunqiu, 春秋) in which Confucius dutifully recorded no less than 37 solar eclipses. It is also quite remarkable that Confucius did not link these natural phenomena with prognostications, contrary to the practice adopted by historians after him, and, as we know, these historians were Confucian scholars. For this Confucius received a few good words even from Lu Xun (鲁迅), one of the major figures in the May Fourth Movement.[12]

Some critics said that Confucius paid little attention to dialogues when compared to Socrates (470–399 BC) and Plato (427–347 BC) and thus hindered the development of science. They cited the following passage from the *Confucian Analects*:

The Master said, "I have talked with Hui 回 the whole day, and he has not made any objection to anything I said, as if he was stupid. After he left I observed his personal conduct and found that he has put what I taught into practice. Hui is not stupid" (*Confucian Analects* II, Wei zheng 为政)[13] and interpreted it as praise from Confucius for his favorite disciple Yan Hui's (颜回) silence. However, one should read the passage as only a remark, if not a mild criticism, made by Confucius on Yan Hui's silence. On another occasion Confucius made the following remark:

"Hui is not assisting me. There is nothing that I say in which he does not show delight."

Confucian Analects XI, Xian jin (先进)[14]

There are several instances in the *Confucian Analects* where Confucius conceded to the contradicting views expressed by his disciples, especially Zi Lu (子路). Confucius changed his plan to meet Bi Xi (佛 肸) a rebellion leader, when Zi Lu voiced his objection. Similarly, he rejected another invitation from Gongshan Furao (公山弗扰) (*Confucian Analects* XVII, Yang Huo 阳货).[15]

There were also some who questioned the methodology employed by Confucius in his thinking and search for knowledge saying that it lacked the deductive method and the dialectic logic of the ancient Greek thinkers.

First, let us remind ourselves that as a scholar and teacher, Confucius has always been noted for his attribute of having an insatiable appetite for learning and an untiring devotion to teaching xue er bu yan, hui ren bu juan 学而不厌, 诲人不倦 (*Confucian Analects* VII, Shu er 述而).¹⁶ Let us look at the very first sentence in the (*Confucian Analects* I, Xue er 学而) that reads: "Zi yue, xue er shi xi zhi, hu yi yue hu? 子曰: 学而时习之, 不亦悦乎," which James Legge renders it as "The Master said, 'Is it not pleasant to learn with a constant perseverance and application?'"¹⁷

The two words "shi, 时" and "xi, 习" are both open to more than one interpretation. "Shi" can mean "normally" (pingshi, 平时) "constantly" (shichang, 时常; shishi, 时时) "at the right opportunity" (heshi, 合时) "at any time" (suishi, 随时), "now and then" (youshi, 有时) etc., while "xi" can mean "to learn" or "to practice." Suppose I make a different choice of meaning of these two words and come out with the following translation:

> The Master said, "Is it not a joy to learn something and have the right opportunity to put it into practice?"

As a solitary sentence I cannot justify that my translation is more correct than James Legge's version. However, if we read the two sentences immediately following this sentence the situation will clarify itself. One is an obvious statement in the form of a question about the happiness of seeing a visiting friend from distant land, the next is a deduction from the two examples cited to state in the form of a question that a junzi would not show anger at another's ignorance. The first sentence would then be referring to something very obvious to the listener. My version seems to be more logical without leaving the reader to wonder why it is such a pleasure to learn with a constant perseverance and application. We can deduce from this interpretation that Confucius was also a practical person.

The *Confucian Analects* informs us that Confucius listened widely, putting aside what was in doubt, and observed much, putting aside what seemed perilous — duo wen que yi duo jian que dai (Confucian Analects II, Wei Zheng 为政)¹⁸ — and that he would put forth questions and would not be ashamed to seek knowledge from one in an inferior position as illustrated by his visit to the state ancestral temple (*ru tai miao mei shi wen* 入太庙每事问, X, Xiangdang 乡党),¹⁹ and an instruction he gave to his disciples (*bu chi xia wen* 不耻下问, *V Gongye Zhang* 公冶长).[20] After listening, enquiring and observing in the process of learning, Confucius said that it was necessary to think, as he realised that learning without thinking was useless. He said:

> "Learning without thought is labour lost; thought without learning is perilous"
>
> *Confucian Analects* II, Wei zheng (为政)[21]

Confucius insisted that one must be honest to oneself about knowledge and acknowledging his or her ignorance was knowledge itself. He once said to his disciple Zi Lu:

> "You 由, shall I teach you what knowledge is? When you know a thing, to hold that you know it; and when you do not know a thing, to allow that you do not know it — this is knowledge"
>
> *Confucian Analects* II, Wei zheng (为政)[22]

Confucius once told his disciple Zi Gong (子贡) about his methodology. A passage in the *Confucian Analects* (XV, Wei Linggong 卫灵公) reads:

> The Master said, "Ci 赐, do you suppose that I am one who has learned many things and kept them in memory?" The reply was, "Yes, isn't it so?" (The Master) said, "No, I seek an all-pervading unity (rule)- yi yi guan zhi 一以贯之"[23]

"Yi yi guan zhi" reminds me of the methodology adopted by the late Dr Joseph Needham. When he embarked on writing an article or a chapter of a book he would first select the biggest table he could lay his hands on. He would then bring together all relevant reference books, journals, and off-prints, together with the notes he made and notes prepared for him by his collaborators. He would lay all that he had already perused on the table, and if space was insufficient he would use chairs and side tables. He sometimes used a chart with lines after lines linking things together in an orderly way. Lu Gwei-Djen (1904–1991) used to call them "Joseph's railway lines." Finally he would proceed to write, linking all the facts in a logical order in a style that has earned him the reputation of a great writer, which is a rare achievement for a scientist. He called this "weaving." To pierce and connect all the pieces with one strand of wool or thread may just as well be described by the same words "yi yi guan zhi," although Joseph Needham probably did not have the same thing in mind as Confucius. In any case, the words of Confucius and Needham's "weaving method" do not differ much from the deductive method of the ancient Greek people other than in name.

A method similar to the dialectic method of ancient Greece seems also to have been used by Confucius. Xi Zezong quotes the following passage:

> The Master said, "Am I indeed in possession of knowledge? I do not know. When I am questioned by ordinary folk, (to begin with) I am hollow and devoid (of an answer). I put the two ends together and exhaust my thinking to get it — wo kou qi liang duan er jie ran 我叩其两端而竭然."
>
> Confucian Analects IX, Zi Han (子罕)[24]

Note the last sentence about taking the two ends or extremities, a structure which has profoundly influenced the Chinese language. Many words are formed by taking the two extremes. For example, big and small give the term for size (daxiao, 大小), high and low for height (gaodi, 高低), cold and hot for temperature (hanshu, 寒署), etc.

3.3. From Mencius to Zhu Xi

The principles of Confucius were interpreted in different ways. Take for example the question regarding human nature that was merely hinted at by Confucius when he said, "In their nature human beings are closely alike, but in their nurture they become apart — xing xiang jin ye xi xiang yuan ye 性相近也习相远也" (*Confucian Analects* XVII, Yang Huo 阳货).[25] Mencius (c. 390–305 BC) stressed the original goodness of human nature, saying that the tendency of human nature toward goodness was likened to that of water flowing downwards — ren xing zhi shan ye you shui zhi jiu xia ye (人性之善也犹水之就下也) (*The Works of Mencius* VI, Gaozi 告子)[26] — when he refuted the interpretation of a contemporary philosopher Goozi

(告子). The latter was saying that there was neither good nor evil in human nature — xing wu shan wu bu shan 性无善无不善 (*The Works of Mencius* VI, Gaozi, pt. I).²⁷ After Mencius, another philosopher Xunzi (荀子) (313–238 BC), who propounded a theory of innate evil in human nature — ren zhi xinger (人之性恶).²⁸ Thus there was more than one school of Confucianism, although Mencius has been accepted by later generations as the bearer of the main-stream. Whatever interpretations they made of Confucian philosophy should not be attributed directly to Confucius but to the interpreters or the particular schools alone.

Let us consider whether Mencius had played a role in hindering the development of science in China in view of the very important position in Confucianism that he occupied. From the May Fourth Movement until the third quarter of this century scholars often searched for negative factors in Confucianism in their attempt to explain why modern science did not develop in China and in doing so they overlooked much that was positive. Mencius is a case in point. Take for example environmental science, a subject that became popular only in the later half of this century. Mencius long recognized its importance when he said the following words to Huiwang (惠王), the King of the State of Liang (梁):

> If the seasons of husbandry be not interfered with, grain will be more ample than can be eaten. If the use of small mesh nets is forbidden in ponds and pools; fishes and turtles will be more than sufficient for consumption. If axes and bills are let into hills and forests only at the proper time, timber and wood will be more plentiful than can be used.
>
> *The Works of Mencius* I, Liang Huiwang (梁惠王)²⁹

Mencius showed that he was not totally ignorant of astronomy when he used it to illustrate the importance of making rational enquiry. He said, "There is heaven so high; there are the stars so distant. If we have investigated their phenomena, we may, while sitting in our places, go back to the solstice of a thousand years ago." (*The Works of Mencius* IV, Li Lou 离娄)³⁰

Those who have read *The Works of Mencius* will probably agree with me that Mencius was noted for his skill in debates. He even tried to be apologetic for his endowment in the art of disputation as we can see from the following passage:

> Gongduzi 公都子 asked, "People outside all say that you, Sir, are fond of disputing. I venture to ask whether it is so." Mencius replied, "How can I be fond of disputing? I am only compelled to do it."
>
> *The Works of Mencius* III, Teng Wengong (滕文公)[31]

This brings out an interesting issue raised by Nakayama Shigeru (中山茂) a little more than 20 years ago.[32] As already referred to earlier in this chapter, comparisons had been made between China and ancient Greece to pick up what was absent in the former but present in the latter to account for the non-development of science in traditional China. One example was the emphasis on rhetoric in the oratorical arts of the Sophists, which gradually developed into logic through Socrates, Plato, and eventually Aristotle (348–322 BC). Nakayama points out that disputation is a difference in character between Western and East Asian civilizations and that this difference in character gave rise to two different styles of learning, one giving emphasis to oratorical skill and the other to writing skill. He attributes this to the early invention and the more general availability of writing materials in China as compared to its Western counterpart, and he also notes the importance of the historian's position in China. We can think of the names of a few great speakers in the Warring States period of China, and Mencius is an outstanding case. Mencius, however, was not proud of possessing such a talent, thus proving Nakayama's point. On the other hand, I would not take this as a negative factor for the development of science in China. Greek civilization has been accorded too much credit while those of the Arab world, China, and India have not received the recognition they deserve. Furthermore, one has to be very careful when one tries to compare two civilizations. Kim Yung-Sik 金永植 has the following to say:

> "The most serious problem, in my opinion, lies in the hidden assumption that frequently underlies those comparisons, namely the assumption that the factors which were significant in the Western scientific development had to be the factors which affect the development of the sciences in China."[33]

Nevertheless we should not underrate the importance of writing and printing and blame a lesser emphasis on the oratorical skill for the non-development of modern science in traditional China. I am reminded of the following words by George Sarton (1884–1956), the pioneer of the history of science as a university discipline:

> The discovery of printing was one of the great turning points in the history of mankind, and it was of special importance to the history of science. It changed the very warp and woof of history, for it replaced precarious forms of tradition (oral and manuscript) by one that was stable, secure, and lasting; it is as if mankind had suddenly obtained a trustworthy memory instead of one that was fickle and deceitful. It is not enough to make a discovery, for if it fails to be transmitted, it is almost as if it had never been; it is not enough to write a scientific treatise, it must be preserved. If it be lost, as were a great many ancient and mediaeval treatises, it is of no use to us. We need the text, a faithful and permanent text, and that became possible only when printing was established by the middle of the fifteenth century.[34]

Sarton is referring to Europe, but his statement on the importance of printing has a general application. The positive aspect of printing should also be taken into account in a comparison between the oral and the written tradition.

The tendency of Confucianism to support those in authority attracted the interest of the ruling house of Han China. The Emperor Han Wudi (汉武帝) (reigned 140–87 BC) turned Confucianism into the orthodox national culture, barring other schools of thought. He appointed Dong Zhongshu (董仲舒) (c. 179–93 BC) as head of a large group of scholars which he had assembled. Dong Zhongshu developed a philosophical theory on the unity of heaven and men identifying natural phenomena with actions or fractions of the emperor. Again one may note that Confucius himself deliberately refrained from associating occurrences of solar eclipse with prognostication. What Dong Zhongshu did illustrate is that certain things done in the name of Confucianism had nothing to do with Confucius himself.

The most illustrious exponent of Confucianism since its official recognition in Han China came 14 centuries after Dong Zhongshu, in the person of Zhu Xi (朱熹) (AD 1130–1200), the author of the "neo-Confucian synthesis" that had a profound influence for many hundred years, not only in China but also in Korea and Japan. His philosophical writings contained his knowledge of calendar astronomy, harmonics, geography, medicine, and some of the fundamental ideas that were also of interest to the Western scientific tradition. Let us take a few examples of the ideas that were of mutual interest in East and West. Zhu Xi touched on the idea of infinite greatness and infinite smallness, saying that being infinitely big there is no "outside" to it, and being infinitely small there is no "inside" in it, in other words the infinitely small is indivisible. He explained the idea of inertia by taking the example of a cart which would require an applied force to set it in motion, but once in motion the starting force would no longer be required. He expressed his observation of relative motion by taking two wheels rotating about the same axis with different speed so that the one rotating more slowly would seem to an observer on the faster wheel as rotating in the opposite direction. He noted the existence of centrifugal force, saying that water in a revolving vessel would not spill even when the vessel was upside down. It is not possible here to deal at length with the wide range of Zhu Xi's knowledge. Fortunately one can refer to a number of publications on this topic, particularly a forthcoming book of Kim Yung-Sik on Zhu Xi.[35]

3.4. Concept of Science in Traditional China

Even today the word "science" does not have exactly the same meaning in Europe. Its nearest German equivalent is "Wissenschaft", which includes all systematic study, such as what we call science and also what we call history, philosophy and philology. We should not be surprised to hear from a historian in Russia that he is doing scientific research. In China, the word "kexue, 科学" only came to be used as the equivalent of the word "science" in the middle of the last century. However, the general concept of "knowledge of the natural world" with or without the idea of "controlling nature or the environment" must have existed in the human mind long before the terms were coined. The definition of this concept varied in the course of time, and also for different civilizations. In 12th century China,

Zhu Xi did not study the natural world independently, but took it as a kind of "cosmic basis" for morality, and he took natural phenomena as analogies when he attempted to solve certain social and ethical problems. In 13th century Europe, natural philosophy was closely bound with theology and astronomy with astrology. Few people even asked what the traditional Chinese considered to be knowledge of the natural world and the ability to change or harness it. Zhuge Liang (诸葛亮) (AD 181–234), under the imagination of the 14th century novelist Luo Guanzhong (罗贯中) and described in the *Romance of the Three Kingdoms*, possessed knowledge that "[t]raversed the heavens in one direction and the earth in another," while having the ability to modify the work of nature, as by changing the direction of the wind. In the mind of the traditional Chinese, Zhuge Liang would be science personified. This was the topic of my earlier lecture delivered in Chinese. I illustrated the method of qimen dunjia (奇门遁甲) for forecasting the time of onset of wind and its direction using astronomical data and calculations.

Zhu Xi lived in a period when the qimen dunjia and two other methods were examination subjects in the Astronomical Bureau. These subjects were often studied in secrecy within the walls of the imperial palace. Traditional Chinese science was based on the concepts of Yin (阴) and Yang (阳), the wuxing (五行), the Hetu (河图), and Luoshu (洛书) diagrams, and the system of the Yijing (易经). While the philosophy of gewu (格物) of the neo-Confucian scholars was investigating natural phenomena from their understanding of these basic concepts, and as in the case of Zhu Xi, attempting to link these phenomena with morality, astronomers within the Astronomical Bureau combined observations with methods derived from these basic concepts not only for weather forecasting but also for the prediction of political, military, and more mundane human affairs. All astronomers, while being educated, must have learned the Confucian classics. They were Confucian scholars in that sense, although they were not necessarily neo-Confucianists. Hence we see that Confucianism did not hinder the development of traditional Chinese science and, on the contrary, it has played an active part in the history of science in China not only in the areas mentioned above but also in the recording and preserving of materials that are indispensable for the historian of science.

3.5. Chinese Medicine and Conclusion

In conclusion, I would like to change the question slightly and ask whether Confucianism can be a stumbling block to science as we understand it today. Here we cannot involve Confucius himself since he lived twenty-five centuries ago. Let us confine ourselves to just one of these principles that forms the foundation stone of Confucianism. This is the word "ren, 仁" consisting of the word "two" with "man" radical, suggesting the proper relation between two persons. It is generally rendered into English as "benevolence," but there is no exact equivalent. Let us take medicine as an illustration.

Confucianism had played an important role in the history of Chinese medicine, particularly in the development of medical ethics and the encouragement of Confucian scholars to study medicine in order to fulfill their obligations of filial piety to their parents and loyalty to their ruler. As we know, filial piety and loyalty are two different manifestations of ren (仁). The story of the legendary Emperor Shennong (神农) risking his own life by tasting 100 kinds of plants to determine their medical quality is another manifestation of ren. The Han medical writing Huangdi neijing (黄帝内经) (Yellow Emperor's Canon of Interior Medicine) said that medicine, being the craft of the sage, was a noble profession and being such the practitioner should have a noble moral character. Confucian influence on Chinese medical ethics cannot be more strongly expressed than in the works written by the Tang physician and alchemist Sun Simiao (孙思邈) (581–682 AD) He said:

> I searched for the reason why medicine was introduced by the wise sages and found that its purpose was to teach every family and inform every individual that it would be neither loyal nor filial if one was unable to cure the illness of the emperor or one's own parents. After stating this high Confucian moral principle, Sun Simiao continues. When a doctor attended his patient, he should compose himself, banish all his desires and approach the case dedicated to the relief of suffering with a compassionate heart. No regard, should be given to the social status of the patient, be it lowly or exalted, poverty-stricken or affluent, be the patient aged or young, ugly or beautiful, being a friend or enemy, being a relative, being a Chinese or a foreigner, being a wise person or a fool; but everyone

should be treated alike, exactly like a close and dear relative. A doctor should not consider his own personal safety, but must regard the sufferings of a patient as his own, grieving as for his own. The doctor must not entertain any desire of just putting on a show, but must be single-minded in his intention to relieve sufferings. Thus a doctor should not avoid difficulties in travelling, nor be concerned with the time, whether it be day nor night, winter or summer. Nor should a doctor be concerned with his own personal comfort, whether hungry or thirsty, tired or exhausted ....[36]

Confucian influence on medical ethics still survives in modern Chinese society. We can see occasionally hanging on the walls of modern clinics or surgeries frames or wooden boards bearing messages that read "yi zhe ren shu 医者仁术 — medicine is the art of ren or the doctor practises the art of ren or "renxin ren shu 仁心仁术 — a benevolent heart and a benevolent art". All these bear the mark of Confucianism. To the Chinese mind practising medicine itself amounts to putting Confucian precepts into practice.

Looking at the Confucian influence on medical ethics we cannot say that Confucianism should ever be regarded as a hindrance to the advance of medicine, be it traditional Chinese medicine or modern medical science. At the most one might say that Confucianism is too idealistic for medical ethics. Confucianism is not science, its objectives were not science, but its principles are not anti-science. If modern scientists give some consideration to the simple word "ren", we may hope that the human race will have less worry on environmental problems and less fear of being confronted with mass destruction. Although some may not be so optimistic because of the apparent lack of the carrot and stick in Confucianism, yet being compassionate and having consideration for others hinders nothing that is good for mankind.

Notes

1. James Legge, *The Chinese Classics*, in seven volumes, *Confucian Analects*, *The Great Learning*, and *The Doctrine of the Mean*; Vol. 2 *The Works of Mencius*, Hong Kong 1861; London 1861: reprinted and revised several times, for example by the Hong Kong University Press. The translated works are hereafter referred to as Legge with the page number in the particular work concerned. For example Legge, p. 100 on *Lunyu* refers

to page 100 in Legge, *Confucian Analects*. Many excellent translations have appeared since Legge's publications. Legge's classical work is referred to here because of its lasting influence in the West.
2. Tr. auct.; see Legge pp. 264 and 265.
3. See Bo Shuren, (1988). "Shitan Kong-Meng de keji zhishi he rujia de kejizhengce" 试谈孔孟的科技知识和儒家的科技政策·*Ziran kexueshi yanjiu* 自然科技史研究, 7(4), 297–304.
4. Tr. auct., see Legge, p. 218.
5. Tr. auct.; see Legge, p. 140.
6. Tr. auct.; see Legge, p. 277.
7. After Legge, p. 150.
8. See Legge, p. 297.
9. See Legge, p. 409.
10. See Joseph Needham (1956). *Science and Civilisation in China*, Vol. 2, Cambridge: Cambridge University Press, p. 15.
11. Xi Zezong (1994). *Kexueshi bajiang* 科技史八讲. Taipei, pp. 79–102.
12. Lu Xun, (1956). *Lu Xun quanji* 鲁迅全集, Vol.1. Beijng: Renmin wenxue, p. 296.
13. Tr. auct., see Legge, p. 149.
14. Tr. auct., see Legge, p. 238.
15. See Legge, p. 321.
16. See Legge, p. 195.
17. After Legge, p. 137.
18. After Legge, p. 151.
19. See Legge, p. 235.
20. See Legge, p. 178.
21. After Legge, p. 150.
22. After Legge, p. 151.
23. Tr. auct., see Legge, p. 291.
24. Tr. auct., see Legge, p. 219.
25. See Legge, p. 318.
26. See Legge, p. 396.
27. See Legge, p. 401.
28. This is the opening sentence in *Xunzi* (荀子) written by Xun Kuang (荀况) a younger contemporary of Mencius. See Legge, p. 28.
29. Tr. auct., see Legge, pp. 130–131.
30. After Legge, p. 332.
31. Tr. auct., see Legge, p. 278.
32. See Shigeru Nakayama (1974). *Academic and Scientific Traditions in China, Japan and the West*. Tokyo: MIT & University of Tokyo Press.
33. See Kim Yung-Sik (1995). "Chu Hsi on matter, motion, etc.: What did a traditional Chinese thinker think about the ideas that were important in the Western scientific

tradition?" Seminar paper delivered at the National Tsing Hua University, Hsinchu, January 24, 1995.
34. Sarton, George (1958). *Six Wings: Men of Science in the Renaissance*. London: The Bodley Head, p. 3. For example Ho Peng Yoke (1985). *Li, Qi and Shu: An Introduction of Science and Civilization in China*. Hong Kong: University of Hong Kong Press.
35. Kim Yung-Sik (2000), *The Natural Philosophy of Chu Hsi, 1130-1200*. Philadelphia: American Philosophical Society.
36. See Ho Peng Yoke and Lisowski, F. Peter (1993). *Concepts of Chinese Science and Traditional Healing Arts: A Historical Review*. Singapore: World Scientific Publishing or Ho Peng Yoke and Lisowski, F. Peter (1997). *A Brief History of Chinese Medicine*. Singapore: World Scientific Publishing.

∽ 4 ∾
EAST MEETS WEST: THE IMPACT ON CHINA AND HER RESPONSE*

LIU TS'UN-YAN

Australian National University

Professor Lim Pin, the Vice-Chancellor of National University of Singapore, in his *Foreword* to the Inaugural Lectures of this Series (1995), mentions that "Professor Wu was a Renaissance Man with a deep knowledge of both Eastern and Western traditions."[1] This well-worded observation has inspired me to think it might be appropriate for me to relate something about the historical background of East meets West, and how such communication affects both sides so far as their cultures and traditions are concerned. As you know, communication is commonly used to mean exchange of information and trade, but at the heart of it is the exchange of knowledge, entailing sometimes the inevitable conflict of ideas and beliefs.

---

* This chapter is a reproduction of the memorial lecture given by the author in memory of Professor Wu Teh Yao in 1998, a great educator and author, a brilliant political thinker and administrator, and a broad-minded leader and devoted public servant not only of China but also wherever he lived and worked. The author began to communicate with him only as late as the spring of 1987, when he invited the author to participate in the forthcoming International Conference of Confucianism scheduled to be held in August of that year at Qufu, Confucius' birthplace in Shandong. The Conference was sponsored jointly by the Institute and the Confucius Foundation of China. The author accepted the tempting invitation for it would gave him a good chance to see a more relaxed and vigorously

Historically speaking, the Western interest in the East extends back some two thousand and several hundred odd years before our time. Herodotus, the Father of History as he is called by the Europeans, when depicting the Greco-Persian wars in his *History* called the Persians and the people of other nations in the region *Barbaros* (barbarians). This was a brief and superficial impression of the East through the eyes of a Western observer. As a matter of fact, in the year 479 BC when the Greeks overwhelmed the Persians at Plataea, it was in the same year that an intellectual giant of the East, Confucius, passed away, though at that time China was still unknown to Westerners. During the 11th century, the crusades began. The Christians had some success in resisting the spread of Islamic forces and influence, but soon encountered the westward invasions of the Mongols. In 1258, the Mongolian army led by Möngke's (T. 1251–1259)[2] younger brother Hülegü[3] ravaged Mesopotamia, took Baghdad, the capital of the Caliphate, and before long the forces of the Mongols controlled the Middle East, the Near East and Eastern Europe. In 1275, in the reign of Kublai Khan (r. 1260–1294),[4] the Venetian youth Marco Polo (1254–1324) arrived in Dadu (Beijing) with his uncle and his father, and he lived and served in the Mongolian-ruled China for 17 years.

After Marco returned to Venice and during the war between the two city-states Venice and Genoa, he was taken prisoner by the Genoese, probably in 1298. His captivity lasted less than a year, and in prison, apparently,

---

rehabilitated China after the stormy revolution, as well as an opportunity to meet Professor Wu and other friends old and new. That was the beginning of a good acquaintance and friendship. In the following year Professor Wu invited the author to Singapore and work in his Institute for a month which he accepted. My job was to read aloud with expression, in *putonghua*, the whole text of the Confucian *Four Books*, for the purposes of video-recording. The project was carried out from early April to early May, 1988 and the recording was later interspersed with Classical music and illustrations, thanks to the efforts of Mr Stewart Arrandale and other technician staff of the Centre of Educational Technology of this University. During the sojourn, the author had the privilege to discuss things of mutual interest with Professor Wu. The author describes the magnanimity of Professor Wu toward his juniors by quoting two lines from the Chinese historical work *Shiji* of the second century BC which says:

> Two strangers encounter each other in the street, each lowering the cover of their carts and talking like old friends.

Shiji, juan 83 (a proverb cited by Zou Yang in his petition to Prince Liang defending his innocence when he was in custody).

he dictated his adventurous stories in the East to a fellow captive of Pisa named Rustichello, who was an able writer of chivalric romances at the time. The latter put Marco's dictations into the stylish language of the district *langue d'oïl*, and produced a book named *Il Milione* (or *The Travels of Marco Polo* as it was called in England), in which the vast amount of anthropological and geographical information about China and the unbelievable riches and glories of the powerful Mongolian Empire, its territories extending across two continents, were vividly described.[5] This would to some extent correct the deeply rooted prejudice of the Westerners toward the East, though only partly. Pondering the problem from the cultural viewpoint, although Marco Polo's work became popular reading for millions of people of different races through translations, his knowledge about the thousands-year-old cultural tradition of the ethnic Han Chinese was minimal, if not completely blank, and the Mongols, being nomad and combative, heeded only the restrains of religion.

Although the mission of the Polos had very little concern with preaching, long before he entered the Chinese land, when the rulers before Kublai Khan, namely Güyüg (r. 1246–1248)[6] and the already mentioned Möngke were holding their court at the *ordo* (tent-palaces) of Karakorum the capital, about 200 *li* southwest of Ulan-Bator, preachers of many sects of Christianity including the Nestorians, the Franciscan, and the Dominican friars, and the representatives of the popes had come to pay tribute to the Mongolian court. John of Pian di Carpine, a papal envoy who in August 1246, had witnessed Güyüg's election to the throne, which was held in an *ordo* about half-a-day's ride south of the Mongol capital.[7] It is said that the elected khan Güyüg revered his Christian advisers and was under the influence of Nestorianism. The historians believe that if Güyüg had not died at an early age of 42, after a rule of only two years, it was possible that the empire might have been converted to the Christian faith. Like Genghis Khan, his grandfather, Güyüg's successor Möngke was a shamanist, who normally took omen by a burnt shoulder-blade of a sheep. But he too showed tolerance to all faiths. Christian churches, Buddhist and Daoist monasteries, and Islamic mosques flourished simultaneously in the same capital-city, where international society truly existed. William of Rubruck, a Dutch friar who saw the court of Möngke in 1254, has left a colorful account of his experience in his famous work *Itinerarium*[8] in which he enumerated the members of the so-called European colony of the city, which included, and I quote, "Frenchmen, Germans, Hungarians, Slavs, and at least one Englishman. They intermingled with Alans, Georgians, Armenians, Persians, Turks and Chinese. All these people worked for the Mongols in various capacities."[9]

When Marco Polo and his group visited China they took the "silk route" by land. They set off from Persia, passing through Afghanistan, the present-day Xinjiang to Suzhou and Ganzhou, the present-day Gansu. Their return trip was by sea. From Quanzhou, their 14 four-masted ships entered the Indian Ocean from the China Sea, passing through Singapore Strait, Indonesia, and Ceylon (Sri Lanka), and finally arrived at the port of Hormuz, then under the rule of Ilkhan of Persia.[10] People nowadays in China are fond of using the word *daqihou* or the macroclimate to mean the general trend of thought, or the tendency of a particular time from which people take indication to act. At Polo's time the *daqihou* was shaped by merchants who wished to trade and earn good money, and by rulers and religious leaders who on the one hand wished to spread their doctrine and proselytize among the heathens, and to persuade the Mongols to unite with them to confront the strong forces of Islam on the other. However, history moved on and three centuries later, when Matteo Ricci (1552–1610),[11] the Jesuit missionary visited China, the *daqihou* at this time was completely different. In Marco Polo's time, navigation in that part of the world by Chinese ships relied on the help of the Arabs' knowledge of the movement of the stars and the sun, together with the use of the Chinese magnetic needle. But at the time of Matteo Ricci's journey, although the last battle of the Crusades had not yet been fought, the power of Islam had already declined, and the Europeans had also gained the upper hand over the Arabs in knowledge of navigation. Latitude and time were determined with the aid of the Astrolabe, originally an ancient invention,[12] now improved for measurement of the elevation of the pole star above the horizon. In 1488, the Portuguese navigator Bartholomew Diaz reached the southernmost point of the African coast, later named as Good Hope. Nine years later and six years after the discovery of America by Christopher Columbus, another Portuguese Vasco da Gama, in 1497, landed in India at Calicut. As a memorial to his discovery of a new route to the East, Vasco da Gama erected a marble pillar there.

The sea route from Europe to Asia was now open for navigation. It also ushered in a new era in human history, with several Western sea powers competing in colonial conquest and exploitation. The efforts the Portuguese made in this respect were the most conspicuous among the early contenders. Their forces reached India, Goa, Ceylon, and Southeast Asia. In 1511, only one year after Goa was made the capital of Portuguese India (Estado da India), the Portuguese commander Afonso de Albuquerque seized Malacca from its native ruler Sultan Mahmud who fled after some fierce fighting. Then the invading forces moving northward tried to knock open the Chinese gate on its southern frontier. The struggles between the rival Western powers seeking privileges and territorial gains from the East became ever more intense.

* * *

In the autumn of 1583, Matteo Ricci, an Italian priest of the Society of Jesus, came to Zhaoqing in Guangdong from Macau. The capable premier of China Zhang Juzheng (1525–1582) had died the year before, and Macau had been under Portuguese rule for nearly 30 years. In his 27 years in China, Ricci had made genuine efforts to promote the exchange of the Chinese and the Western cultures, and his contributions on this account were tremendous. Before he entered China he had spent more than one year in Macau studying assiduously Classical and spoken Chinese, and very soon he had mastered the rules of this exotic language. When he moved to Shaozhou (1589) in the northern part of Guangdong where he stayed for more than five years before he moved again to Jiangxi and then to Nanjing (Nanking) and further north, there was tremendous improvement in his spoken Chinese. The spoken Chinese which he acquired was probably a kind of Mandarin or *guanhua*, an artificial vernacular language prepared for the communication among scholar-officials who originally came from different areas and spoke a different *patois*. It was reported that about this time Ricci had translated the *Sishu* or the Confucian *Four Books* into Latin, the manuscripts of which he sent to his colleagues in Rome for study. His manuscripts were never published, but were polished, revised, and edited at different times by co-workers and followers. Remnants of them may still be found in a much later work the *Confucius Sinarum Philosophus* published in Paris in 1687 with a dedication to King Louis XIV written by Philippi Couplet.[13] Another contribution of Ricci in the field of sinological studies is that he was the first to have invented a set of Chinese Latinized alphabets known as *Daxi zimu* or the *Alphabets from the Great West*, also known as *Xizi qiji*, the *Miraculous Signs of the Western Words*, in which each of the Chinese characters is systematically split into two parts, the *zifu* (literally "word father"), equivalent to our understanding of the *initial*, and the *zimu*, equivalent to our understanding of the *final*.[14] Ricci's original work is no more extant. Luckily some slender evidence of it is still preserved. In the *Bibliotheque Vaticane* there are three fragments of 1605 on which Chinese characters stand side-by-side with their Latin Romanization in columns. The contents have been proved to be identical with four passages from Chinese essays composed by Matteo Ricci and carved on various ink tablets made by the famous Cheng Dayue, alias Cheng Junfang (1541–1616), who manufactured graceful ink sticks and ink cakes on which pretty designs were engraved in relief. These original essays and the embossed work are contained in Cheng's own illustrated album of printings the *Chengshi moyuan*.[15] Of these four articles written by Ricci in Chinese, one was dedicated to Cheng Dayue himself, for he, a successful manufacturer and an art connoisseur from Shexian in Anhui, a region noted for several hundred years for the production of ink and paper, was one of Ricci's best friends.

We shall never forget the great efforts made by Ricci to introduce the Western sciences to China, and it is no exaggeration to say that it was due to his exertions that Western science and Eastern science, rather than the traditional pseudo-sciences such as astrology and sorcery, met. Ancient Chinese political philosophy, even before Confucius's time, despised clever skills and devices, condemning them as overly subtle and therefore tantamount to luxury and extravagance. The Daoist philosophy of blurring the distinction between being and nonbeing tended to knock back the desire for precision, though of course Confucius himself demands the rectification of names.[16] In late Ming, however, because of the threat of the Manchus on the northeastern front, and the success of several kinds of foreign cannons used during the battles against the Japanese invaders in Korea (1593), there was a need for a different mentality, and Ricci was determined to push forward appropriate changes.

From Zhaoqing in 1583, the mission of Ricci was not plain sailing. There were xenophobes who disliked foreigners whatsoever and slanders and false accusations against him and his mission were common. At first he and his colleagues Michel Ruggieri (1543–1607) dressed themselves in Buddhist attire, assuming that it was the proper dress for preachers universally. But when they were to inaugurate their newly built church on a small piece of land granted by the Chinese authorities, the prefecture-governor, Wang Pan, presented to the church two wooden boards. One was a horizontally inscribed board for the gate, reading "Xianhua Si" (the Flowery Immortal Monastery); the other, to be hung in the hall, bore the four characters *Xilai jingtu* or "Pure-land preaching from the West" engraved on its surface. Now this word "West" does not mean the Atlantic seaboard, but the land of Amitaba, for the people took their teaching for that of a certain sect of Buddhism, the religion they were more familiar with. This obliged Ricci and Ruggieri to relinquish their monk costume as soon as they arrived in Shaozhou, and to adopt that of the Confucian scholars in order to gain the minds and hearts of the socially much-esteemed Chinese intellectuals. The Chinese title for Catholic priests has since been *siduo* or "the one who rings the bell to warn the ignorant," apparently drawing on the passage from the *Confucian Analects*. "Heaven is going to use your master to ring the tocsin" (3/24).[17] Each priest took a Chinese name, including a courtesy name *(zi)* or a style *(hao)*. For example, Matteo Ricci's Chinese name is *Li Madou* and his courtesy name is *Xitai*. Some modern sinologists have also adopted this habit. Joseph Needham's Chinese name is *Li Yuese*, and he also has a style Shisuzhai daoren, *shisu* being a transliteration for Joseph.[18] This may be understood partly in terms of Ricci's belief that it was necessary to gain complete acceptance by the open-minded Chinese scholar-officials who as a class were the pillars of the state.

When Ricci was a student in the Rome College from 1572 to 1578, he learned mathematics, geography, and cartography from the German Jesuit astronomer and mathematician Christopher Clavius (1538–1612), one of the most distinguished scientists of his time.[19] His erudition gave him much advantage to attract and win over some of the Chinese literati who had some basic or even specific knowledge of traditional sciences not prohibited by the dynasties, such as astronomy and the compilation of the calendar. For people in the street, the display of clocks and prisms (the *sanlenjing*, a glass or crystal body with triangular ends and rectangular sides which broke up white light into rainbow colors) and the playing of the clavichord, the musical keyboard instrument, were occasions of interest and entertainment. Ricci was also fond of showing biblical pictures to the native. Four of them, skilfully copied and engraved from the original by Chinese artisans, are contained in the aforesaid *Chengshi moyuan*. However, the most astonishing display was the *Yudi shanhai quantu* or the *Universal World Map* which was later engraved in woodblocks and printed in 1584 by the prefecture-governor of Zhaoqing. It was also the prototype of Ricci's *Mappa Mundi*, revised editions of which, printed at different times, are kept in several well-known libraries around the world.[20]

The Chinese began to make maps and atlases at a very early stage of their history. Records of such activities are numerous in the Bibliographical Treatises of various dynastic histories, and details of them are scattered in related biographies and in individual collected works. But few specimens are still extant. When China was reunited after the end of the division period of the Three Kingdoms, Pei Xiu (224–271 AD) presented to the court an atlas of China in 16 sections. In its preface, he gave six fundamental rules which laid down the grid system in Chinese cartography.[21] The atlas was preserved until the late 9th century. One other relic of this kind still preserved is a slab of stone on which a sketch of a map entitled *Hainei huayitu* (*The Map of China and the Barbarian Lands within the Four Seas*) is engraved. The original map was huge: its width was three *zhang* (one *zhang* being approximately equivalent to three-and-one-third meters) and its length was three *zhang* and three *chi* (one *chi* being approximately one-third of a meter). One hundred *li* of the land was represented by one *cun* or one-third of a decimeter in the drawing. In the Annuals of Emperor Dezong (r. 780–804) in the *Dynastic History of Tang* (*Jiu Tangshu*) compiled by Liu Xu, it is recorded that "in the 10th month of the 17th year of Zhenyuan (801), the Prime Minister Jia Dan presented to the throne the *Hainei Huayitu* together with a work entitled *Gujin junguoxiandao siyishu* (A Geographico-Political Account of the Princely States, Prefectures, Counties, Circuits and Barbarian Countries Past and Present) altogether 40 *juan*."[22] Jia Dan was a very good geographer. In 844, when the Kirghiz people (a Turkic people living in what is now northeast Russian Central Asia) sent an envoy to the Tang court, the ministers could not explain their altered name in the document. An edict came down from the Emperor Wu Zong (r. 841–846) asking for detailed information, and it was only by reading Jian Dan's work that the answer was found. The sketch of Jia Dan's map on stone, carved and erected in 1137 in Tungusic Jurchen occupied Shandong, is kept in the Forest of Steles (*Beilin*) in Xian.[23]

Although the original edition of Ricci's map is no more extant, a representation of it as well as two other world maps (both of zenithal projection centered on the North and South poles and divided into 360 degrees) are found in Zhang Huang's (1527–1608) huge encyclopaedic work, the *Tushubian*. These two world maps appeared in the 1602 edition with Ricci's map, which probably were also from the original. Zhang Huang was a contemporary of Ricci and had met him in 1595 at Nanchang, the provincial capital of Jiangxi. Zhang was an orthodox Confucian scholar of the time, his short biography is found both in the *Mingshi* and in Huang Zongxi's *Mingru xuean* or the *Records of Ming Scholars*.[24] As you know Ricci's *Mappa Mundi* had gone through several revisions. The revised edition of 1600 is reproduced in Guo Zizhang's *Qiancao*, a miscellany of writings compiled by the author after concluding his service as governor of Guizhou province in 1608. The 1602 and 1603 editions were published with the assistance of Li Zhizao (1565–1630)[25] and the 1604 edition was published in collaboration with Li and Xu Guangqi (1562–1633).[26] Li Zhizao translated and printed the map in Chinese; it could be mounted in sections on portable screens and used as domestic decoration. It became so popular that when the Emperor Shenzong (r. 1573–1619) demanded to see it the eunuchs had to resort to reprinting it, as it was learned that its wood-blocks had been shipped to the south.[27]

In drawing the original, Ricci benefited immensely from two predecessors' works, the memorable world chart of Gerardus Mercator of 1569 and the Atlas of Abraham Ortelius of 1570. But to bring the vast land of China and Eastern Asia into his map, however, he had to rely on some local sources. The Chinese work he might have made use of, and incorporated into his *Mappa Mundi*, was the *Guangyutu* compiled by Luo Hungxian (1504–1564),[28] a zealous adherent of the philosophy of Wang Yangming (Shouren, 1472–1529). Thanks to Wang's spirit of acquiring pragmatic knowledge, it is said that the various maps of provinces and of the coast and rivers displayed in Luo's work were found to be very helpful for defence against the invading Japanese pirates rampant during the mid-16th century. Luo's work, however, was modeled after the *Yuditu*, another map originally measuring seven *chi* length by seven *chi* width compiled by Zhu Siben (ca. 1273–1337), a Han-Chinese geographer and contemporary of Marco Polo. In the preface to his work, Zhu informs us that his map was compiled between 1311 and 1320. It also reveals that Zhu, though a learned scholar of geography of the time, "still had difficulty in providing trustworthy information about the land southeast of the 'Swallowing Sea' (i.e. South China Sea), northwest of the deserts, and other foreign states." He said, "For although tributary envoys come from time to time, their lands are too far away for investigation. Either they give no details, or what they talked about is complete nonsense and unbelievable. Places in this category are left blank in my work."[29] Zhu's work is no more extant but its essentials must have been incorporated into Luo's work which was named *Zengbu guangyutu* or the *Yuditu*, revised and enlarged.

Xu Guangqi and Li Zhizao were the two Ming scholars-officials who had shown high respect for Ricci for both his personality and scholarship. They both learned Western science from the discussions with Ricci and assisted him to put the Western works into stylish Chinese for publication from his dictations. As a high official who rose up the ladder of success to a premiership in late Ming, and with the memory of the famous Catholic Library standing on his family land at Zikawei in Shanghai over the past 300 years, Xu seems to have enjoyed more fame among the populace. Working with Ricci these two Chinese scholars published a considerable number of scientific works and earned the enviable reputations as pioneers who lifted the curtains of modernization. Among Xu's publications, the translation of Euclid's *Elements* is perhaps the most well-known work of the kind ever mentioned in a modern textbook of Chinese history. The translation was revised several times and its final form was put to print in 1611, about one year after Ricci's death. To start disseminating scientific knowledge at this time does not seem to be too late, as we know the most important translation of this work in Latin is that of Commandinus, dated 1572. Xu Guangqi also printed several works on trigonometry. Two of them were his own writings, comparing angular measurements in ancient Chinese books with newly imported theories.[30] His treatise on Western hydraulics, written from Sabatino de Ursis's (1575–1620) dictation, is included in his *Nongzheng quanshu*, or *A Complete Book on Agricultural Management*.[31] Li Zhizao's famous work was his *Hungai rongxian tushuo*, a translation of Father Clavius' *Astrolabium*.[32] I have briefly mentioned that the astrolabe is an instrument used for the taking of altitudes of celestial bodies from which time and latitude may be deduced. It was used in navigation by the seamen at this time until it was replaced later in the mid-18th century by the sextant. Praising the work of Li Zhizao, Ricci remarked, "From the illustrations and diagrams of the book, we are able to know that Chinese people are talented enough to learn our science and can achieve fruitful results."[33]

* * *

The time when Matteo Ricci and his mission visited China, was not an ordinary one. In Europe, the several branches representing the Protestant Revolt now had grown full-fledged. Members of the Society of Jesus, founded by the Spanish soldier Ignatius Loyola in 1534, only 17 years since Martin Luther posted his 95 theses on the church door at Wittenberg for debate, had been extremely active and progressive. The Jesuits, who were reformists within the Catholic Order, not only intended to regain their lost ground in Poland, Bavaria, Belgium, and the Southern Netherlands but also tried eagerly to convert the people of India, China, and Japan, even went to America to proselytize among the indigenes. They were people full of youthful spirit and were not afraid of difficulties. While moving round China from Guangdong and Jiangxi to the two capitals Nanjing and Beijing, Ricci made friends with a large number of intellectuals of the highest calibre whom he believed to be representative of the scholar-officials and gentry of the time. People like Xu Guangqi, Li Zhizao, and Yang Tingyun (1557–1627), who had been converted and baptised, were the advocates of modernization and science; Jiao Hong (1541–1620), the bibliophile and historian, was one of the leading scholars of the time; Li Zhi (1527–1602), the nonconformist with remarkable intelligence whose words against bogus-Confucianism have continued to shine through generations down to the present day; the three Yuan brothers (Zongdao (1560–1600), Hongdao (1568–1610), and Zhongdao (1570–1624) were essayists who cherished a literary life and a style of natural simplicity; Li Rihua (1565–1635), the calligrapher and art critic, whose diary, the *Weishuixuan riji* or *The Diary* from the Watertasting Studio, records memorably their mutual friendship — all such acquaintances convinced Ricci about the greatness of China, that Confucian scholars were outstanding, and that all the government officials were *philosophes*. He could not quite remember that for the multitude of so-called scholars, memorization of the books laid down by the sages and men of worth and the composition of "eight-legged" essays were the stepping-stones to success.

Living in an exclusive society like China, in which only a very small percentage of people had even a vague knowledge of the outside world, some degree of anti-foreign feelings was inevitable. Being a nation possessing an uninterrupted written history over 3000 years which was highly sophisticated, some arrogance and self-centredness were an almost inevitable consequence. With the help of influential and open-minded scholars, and the indefatigable efforts made by Ricci himself, the missionary work in a number of cities was carried out fairly smooth. During the last few years of his stay in Beijing, Ricci erected a church on the land bought in the southwestern corner of the inner-city. When he died in May 1610, Emperor Shenzong granted him a burial place in the suburb as an honor. But the seeds of hatred had been sown, professional jealousy from followers of different faiths, such as the Buddhists and the antagonistic feelings of the diehard traditional scholar-officials never ceased. Ricci was not polemical by nature. However, in his *Tianzhu shiyi* (*The True Teaching of God*) written in 1603, he attacked the Buddhist belief in *saṃsāra* (transmigration of souls and the eternal cycle of birth and death) and their vow to abstain from killing living beings. This hurt the feelings of the Buddhists. In 1609, his reply addressed to Yu Chunxi (included in his *Bianxue Yidu*), an official and a Buddhist devotee, made his position even clearer. Yu was a native of Hangzhou. Monk Zhuhong, also known as Master Yunqi (1532–1612), a Buddhist leader of the Pure land Sect who also lived in Hangzhou, saw Ricci's letter and he wrote four articles "On Heaven" to refute him in his *Zhuchuang sanbi* (*Second Sequel to Random Writings under a Bamboo-window*). The work was published after Ricci's death. Zhuhong was normally quite friendly with the Confucian scholars, and he tolerated Daoist priests.[34] But he viewed Catholicism as heterodoxy and thought he must clarify the issues lest many of the scholar-officials go astray.

The calculation of the time of the eclipse of the sun was another controversial case in point. It sounded silly and trivial but it was very serious, for the annual publication of the Imperial Calendar was a state affair, the divination based upon it would affect the future of the dynasty. Now that the Office of the Directorate of Astronomy (Qintianjian) was occupied by two schools of experts, one followed the calculation of the *Datongli* which was a modified version of the traditional calendar *Shoushili* of Yuan time. (The origin of the term *shoushi* [giving the people the seasons] is found in the first book of the *Book of History, Shangshu*.) The other school *Huihuili* or the Muslim calendar, also inherited from Yuan. On the first day of the 11th month in the 38th year of Wan Ii, the cyclic being *renyin* (December 15, 1610) the time of the eclipse of the sun and of the last encroachment made by the moon on the sun's rim calculated by both calendars proved to be erroneous. Li Zhizao was ordered to come to Beijing from the Southern Capital to revise the calendar, and the Jesuits Diego de Pantoja (1571–1618), Sabatino de Ursis, and others, who were already in Beijing, were invited to assist. This was a heavy blow to conservatism. In September 1616, only six years after Ricci's death, the counter-attacks came. Shen Que (d. 1624),[35] the Vice-Minister of Rites at the Southern Capital Nanjing, memorialized the court requesting that the missionaries be expelled immediately and forbid the spread of foreign teachings in China. Among the accusations he itemized in his three memorials, one was the term *Tianzhujiao* (*The Doctrines of the Heavenly Master*) and *Daxiyang* (*The Great Western Ocean*) used in the sermons. These, he believed, were a great insult to the sublimity of the Chinese emperor and to the country. Others related to the introduction of the Western ways of calculating calendar which were unorthodox; opposition to the traditional worshipping of ancestors, which was nonfilial; and other things concerning the church's illegal acquisition of lands in the vicinity of the tomb of the First Emperor, the founder of the dynasty. Like Monk Zhuhong, Shen's memorials emphasized that, "in the past twenty years they have made a wide range of acquaintances", and that the extreme danger at the time was that "they have got hold of a number of scholars and gentry, not to speak of the populace. This is regrettable." He added, "Now that scholars and gentry look upon these things as normal and routine, many of them seem to be happy with such unworthy incidents and have forgotten the future and the grand design."[36] The Jesuit-leaders at Nanjing, Alfonso Vagnoni (1566–1640) and Alvaro Semedo (1585–1658), and several Chinese Christians were arrested and thrown into prison where they underwent more suffering and humiliation. The two missionaries were expelled and sent back to Macau the following year, though they still managed to return to China to work when the storm temporarily subsided, each assuming a new Chinese name.

The manner in which Ricci chose to carry on his work was distinctive. He wished to avoid the stereotype way of introducing Christianity and was inclined to agree that the word *shangdi* (Lord on High) in the Chinese Classics the *Book of History* and the *Book of Odes* was no different from the God in the *Bible,* and that the sacrificial offerings to Heaven, Confucius and ancestors were merely a custom or an institution of the Chinese. When he took charge of the missionary works he did obtain some consent, or tacit consent, from the Rome authorities, hence his promotion of the missionary work was fruitful. This being the case, his approach actually met with opposition of various degrees both inside and outside the Society, and from the other religious Orders. For example, Nicolo Longobardi (1565–1655), a devoted Jesuit and first-class mathematician whom Ricci proclaimed to be his successor as the superior of the mission in China, had never uttered any words opposed to Ricci when he was alive, but turned against him after his death. This kind of conflict, emerging after the attitude of the papal court had changed, was the crux of the so-called rites controversy. In 1705 and 1720, envoys were sent to China by Pope Clementi, declaring his decision to ban the Chinese rites (a decree dated 1720 from the Manchu Emperor Kangxi [Xuanye, r. 1661–1722] to inform the priests who served at the inner court of his displeasure is displayed in the Leshoutang or the Hall of Longevity Bliss in the Archives Department of the Palace Museum, Beijing. The paper is dotted with some characters in vermilion ink which were written by Kangxi). In 1742 the papal decree was reconfirmed by Benedict XIV. The epoch of Matteo Ricci seemed to have gone, never to return. History informs us that it was to take over 300 more years before Ricci's *modus vivendi*, special concern for the peaceful coexistence of people, his generosity and tolerance, his adaptation to a new environment and willingness to think of the other side, were to be reconsidered. A decree of the Vatican published during the third year of the Sino-Japanese war on December 8, 1939, authorized Catholic Christians to observe the ancestral rites and to take part in the ceremonies honouring Confucius, albeit the question whether God is *shangdi* remains unresolved.

Compared with the new group of sinologists who rose like blustering wind during the second half of the 19th century, Matteo Ricci could not be counted as a professional sinologist, although these sinologists of the much younger generation were also non-professional. Those who began with the career of evangelist may be regarded as Ricci's colleagues, others started out as consul, diplomat, or interpreter; though some of them were to be offered a Chair at university when they returned to their native countries. The subtle influence exerted by Ricci and his sympathetic colleagues on European thought which raised stormy debates and changes a century later would not have been expected by them. What they said and wrote, such as there was a sort of "natural Christianity" in the Chinese that they had from early times enjoyed a special share of grace were governed by the most perfect institutions, did not find general acceptance. But after 100 years or so, when European scholars and lawyers rediscovered the concept of Natural Law from Greek philosophy (quite similar to the Chinese term *tianli* or heavenly principles, or *liangxin*, the conscience), great thinkers of the time like John Locke, Montesquieu, Voltaire, and others rose to advocate natural religion, were critical of authority, and even turned to the East for inspiration. Looking at developments from a wider angle, we could say that the people who signed the American *Declaration of Independence* (1776) proclaiming that they wanted to assume "the separate and equal station to which the Laws of Nature and of Nature's God entitled them," and the French *Declaration of the Rights of Man and of the Citizen* (1789) which aimed "to preserve the natural and inalienable rights of man," drank from the same stream. As for the appreciation of things from the East in their daily lives, such as the love for the delicate things of fragile porcelain, the vaporous hues of Chinese silks, carpets, lacquer-ware and the "Chinese Garden," all demonstrate the attraction the culture of the East held for those of the Rococo period.[37]

* * *

If we consider that the time of Marco Polo's visit to China was the first period of Europeans from the West meeting the Chinese in the East, and Matteo Ricci's epoch the second period, followed by James Legge (1815–1897),[38] the Protestant clergyman of the London Missionary Society from Scotland who came to the Far East around the time of the Opium War may definitely be regarded as the representative of a third period. The reasons why we consider him so is that, in the first place, he was a priest, and in the second half of the 19th century there were many priests, or consuls, or merchants in China who, like him, were interested in learning Chinese. Second, he endeavored to be a competent sinologist, and for that purpose he had translated a considerable number of Chinese Classical works. Such efforts was believed to be absolutely necessary by him and his contemporaries, if one were to obtain a thorough understanding of the Chinese, their thought, their beliefs, their way of life, and their institutions. And third, in his later years, after he had translated and published many Chinese Classics, he was made the Foundation professor of Chinese at Oxford (1876). Although he was not the first to have occupied such a Chair either in Europe or in England, he had the most publications and exerted the most profound influence on the academic world, at least in the field of translation. During the 1960s a large collection of his work was reprinted and the University of Hong Kong held an international conference to celebrate his centenary. By taking him as representative, we can afford to pay less attention to some of his contemporaries.

James Legge was not only a Protestant but was also a non-Conformist, that is, of the reformists opposed to the rigid establishment then represented by the Presbyterian Church. He arrived at Malacca when the cannons of the Opium War were still roaring (the Dutch wrested the city of Malacca from Portugal in 1641, but ceded it to Britain in 1824). The theoretical geographical area of the activities of the London Missionary at the time included Guangzhou and Macau. However, the fact was that Macau had been monopolized by the Portuguese and the Catholics as their headquarters, and China would not permit any British subject to live in Guangzhou except the staff of the British East India Company. Legge's predecessor, Robert Morrison (1782–1834), the pioneer Protestant evangelist who came to the Far East some 35 years before Legge, died in Guangzhou while working as an interpreter for the East India Company, for China was not accessible for preaching; Malacca was then the only suitable place for their base. Had it not been for the concluding of the Treaty of Nanking (1842) and the ceding of Hong Kong to Britain, most likely Legge would still have had to use the place as his operation base, and follow Morrison's footsteps to serve as the principal of the Anglo-Chinese College founded by him and take care of the *Bible* printing-house. He would not have been able to move the base to Hong Kong as he did in 1843.

As you know Matteo Ricci had stayed in China for 27 years, Legge spent nearly 26 years of his life in Hong Kong from 1843 to 1873 except for those four-odd years in which he returned twice to England for health or other reasons. The five huge volumes of *The Chinese Classics* he translated, including the *Four Books*, the *Book of History*, the *Book of Odes*, and the *Spring and Autumn Annals*, together with the *Zuo Commentary*, were all published the year before his last departure for his homeland (there are actually eight volumes as three of them are divided into two parts and bound as two separate volumes). This work was not simple, even the printing with types of both languages set side-by-side was a gigantic job. No wonder it took 11 laborious years to complete. We cannot but be amazed by the wide knowledge of the traditional Chinese culture of the translator, this clergyman who came from the West, and his incomparable perseverance. Some have claimed that Legge in his translations had the assistance of Wang Tao (1828–1890),[39] a talented native scholar from Suzhou, who was suspected by the Qing authorities of having had some sort of involvement in the Taiping rebellious activities at the time, and had fled his country to Hong Kong for refuge. Wang Tao arrived in Hong Kong in October 1862, where he soon became a good friend and assistant to Legge. For many years their collaboration was quite admirable, and this we cannot deny. As you know their cooperation began with the *Book of History*, the third volume of Legge's *Chinese Classics*, but before it the first two volumes, the three of the *Four Books* and the *Works of Mencius* were already published. Wang Tao's assistance can only be seen throughout the last three volumes, and some remnants taken from Wang's manuscript notes called the *Liji jishi* (Collected Commentaries to the *Book of Rites*) and the *Zhouyi jishi* (Collected Commentaries to the *Book of Change*) are also found in Legge's translations of these two classics. My statement here is of course not intended to detract in any way from the merit of Wang Tao's contributions in Legge's work.

Dr Joseph Edkins (1823–1905) of Shanghai recorded that Legge "had great advantages in the constitution of his mind." He wrote, "Once as he and I paced the deck of our vessel on his second voyage to China, we occupied ourselves with repeating whole books of the *New Testament*. I remember he easily acquired the *Epistle to the Hebrews*. He was able to prompt me, I was unable to prompt him."[40] Other sources inform us that Legge had a good command of Latin, was partial to the magnificent style of classical language, and therefore, even though he had only a few months training in the Chinese language under Professor Samuel Kidd of the London University before undertaking his journey, as soon as he arrived in Malacca he was eager to give it a try. If you care to read carefully the *Prolegomena* to each of his translated classics (none of them is shorter than 120 pages and one extends as far as 208), we shall see that not only was he well provided with supporting material but was also often prepared to make changes and alternations and was never afraid to improve his work. Besides the help he received from Wang Tao and others, Legge already indicated very clearly that his works were not unaided. In each case he would never fail to consult the translations produced by earlier scholars, whether in Latin, or in English, French, German, or Italian. By taking one existing work as a model, and adding to his own deliberations and discussions with Wang Tao and others, the chances of committing errors were certainly reduced. The two exceptions were the *Zuo Commentary*, a Russian translation, which was unavailable, and the *Book of Rites*, for which Legge had little reference material. It is by pondering over the successful translation of these two works one may come to appreciate his great contributions.

Whether he inherited the idea from Matteo Ricci or not, in Legge's translations of the *Book of Odes* and the *Book of History* the term *shangdi* and God are equated. When these works were published as the third volume of the *Sacred Books of the East*, in June 1880, no less than 23 gentlemen addressed a protest letter to the editor, Professor F Max Müller (1823–1900). This being true, the fact that Legge and Ricci lived in different times and this, we may like to add, was very unfortunate for him. Let us recall that when he first came to the East, it was the time of the Opium War. In the year of his death (1897), Taiwan and Penghu (Pescadores) had been ceded to Japan, and after that came the time that Germany occupied and then leased the Jiaozhouwan (Kiaochow Bay), an inlet of the Yellow Sea. To follow suit Russia leased Lushun (Port Arthur) and Dalian (Dairen), Britain took another port, Weihaiwei, as a naval base to counter Russia, and France had Guangzhouwan (Kwangchow Wan) as her Fort Bayard in the south. And there was the civil war known as the Taiping Rebellion which lasted over 15 years, the occupation of the capital by the allied forces of Britain and France in 1860, and the heavy loss of territories China suffered over the years on her northeastern frontier from Russia and her southwestern frontier from Britain and France. All of these showed that the country was on the verge of disintegration, could hardly qualify as a sovereign state.

The attitude of the Westerners at that time was so different from that of their forerunners in the late Ming and early Qing. For, although the Jesuits might not have believed China was superior to the West and treated the Chinese as their betters, they did treat them as equals, and they did cherish the idea of harmony and friendship. During the time of James Legge, it may be said — even of those clergymen who turned professors after they returned to their native lands — that the idea they cherished was to give instruction to the backward and ignorant; they believed China needed their help to find salvation. While dispensing the gospels (the equivalent in Chinese is the Voice of Blessing), they boasted in church and strutted self-satisfied in public. But in their hearts they could not help but think this was a savage country, a sinking vessel beyond redemption. The fact is that not all they believed was untrue. China definitely had her faults and had only herself to blame. The harsh criticisms made by her neighbors may have served as a timely warning. The relationship between two nations is not very different from that between two persons. Friendship is reciprocal. The invaders may strut with heads in the clouds, but there is something which is liable to rebound. Sometimes remorse is felt only after the passing of generations. I have mentioned briefly Germany's occupation of the Jiaozhouwan. Professor Herbert Franke of Munich University wrote in 1968, "German Sinology was also furthered by politics to a certain extent after the territory of Kiaoutschou was leased by the German Empire in 1898. But the loss of the outpost through the Treaty of Versailles was soon shown to be a piece of good fortune, since relations between Germany and China after 1919 thereby escaped the stresses which tended to accompany the imperialist attitude of western states towards Asian peoples. Germany's withdrawal from the struggle for power in east Asia had nothing but a favourable effect."[41]

China has gone through tremendous changes since the end of the Second World War. The shackles and fetters imposed upon her over 100 years were removed, though not without a heavy price. The time of blindly eulogizing China for her unprecedented and violent Cultural Revolution is over. The domino theory proved inconsequent even after the tumultuous times followed the conclusion of the Vietnam War, and China has been readmitted to the international arena for peace. It is lucky for China and the Chinese people, who have not lost their special share of grace, as Matteo Ricci had so happily pointed out. They have braved so many calamities and difficulties and have regained the strength to rebuild their homeland. Both Ricci and James Legge were said to have been versed in the study of Chinese Classics. Had they really grasped a true understanding of the Chinese mind? What was the ultimate attitude of the traditional Chinese toward the world? How would the Chinese like to treat their neighbors, and be treated by them? The following passage, quoted from Legge's translation of the *Book of Rites* (*Li Chi*), may be important for China's neighbors to hear:

> When the Grand Course was pursued, a public and common spirit ruled all under the sky; they chose men of talents, virtue, and ability; their words were sincere, and what they cultivated was harmony. Thus men did not love their parents only, nor treat as children only their own sons. A competent provision was secured for the aged till their death, employment for the able-bodied, and the means of growing up to the young. They showed kindness and compassion to widows, orphans, childless men, and those who were disabled by disease, so that they were all sufficiently maintained. Males had their proper work, and females had their homes. (They accumulated) articles (of value), disliking that they should be thrown away upon the ground, but not wishing to keep them for their own gratification. (They laboured) with their strength, disliking that it should not be exerted, but exerting it (only) with a view to their own advantage. In this way (selfish) scheming were repressed and found no development. Robbers, filchers and rebellious traitors did not show themselves, and hence the outer doors remained open, and were not shut. This was (the period of) what we call the Grand Union.
>
> *Li Chi*, Ch. VII, *Li Yun*[42]

Legge praised the chapter from which this passage is taken as "one of the most valuable in the whole work."[43] He believed those words recorded the utterance of Confucius, without the prompting of an interlocutor. Should what he said be correct, and should a modern Herodotus like to visit the present-day China where the trend of studying Confucian texts and thought has been seriously taken up again, might he not be politely informed that the passage we have just heard is socialism with Chinese characteristics?

Notes

1. *Wu Teh Yao Memorial Lectures*, The Centre for the Arts, National University of Singapore, Singapore, 1995, "Foreword", p. 1.
2. The Emperor Xianzong.
3. Biography of Xuliewu, *Xin Yuanshi*, juan 108; B. Spuler (1939). *Die Mongolen in Iran*. Leipzig: J.C. Hinrichs.
4. The Emperor Shizu.
5. Leonardo Olschki (1960). *Marco Polo's Asia*. Berkeley: University of California, pp. *48ff*.
6. The Emperor Dingzong.
7. I. de Rachewiltz (1971). *Papal Envoys to the Great Khans*. London: Faber & Faber, pp. 98–102.
8. *Cf* W.W. Rockhill (trans.) (1900). *The Journal of William of Rubruck*. London: Hakluyt Society.
9. I. de Rachewiltz (1971). *op. cit.*, p. 134.
10. Leonardo Olschki (1960). *op. cit.*, pp. 29–31.
11. Wolfgang Franke (1976). "Matteo Ricci". In *Dictionary of Ming Biography*, L. Carrington Goodrich and Chaoying Fang (eds.), pp. 1137–1144. New York: Columbia University Press.
12. Invented probably by Hipparchus (150 BC).
13. Henri Cordier. *Bibliotheca Sinica*, Vol. 11, pp. 1392–1394.
14. Luo Changpei (1934). "Yesuhui shi zai yinyunxueshang de gongxian". In *Bulletin of the Institute of History & Philology*, Academia Sinica, No. 3, Pt 3, Peiping, pp. 267–338.
15. Chen Yuan (1927). "Mingji zhi ouhuameishuji luomazi zhuyin". Tongxian; Henri Cordier, *op. cit.*, V, p. 3677.
16. Simon Leys (trans.) (1997). *The Analects of Confucius*, 13:3, New York: Norton, pp. 60–61.
17. Ibid., 3:24, p. 13.
18. Ho Peng Yoke (1983). "Dui Liyuese he *Zhongguo kexue jishushi* de renshi". In *Bulletin of the Institute of Modern History*, Academia Sinica, No. 12, Taipei, p. 425.
19. Fung Kam-Wing (1997). "Christopher Clavius and Li Zhizao", a paper read at the XXth International Congress of Science, July, 1997 at Liege, Belgium.
20. Hong Weilian (William Hung) (1936). "Kao Limadou de shijieditu", *Yugong*, V: 3–4, Peiping.
21. *Jinshu*, juan 35.
22. *Jiu Tangshu*, juan 13 and 138.
23. Zhang Guogan (1962). *Zhongguo gufangzhi kao*. Beiging: Zhonghua, pp. 77–78.
24. *Mingshi*, juan 283 and *Mingru xuean*, juan 24. Zhang, a great Confucian scholar from Jiangxi, was the head of the White Deer Grotto Academy around 1592. See L. Carrington Goodrich and C.A. Tay (1976). "Chang Huang". In *Dictionary of Ming Biography*, Vol. I, pp. 83–85, New York: Columbia University Press.

25. Fung, *ibid.*; Chen Yuan (1980). "Zhexi Li Zhizao zhuan". In *Chen Yuan xueshu lunwenji*, 1, pp. 71–79. Beijing: Zhonghua; Paul Teh-lu Yap and J.C. Yang (1943–1944). "Li Chih-tsao". In *Eminent Chinese of the Ch'ing Period*, Arthur W. Hummel (ed.), pp. 452–454. Washington; Leung Yuen Sang, "Qiusuo dongxi tiandijian" in *Ruxue guoji xueshu taolunhui lunwenji* (International Conference on Confucian Studies), Vol. II, Qilu shushe, Jinan, 1989, pp. 1127–1147.
26. *Mingshi*, juan 251; J.C. Yang (1943–1944). "Hsü Kuang-chi". In *Eminent Chinese of the Ch'ing Period, ibid.* pp. 316–319.
27. Chen Yuan (1980). "Zhexi Li Zhizao zhuan", *ibid.* p. 76.
28. *Mingshi*, juan 283, *Mingru xuean*, juan 18; Huang, Stanley Y.C. (1976). "Lo Hung-hsien". In *Dictionary of Ming Biography, ibid.*, Vol. I, pp. 980–984.
29. Zhang Guogan, *ibid.*, pp. 123–124.
30. See *Siku quanshu zongmu*, juan 106 under "*Celiang guangyi*".
31. *Siku quanshu zongmu*, juan 102.
32. See note 18, also *Siku quanshu zongmu*, juan 106.
33. See note 19.
34. For the thought of Zhu Hong, see Leo Hurvitz (1970). "Chu-hung's One Mind of Pure Land and Ch'an Buddhism". In *Self and Society in Ming Thought*, William Theodore de Bary (ed.), pp. 451–481. New York: Columbia University Press.
35. *Mingshi*, juan 218; Lienche Tu Fang (1976). "Shen Ch'iieh". In *Dictionary of Ming Biography, ibid.*, Vol. II, pp. 1177–1179.
36. Lienche Tu Fang (1976). *ibid.*; the *Nangong shudu* is included in the *Poxieji*, Japanese edition, 1855. Read also Chen Yuan, "Zhexi Li Zhizao zhuan", *ibid.*, p. 75.
37. Adolf Reichwein (trans. by JC Powell) (1925). *China and Europe: Intellectual and Artistic Contacts in the Eighteenth Century.* London: Kegan Paul, Trench, Trubner & Co., pp. 23–72.
38. Lindsay Ride (1960). "Biographical Note" attached to the reprinted edition of *The Chinese Classics.* Hong Kong: University of Hong Kong Press, pp. 1–25.
39. Roswell S. Britton, "Wang T'ao" in *Eminent Chinese of the Ch'ing Period, ibid.*, pp. 36–39; H. McAleavy (1953). *Wang T'ao.* China Society Occasional Papers No. 7, London.
40. Quoted in Lindsay Ride, *ibid.*, p. 20.
41. Herbert Franke (1968). *Sinology at German Universities.* Germany: Franz Steiner, Wiesbaden, pp. 12–13.
42. *Li Chi*, Vol. 1, New Hyde Park, New York: University Books 1967, pp. 365–66.
43. *Op. cit.*, Translator's *Introduction*, p. 24.

ରେ 5 ଯେ
ACROSS TRANSLINGUAL LANDSCAPE: CRISIS AND INNOVATION IN CONTEMPORARY CHINESE CULTURES*

LEO OU-FAN LEE

Harvard University, USA

"It is in one's own language that one is bilingual or multilingual."

Gilles Deleuze

The modern Chinese writer Lao She wrote a novel about Singapore, Xiaobo de shengri (Xiaobo's birthday), in which the hero is a young boy of Chinese origin who is confused about his identity: he is not sure whether he is Fukienese, Cantonese, Indian, Malay, white, or Japanese. His father, who originally comes from Guangdong, owns a Chinese goods store which is guarded by an Indian janitor, but he cannot find either China or India in the map of Singapore. His father also harbors prejudices against Chinese from other regions, such as Fukienese and Shanghainese. Still, his father hires a teacher from Shanghai to teach Xiaobo Chinese (guoyu), whereas his brother learns a different language, "guizihua" or "devil's tongue" (i.e., English) which confuses him even more. His favorite toy is a sash made of tom silk: if he puts it on his head as a turban, he becomes Indian; if he puts

---

*This chapter is a reproduction of the Wu Teh Yao memorial lecture given by the author in 1999.

it around his waist, he becomes Malay. His favorite pastime is to play with other kids in the garden — Fukienese, Malay, and Indian — and they all communicate with one another in Malay. When his brother threatens to report this "misdemeanor" to their father, Xiaobo replies: "I can turn them all into Chinese when we play — isn't that enough?" Besides, children do change colors, like birds. So "when Indian children grow up, they become Chinese."[1] Thus in one stroke Xiaobo solves the race problem in Singapore.

This remarkable episode from Chapter Two of the novel is relevant to the issues discussed in this chapter. More than half a century ago, Lao She already saw a multiracial and multilingual society in the making in Singapore. The idyllic scene of Xiaobo playing with other children could be interpreted as representing a kind of utopia, which comes quite close to the vision of the present-day Singapore, according to Wong Yoon Wah.[2] But there are also certain things left unsaid in Lao She's story. In this idyllic portrait, Lao She obviously chose to emphasize racial harmony through difference and deemphasize the potential tension such difference may cause. One element is language. It is clear that in Xiaobo's family they all speak Cantonese, not Mandarin. Xiaobo surmises that "anyone who doesn't speak Cantonese or Fukienese and wears foreign clothes must be Shanghainese." But so do the "foreign devils," who also wear foreign clothes but speak a different, and equally incomprehensible, language. "Perhaps all foreign devils come from Shanghai?"[3] Why then could one of them become his Mandarin language teacher? Xiaobo's language confusion is also a mirror of a larger issue of multilingualism whose implications on contemporary Chinese culture need to be unraveled.

In the story, Lao She has chosen to focus on the oral side of this language babel. Since it is a story about children, little is said about the written language. For instance, the Shanghai teacher hired to teach Xiaobo how to read and write Mandarin, in addition to speaking it? Perhaps so. Like the Shanghai teacher, Lao She himself got a job teaching Chinese at a local school when he landed in Singapore in 1929. Lao She was probably hired to teach "Zhongwen" — that is, Chinese in both oral and written form, both language and literature or language through literature. As is well known, in traditional Chinese curriculum for children, the written word (wen) carries more weight than oral speech; the two sides were definitely not the same.

Lao She spoke perfect Mandarin — perhaps too perfect, because as we know, he came from a Manchu family in Peking. His Mandarin must have contained a very pronounced Peking accent that distinguished his speech from the usual Mandarin spoken by others, such as Xiaobo's Shanghai teacher. The latter's speech can be called Putonghua — a more common and generalized Mandarin, a term now adopted officially in the People's Republic — as opposed to the pure native Pekingese or "Jingpianzi" that Lao She spoke. To be sure, the differences between Mandarin and the Peking dialect is far less noticeable than, say, between Mandarin and Cantonese. Still, such a differentiation must be made in order to see Lao She's linguistic advantage over other modern Chinese writers, such as Lu Xun, who came from the south. Mandarin, as we all know, is a northern tongue close to Pekingese, and all southerners have to learn it with effort, especially perhaps people from Guangdong — hence the popular derogative saying, "fear not heaven or earth; fear only when a Cantonese tries to speak Mandarin." Lao She also enjoys a distinct advantage in writing Mandarin, as the natural rhythm of his native speech can be easily transposed into his written prose. This easy colloquialism in both dialogue and narration is a endearing hallmark of Lao She's fictional style, especially to readers of his native place, Peking. His stories can also be read aloud, much as storytellers did in traditional China. (For that matter, Lao She's favorite English author, Charles Dickens, also used to read his stories aloud to friends at home before they were serialized in newspapers and printed as books.) For Chinese readers from other regions, however, perhaps this colloquial flavor would not be so noticeable and appreciated.

We must be aware of the fact that guoyu as the written national language was a cultural construction, which began with Literary Revolution in 1917, when Hu Shi formally promoted the use of baihua or the modern vernacular as the language of the New Literature. Central to Hu's argument is that baihua reflects living speech. In his opinion there is no difference between writing (wen) and speech (bai): what you speak is what you write. This intended transparency can be persuasive as theory or polemics but it certainly does not measure up in practice. The modern Mandarin as written is not exactly the same as spoken when we come to Hu Shi's major area of concern, modern Chinese literature. Critics of the time already pointed out that even the written form of May Fourth baihua had become increasingly "intellectualized" with its somewhat Europeanized syntax and a vocabulary containing a wealth of foreign words and expressions. It is certainly a far cry from the colloquial speech of any Mandarin speaker. In other words, written baihua soon became the privileged language of intellectuals, as elitist as the classical language or wenyan it was supposed to replace.

Hu Shi's linguistic ambitions also go beyond the literary domain. In one of his famous essays he coins a pompous slogan: "guoyu de wenxue, wenxue de guoyu" or "a literature of national language, and a literary national language"; presumably the latter can only come from the former.[4] If so, New Literature is given an enormous mission, to create a language that can serve as a unifying tool for nationalism and nation-building. In this sense, Mandarin is indeed guoyu. To Hu's joy, written baihua was quickly adopted by the Nationalist government: the Ministry of Education decreed in the early 1920s that the modern vernacular would be used in all primary school textbooks. However, in literary practice, the uses of the modern vernacular proved to be far more complicated. Though widely adopted by writers, its linguistic state remained unstable. Moreover, the publishing scene in the early Republican era was by no means confined to writings by May Fourth authors. There were certainly many readers who preferred other journals and newspapers and other works by writers not associated with New Literature, for instance, those of the so-called Butterfly School of fiction which incorporated more idioms from the south, particularly the Lower Yangtze River region.

How to write in a proper modern vernacular style? If according to Hu Shi the modern baihua is a living speech, not a dead language like wenyan, then it must reflect the living speech patterns of Chinese people of all regions, which would surely include regional dialects. Suffice it to say here that the use of dialects in modern Chinese literature, especially fiction, was never a settled matter. Hu Shi acknowledged its liveliness but did not actively promote its use. The reason for this may have something to do with the political background, for the promulgation of guoyu had become a national issue and as such no regional patois must be put in a position to challenge its authority.

Thus for better or worse, the bulk of modern Chinese literature was created largely in a "Mandarin mode," that is, its narrative and descriptive style basically reflects the living speech of the northern region. It leaves a large lacuna unfilled: local idioms of other regions are in a way short-changed. When we read Lu Xun's stories, it is hard to imagine that Ah Q or Xianglin's Wife was speaking with a southern (Shaoxing) accent. A few local idioms can be spotted in Lu Xun's prose, but in general he adopted a modern vernacular based on Mandarin, which befits the speech patterns of intellectuals more than it does peasants. This is also true of most May Fourth writers. It would be difficult to reproduce in written form the tonal variations of local dialects anyway, not to mention the lack of written forms for certain dialectical expressions. When May Fourth writers wanted to express locality or local color, they resorted to thick description (as in Shen Congwen's fiction) or to inserting a few local terms in the characters' dialogues. Seldom do we find sustained narratorial voices using a local dialect. The issues involved are both linguistic and ideological. Most Chinese dialects do not have written equivalents, and words have to be coined which most readers do not understand. With the increasing prevalence of Mandarin as guoyu, it has come to be taken for granted that excessive use of dialects is not a good thing. Years later in Taiwan in the 1970s, the talented writer Wang Zhenhe wrote some of his stories with a heavy usage of the Taiwanese dialect for both mimetic and artistic effect, thereby generating great controversy among readers and critics. Wang's stories heralded a burgeoning literary movement for Taiwanese nativism (xiangtu wenxue), which advocated the authentic depiction of Taiwanese reality, including the use of its dialects as a counter strategy against the hegemony of the Mandarin as required by the Mainlander-dominated Nationalist government. This literary movement paved the way for the political self-empowerment of native Taiwanese in recent times.

* * *

On Mainland China, the fate of the modern vernacular underwent a different transformation. Instead of dialects, the crucial element in the new revolutionary literature was politics and political language. For some 30 years after Liberation, Maoist rhetoric suffused all texts, literary or otherwise. Thus when Mao died in 1976, a stylistic reaction was soon underway among writers of a younger generation who turned their own experiences as youths sent down to the countryside into a new quest for cultural creativity and renewal. Under the heading of "searching for roots," writers like Han Shaogong, Zheng Wanlong, Ah Cheng, and many others argued openly that the heavily politicized language used by the Party, which permeated everyday life, must be renounced. The genuine roots of Chinese culture must be sought elsewhere, in remote regions where the local languages still preserve certain old expressions that are untainted by political ideology. Han Shaogong's own linguistic quest has led him to his most recent novel, titled *Maqiao cidian* (*A dictionary of Maqiao village*), which organizes its many strands of plot in a dictionary of local words and expressions.[5] Locality therefore becomes a subversive site against central authority, and language its most powerful weapon.

Other younger writers went even further. The critic Li Tuo, in commenting on the writings of Yu Hua, has openly announced that the long-established peasant style first established in Yan'an by Mao is now dead; in its place is a new fictional language that is artistically experimental and utterly "self-conscious."[6] Li calls this a new language revolution which not only deconstructs the Maoist tradition of "workers–peasants–soldiers" literature but also lifts contemporary Chinese fiction to a new plane even beyond May Fourth realism. Despite its bravado, Li's claim indeed marks a significant departure: since the early 1980s, fiction and poetry produced on the Mainland has become not only depoliticized but also has become more open and variegated in style. The mimetic function of early May Fourth baihua has been extended to new "metaphysical" frontiers just as everyday reality itself has lost its old political meaning. For all its flaunted experimentalism and Western borrowing (from Kafka and Garcia Marquez, in particular), this new genre of literature has certainly enriched the modern Chinese baihua, just as Taiwanese writers like Wang Zhenhe have done by their purposeful use of native dialects.

Still the Shanghai woman writer Wang Anyi has argued that for better or worse Mainland writing had come closer to Hu Shi's ideal of "yanwen heyi" or the unity of speech and writing, the oral and the written, than Taiwanese literature.[7] According to her, Mainland writing has become increasingly colloquial as it has incorporated a large number of dialects and local idioms, especially from the northern regions. In Taiwan, on the other hand, the language of creative writing has become more "technical" and follows stricter syntactical structures.[8] The resulting effect is a separation of writing from speech together with a heightened stylistic consciousness. As such it is further removed from the May Fourth baihua tradition. However, as noted earlier, the experimental writing from a younger generation on the Mainland is equally oriented toward fictional technique. Despite differences of content and style, a consciousness of technique and of fictional language's capability of self-referentiality can be regarded as their shared characteristic. A baihua literary tradition built on the ideal of linguistic transparency, in which the oral vernacular is supposed to be reflected directly in written form, is destroyed forever.

If even in the "core" areas of Mainland China and Taiwan the written baihua no longer has a set standard, especially in creative literature, it would be futile for writers in the "peripheral" areas such as Malaysia and Singapore to imitate the speech patterns of north China or the peasant idioms. The Malaysian-Chinese writer and critic Huang Jinshu has argued that a contemporary writer from such regions can no longer follow the May Fourth baihua tradition; they must fall back on the technique of language as the only recourse — something to be worked at consciously. The problem with Chinese literature in Malaysia (Mahua wenxue), in his view, is not that it is too technical but that it is not technical enough.[9] Moreover the written Chinese in Malaysia is bound to be impure as it stems from a multilingual environment in which the inclusion and impact of foreign languages is inevitable. At the same time, the pull of oral dialects in such an environment makes writing in Mandarin less natural and more effortful. If a prevalent dialect has no written equivalent, is it still possible to create a written literature in Chinese? With his implicit nationalist vision, Hu Shi never thought of such a possibility.

We can push the argument even further: What if the local Chinese writers in these regions are capable only of spoken Chinese (dialect) but not written Chinese? What if, through birth or education, one's written language is English to begin with? This is indeed the fate of the so-called Baba and "Nyonya" writers for whom Chinese, in both written and spoken (Mandarin) forms, has become an alien language. In short can a writer of Chinese origin write about Chinese life in a foreign language such as English? The answer is yes. But the consequential question that seems to beset a number of Malaysian-Chinese and Singaporean-Chinese writers who write in English is: how authentically? Would there be a language barrier created by the intrinsic properties of the languages themselves? Does it require a "cleansing process" — "to clean out their traditional connotations whenever they intrude inappropriately into the texture and feel of the writing" (in the words of Wong Phui Nam)?[10] Would a non-English writer who writes in English inevitably become a "miscegenated" being? Interestingly, such issues have never been raised, as far as I know, by Chinese-American writers who have accepted American English as given without much self-reflection.

Allow me to quote the testimonial of one such writer, Catherine Lim, who began writing short stories in English about life and people from her childhood. "I wrote about an old Chinese woman who had a dream of the Goddess Kuan Yin. I wrote about another old woman whose daughter-in-law was threatening to throw out all the ugly ancestral tablets." At first, Lim was quite confident. "The stories bubbled with Chinese-ness. And they were written in English, an alien and alienating language! This language, the only one I was competent to write in, was proving no obstacle at all. It was submitting graciously to the demands of my local subjects. Then — surprise of surprises! — I discovered that the very language I had thought inappropriate because too lofty for my humble subjects were actually quite inadequate to satisfy the linguistic demands of these subjects. In the matter of Chinese curses, for instance. Now Chinese curses just cannot be reproduced in English without losing some of their power."[11] Lim found it necessary to create new words in English in order "to capture Chinese concepts and throw in such local terms as "kampong" and "malu" and "gila," and "suay": never mind about explaining what each meant as long as they conveyed the rhythm of local small town life and gave a whiff of local small town smells.[12] What, then, would be the next step? Singlish — an intentionally impure English with Singaporean characteristics? Or should she still preserve the basic syntactical structure of English? A comparable strategy was used by May Fourth writers when they wished to evoke the color and smell of small town life by coining new dialect terms within the general grammatical confines of written Mandarin. The result is a kind of local tokenism that does not do full justice to a particular locality. On the other hand, however, it could be a heavily dialecticized prose that defies understanding and baffles the general reader. There is no easy solution except through incessant striving in technique and style.

Instead of debating the issue of whether Mandarin or local dialect or English should be considered a primary language or "mother tongue" in a multilingual society such as Singapore, I would rather bring the matter out of the local context and, for comparison, cite the example of a writer from a totally different era and place, Franz Kafka, the Jewish writer who lived in the Czech capital of Prague and chose to write in the language of what was known as "Prague German." The famous French theorists Gilles Deleuze and Felix Guattari have written a book on this matter, titled *Kafka: Toward a Minor Literature*. What, then, is a "minor literature?" According to Deleuze and Guattari, "a minor literature doesn't come from a minor language; it is rather that which a minority constructs within a major language."[13] As such it would apply to both Kafka's works and to works written by people like Catherine Lim who lived outside the Chinese culture zone, whether in Chinese or English (since both are acknowledged to be "major" languages). What Deleuze and Guattari chose to emphasize is not only the language itself but the linguistic and cultural environment in which such a literature is created. They have attributed three characteristics to such a minor literature, based on the example of Kafka. First, it is by definition "de-territorialized," in which "everything is political" and "everything takes on a collective value." Second, it is also "literature that actively produces a solidarity in spite of scepticism." Third, "if a writer is in the margins or completely outside his or her fragile community, this situation allows the writer all the more the possibility to express another possible community and to forge the means for another consciousness and another sensibility."[14]

Asian-American writers would readily agree to such a definition, but would it be appropriate for Chinese or English writing produced in Malaysia, Singapore, or even Hong Kong? How do writers in these regions "express another possible community"? How to forge the means for another consciousness and sensibility? Deleuze and Guattari consider it to be a problem for all of us who live in the contemporary age: "How to tear a minor literature away from its own language, allowing it to challenge the language and making it follow a sober revolutionary path? How to become a nomad and an immigrant and a gypsy in relation to one's own language? Kafka's answer: steal the baby from its crib, walk the tight rope."[15] It is certainly easier said than done. Such an act presumes the recognition of "marginality" — without any sense of self-inferiority vis-à-vis the "major" language and mainstream culture — that enables a writer to be actively engaged in a critical dialogue with them. At the very least, it forges the means for a kind of multicultural consciousness based on a bilingual sensibility.

The issue of "de-territorialization" is also more complicated in the present Pan-Chinese sphere — Mainland China, Taiwan, Hong Kong, Singapore, and the Chinese Diasporas in North America — than in Kafka's Europe, especially when we extend our discussion to language use outside of serious literature. In this popular domain, we are indeed crossing multilingual landscapes, as there are enormous variations of Chinese language use, both oral and written, from region to region, which seem to pose a frontal challenge to centripetal dominance of Mandarin. The phenomenon reminds us again of one more remark by Deleuze: "The more a language has or acquires the characteristics of a major language, the more it is affected by continuous variations that transpose it into a 'minor' language."[16] In reality, this phenomenon is caused by media and migration: the constant mobility of peoples and growing popularity of new audiovisual products (movies, television, compact disks, VCDs and DVDs, as well as computers and the internet) in everyday life. The following discussion will therefore, switch to a "minor" key as a more personal and informal voice is adopted without belittling its major impact and importance.

* * *

This Pan-Chinese world I would like to describe certainly cuts across national boundaries. Obviously, problems of "identity politics" are involved which differ markedly from the identity politics in the United States in which the key issues are race and gender. Rather, they are manifested and symbolized in languages. It seems that in all these areas except the northern regions of Mainland China dialects are thriving alongside Mandarin and English as spoken languages; in fact, there is increasing assertiveness of both orality and dialect power. As is well known to all, the regional dialect in Guangdong is Cantonese, which continues to be widely used in Hong Kong despite its "return to the motherland" in 1997. In present-day Taiwan, the Taiwanese dialect (or southern Fukienese) is assuming public and near official status, especially in urban business circles and in the countryside, whereas Mandarin is used in official circles and in the more cosmopolitan city of Taipei. In Hong Kong, Singapore, and the "Diaspora" communities in Australia and North America, this situation of dialect plus Mandarin is further complicated by the prevalence of English (and Malay in Malaysia). This multiplicity of spoken tongues and the constant shift from one to the other within the same daily discourse has become a habit, sometimes out of necessity and other times as a way to indicate one's ancestral origin or ideological loyalty. A Singaporean uses the Fukien dialect when speaking to a Taiwanese tourist, but shifts to Mandarin when meeting with a visitor from Mainland China. A Hong Kong businessman speaks with a Mainland colleague in Mandarin, or English with an American officemate, but shifts with relief to Cantonese when talking with someone local or in Canton. A Taiwanese restaurateur in Los Angeles greets a Chinese-looking customer first in English; then quickly shifts to Mandarin or Taiwanese.

For some residents in the Chinese diasporas, their command of written Chinese is no longer so assured after long period of residence. This disequilibrium between the oral and the written is of no major concern except for writers and linguists, but even so the implications for contemporary Chinese culture are immense. While they may still be vaguely called Chinese because of their ancestral origin, their Chinese-ness has taken on an "inter-national" and multicultural character. Traveling in such "trans-Chinese" and translingual landscapes I have been engaged in a kind of practical (that is, not entirely academic) research in order to negotiate my way through these regions and capture their different cultural sensibilities. Over the years, through personal observation, conversations with friends and colleagues, and reading a fair amount of the written materials in the public domain (mainly newspapers and journals in Chinese), I have come to treasure this experience which I present here for both self-reflection and as a test case for further study and debate.

It would seem that anyone interested in meaningful dialogue in these areas needs a spoken knowledge of two or three Chinese "languages" in addition to English. To be attuned to the nuances of such a polyglot world has become almost a pre-requisite to appreciating such diverse sensibilities. Obviously the task entails other ramifications. A dialect such as Taiwanese is being turned into a major language with near official status in Taiwan. On the other hand, dialects including Taiwanese are also undergoing a process of "de-territorialization" by migration and Diaspora, which make them more centrifugal and more mixed. Cantonese spoken in Toronto and Montreal may sound the same as in Hong Kong or Canton, but different diasporic contexts serve to create different linguistic tensions between Cantonese and the major languages there (Canadian English, and/or French). Even in the case of Mandarin use on the Mainland, it has been sufficiently "de-territorialized" into a generalized "common language" or putonghua, its purity and homogeneity inevitably compromised by regional accents in different areas. Another form of de-territorialization can be found in the Mandarin spoken by Taiwanese and Hong Kong residents doing business on the Mainland, who carry their own "minor" accents. In daily practice, the so-called standard Mandarin "accent" (as it is still taught in the Chinese classes in American universities) has become increasingly irrelevant.

Finding my way through this multilingual maze, I notice that my own spoken Mandarin, a near native language, has been subjected to different receptions in different areas. In Beijing, I was taken to be a native, but not quite, since I do not exhibit the expected idiomatic and tonal nuances. In Taiwan I have been taken as a Mainlander because of my "Peking accent" despite the fact that I spent more than a dozen years in Taiwan but no more than six months in Beijing altogether. In Hong Kong, my half-baked Cantonese was laughed at by natives many years ago, when I struggled to learn it in order to teach more effectively, but was recently found acceptable though I speak less well than before due to lack of practice. This state of my language competence places me as a half outsider in all three areas, and my own sense of an outsider's status has also varied when at different times I found the local language pleasantly familiar or intolerably alien. In Singapore, my unrehearsed remarks on the definition of "mother tongue" to the local press were greeted by one local commentator (in English) as revealing a Mandarin-speaking bias, although I am known to favor dialects for reasons of my own. Growing up in Taiwan, I was a victim of the Guomindang government's compulsory Mandarin-speaking policy in the classroom: I was educated not to speak Taiwanese. However, through classmates in the small town of Hsinchu, I acquired a passive understanding which is now losing its hold. But the dialect to which I still feel a warm empathy is Hakka, a minor language which has been used to great effect in Hou Hsiao-hsien's films, such as "A Time to Love and a Time to Die" (Tungnian wangshi). Why am I instinctively drawn to Hakka? Is it due to personal memory since at high school I had many Hakka-speaking friends? Or is it because Hakka is a kind of diasporic language to begin with — a language of "guests", of a migrant people who are never at home anywhere, hence a fitting metaphor for my own existential condition?

Unlike India, the written Chinese language seems to remain the same everywhere, at least on surface. But there are equally daunting complexities and variations in the daily use of written Chinese. The second generation of Chinese immigrants in America are losing their grip on the Chinese language: they can only maintain a speaking knowledge of their mother tongue, so as to communicate with their parents at home. As years go by, their memory of the written forms; becomes dim, consisting perhaps of a few Chinese characters (often those of their names and their parents). This means that the written ideograph is as much a system of incomprehensible signs to them as to any other persons of non-Chinese backgrounds. Gradually, English assumes the place of dominant language, their new "mother tongue" and a decisive clue to their Americanization. The traits may also be observed in youngsters of other immigrant groups. However, on the other shores of the Pacific, written Chinese continues to hold sway.

In the case of reading, there is not only a great divide between the "jiantizi" (simplified characters) used in China and Singapore and the "fantizi" (the unsimplified) used in Taiwan and Hong Kong but also a further "localization" when dialects are written into it. For instance, fictional narratives in Taiwan nativist (hsiangtu) literature are sprinkled with dialect expressions in written form which make little sense in Mandarin unless the reader knows how to pronounce them in Taiwanese. In Hong Kong newspapers, some essays and cartoons are composed almost entirely of coined words in Cantonese which do not exist in the normal dictionary. To compound this audio-visual mixture in popular cinema, several films by the comedian Chow Sing-chi not only have Cantonese dialogue in their soundtracks but also carry subtitles in written Cantonese, i.e., coined script. The version intended for Taiwan audiences is dubbed in Mandarin, which practically loses all the racy double-entendres in the Cantonese version, not to mention the hilarious accompaniment of Cantonese subtitles. The function of subtitles here is not merely one of listening aid but some kind of comical meta-commentary. Thus, a member of the local audience who can both listen and read Cantonese derives double-pleasure as compared to someone like myself who is illiterate in reading Cantonese but can only comprehend roughly half of the dialogue. I must have also lost half the fun.

One could argue that this case is not so unfamiliar. Some British films with dialogues in heavy local accents also carry subtitles in English. But the subtitles are in Standard English only, and English, like most Western languages, is a phonetic language which seldom gives "ideographic" significance or pleasure. On the other hand, written Chinese is both ideographic and phonetic: in its long evolution each Chinese character is laden with an accretion of references in both sight and sound. Therefore it leaves much room, even before we reach the syntactical level, for "audio-visual" puns and jokes built upon cross-references between writing and speech. Chow Sing-chi's films are but a mundane example. More elaborate puns can be obtained by writers who substitute different words for words with the same sound, for instance, in the implicit puns and riddles directed at political leaders. One well-known riddle has "a monk who holds up an umbrella": the answer refers to his having no hair ("wu fa") — the character for "fa" has the same sound as the character for law — and to his holding an umbrella that shields him from the sky, hence "no sky" (wutian). It conjures up the image (and metaphor) of a despotic figure who obeys no laws and who defies sanctions from heaven — in this case, a barely concealed reference to Mao Zedong.

Such standard wordplays based on cross-references between writing and speeches have been in use for more than a millennium in traditional China. In modern times, the game is further complicated, however, by the intrusion of regional dialects as well as Standard English. Again Hong Kong provides a most illuminating example. A postcolonial critic may well make an "intervention" at the linguistic level by reflecting on a few simple everyday words of consumption: the word compound "siduo" is originally derived in sound from the English word "store," which came into use together with such colonial words as "taipan" and "go-down" and "Ah Sir" (when a policeman addresses his superior). "Basi" for bus and "disi" for taxi are commonplace terms used by everyone, even outside Hong Kong. When the Hong Kong term for taxi is transplanted onto China, it is combined with the local term for small van "mianbao che" (literally bread-shaped car) to coin a new term: "miandi" or "bread-shaped taxi," which used to be the cheapest taxi in Beijing until a few years ago. To hail a taxi, in the local Beijing idiom, is to "dadi" — an abbreviation which literally means "to beat up a taxi!" While the Western colonial origins of such daily words recede in people's consciousness when they speak, the written form of the same terms may tell a slightly different story: these new terms may look very odd in the company of regular words in a written Chinese sentence, jarring its semantic normalcy by juxtaposing the familiar with the outlandish. (This in turn makes an interesting comparison with the massive intrusion of Western terms into modern Japanese, which is **not** an ideographic language.) During the first days of a visit to Beijing a few years ago and staying at one of the newly constructed "multinational" hotels (the Hilton), I was at once struck by the familiarity of interior decor and the unfamiliarity of the local language, even in the hotel lobby. Here is a typical sentence describing a daily occurrence that I hastily jotted down in my diary:

At the hotel entrance, I see a "dakuan" (rich man or big shot: the word "kuan" also means cash) cramming into a "miandi" together with his "xiaomi" (literally "little secretary" with the character "mi" written as "mi" or "honey" — a purposeful change of word, so I was told, because these secretaries serve also as mistresses), who talks constantly over a "dageda" ("big-brother-big" or cellular phone).

As I tried to "translate" this sentence with the help of a local friend, a host of references came to mind: not only the verbal punning of "mi" and "mi" or the local exoticism of "dageda" but also, for a curious eye (if not ear), the implicit link between "dage" or literally "big brother," an address often used in Mafia language, and "xiaomi," which is easily equated in my mind to "little sister" or "xiaomei." The combination brings out not merely the familiar familial address but, more seductively, the intimate address in countless traditional chivalric and romantic novels. (I intentionally suppressed all Freudian fantasies about the "degeda.") How a few words refract a rich array of cultural meaning!

These common words in the contemporary vocabulary give us a palpable sense of living reality — the reality of cultural interaction between these regions which accompanies their economic activities. The task of deciphering their interrelatedness is what I would call translation. (The English word "translation," as Salman Rushdie reminds us, comes etymologically from the Latin for "bearing across."[17]) It is not only an act of transferring meaning but also a way to get in touch with these realities by manoeuvring the cultural codes behind them. As an interpretive act it involves the dual task of excavation and extension: the former is generic and genealogical, by going back to the possible literary and cultural resources; the latter is spatial and territorial, as it moves horizontally from one region to another in order to establish some linkages. Hence the process of translation is also "dialogical" as it constantly mediates between a language and its immediate cultural background and between one language community and another.

* * *

Just as the experience of speaking becomes bilingual or trilingual, the reading and writing experience is also likely to be "pluralistic." The meanings of the "local" and the "global" in this case take on, if you like, a specifically "trans-Chinese" dimension. To illustrate, let me begin from the receiver's end (reader) before moving on to the producer's (writer) on this variegated trans-Chinese map of print culture.

First, "Pluralism" in reading means the choice of several reading matters, sometimes from several different genres, which we do everyday: a newspaper in the morning, professional books during the day, and perhaps a novel at bedtime. But this multigeneric reading experience is complicated by bilingualism: e.g., a Chinese newspaper in the morning, professional materials in English, and a Chinese novel at bedtime. A person living with such a habit therefore habitually negotiates two language worlds as he/she typically divides his/her daily life into two halves: life at work and life at leisure. A Taiwan businessman working for a multinational company (hence bilingual) sojourns in Los Angeles and reads during his after-hours a copy of the *Shijie ribao* (*World Gazette*), a Chinese-language daily which is the North American branch of a major newspaper (*The United Daily*) in Taipei. The newspaper also makes him think about home and family in Taipei as it has pages of "domestic" news about Taiwan.

We could also talk in terms of a "cross-local" process of "de-territorialization." For a Monterey Park resident who has migrated from Taiwan, the *World Gazette* is a "local" newspaper in a double sense: with one locality (L.A.) inscribed upon another (Taiwan). But the paper is also read by recent immigrants from the People's Republic who knowing little English have no other recourse for news but to reading the same newspaper from Taiwan, since it is the only show in town.

For them, it is no longer a familiar reading experience because they have to filter through Taiwan reporting about the Mainland. In so doing, they also reluctantly enter into a passive discourse with Taiwan culture. On the other hand, a Taiwan businessman in Beijing also has no access to news about Taiwan except by reading the "Hong Kong/Taiwan" page of the *Beijing wanbao (Beijing Evening News)* in simplified characters and small print. And a Hong Kong clerk may be perfectly happy following his/her daily columns in the local newspapers — a most localized experience — until some of his/her favorite columns begin to talk about Taiwan and China or the immigrant experience in Canada. This "cross-local" process is especially pronounced in a language that incorporates foreign words and phrases in "local translation," as demonstrated earlier. Again, the conflict between the familiar and the unfamiliar occurs not only at the verbal level but in the reading process as well. Reading different newspapers from different areas therefore entails another form of "de-territorialization" not only between English and Chinese but between one form of local or "territorial" Chinese and another.

As a sometime columnist for a Hong Kong Chinese newspaper, I have been writing essays aimed at two or three reading publics. I call this "cross-writing" in one sense because by writing I am crossing imagined boundaries between these communities. But in another sense I also attempt to evolve a "cross-writing" style by mixing territorial genres in Chinese and sometimes also carrying on a kind of bilingual dialogue between Chinese and English through selective translation — all within the same piece of work. This is definitely easier said than done. Several questions arise in my own mind. Is it merely a playful experiment or a symptom of some deep-seated "schizophrenia?" If so, is not "cross-writing" a very unstable state of affairs in which one is constantly negotiating a way out of a cultural paradox but cannot? My implied answers to these questions are by no means certain. Leaving aside English for the time being, I discover that my intended audience has in fact dictated my wording and style, all within a vaguely defined genre of essay-writing. The issue of circulation becomes complicated when an essay intended for a certain territorial readership is reprinted elsewhere: if I address a "local" issue in a Hong Kong newspaper column, does it lose its authenticity when reprinted in a Mainland journal? I do not know. But I find it safer to adopt a honest writing identity — an overseas writer who is also a professor at an American university. This is by now a most familiar pose, since the academic institution has become almost a universal site of employment for writers and intellectuals everywhere.

* * *

The technique I have used in my own essays at "cross-writing" is the usual academic "trick" of irony, an avowedly Western literary legacy. It provides me with a convenient distance from which to relate to the subject or locale at hand. It also provides a double-persona of both insider and outsider, of both being there and not being there. The vision and perspective derived therefrom become intentionally peripheral, since there cannot be any one center of gravity or centripetal pull in my cultural map. The "style" (if I work hard at it) also becomes ironically "intertextual." It means, concretely, that I comment upon the "text" at hand — a certain event or issue, a book or a poem by an author from one area — by relating it to another "text" elsewhere or in another era, and in so doing I hope to strike a distance in time and space. But an ironic effect can only be achieved by mocking my operation itself, together with my "self" as author/commentator. In cross-writing, therefore, the instabilities of tone and voice are precisely the ground of its formal flexibility and perhaps intellectual strength as a form of cultural or multicultural criticism. It is a mixed genre by definition, in which the "style" becomes a matter of "translation" from one cultural background and/or zone to another. Still, like any kind of writing, the final test is in the language itself — a test I have often failed. It proves all but impossible to negotiate my way through local idioms, translated foreign terms, classical references, academic phrases, etc., while maintaining a personal style of irony. Perhaps the effects of heteroglossia and formal polyphony can be achieved only in a Dostoevsky novel, not a short personal essay. I have also realized that through all these years of writing I have not yet mastered baihua, be it Mandarin or modern Chinese.

Most recently, I decided to try something even bolder — writing essays in English as a self-pronounced foreigner. This came about as a result of my reflections on my writings in Chinese. Since it is, but a form of experimenting with diverse cultural sensibilities within the Pan-Chinese world, why not cross the border of this world and reach out into another; the reading public in English. This experience brings me to a new appreciation of the works of the internationally renowned writer, Salman Rushdie.

In a famous essay entitled, *Imaginary Homelands,* Salman Rushdie has the following self-reflection on his status as an expatriate Indian-British writer: "Our physical alienation from India almost inevitably means that we will not be capable of reclaiming precisely the thing that was lost; that we will, in short, create fictions, not actual cities or villages, but invisible ones, imaginary homelands. Indias of the mind."[18] Rushdie wrote these words as a partial explanation of the many factual mistakes, unintended and intended, contained in his novel, *Midnight's Children.* I think that he also, very intentionally, implies that for an expatriate writer separated by a great distance in time and space from his homeland, the proper genre to reclaim his imaginary homeland is fiction. Rushdie's case seems borne out by several expatriate Chinese writers as well: Pai Hsien-yung wrote a series of stories about Taipei residents in America, which also reclaims in fiction form memories of a past generation of Guomindang Mainlanders. But a more intriguing case for my purposes is Lin Yutang, who never wrote any fiction in Chinese but was instrumental in establishing the modern essay (xiaopin wen) as a most popular genre in the 1930s with two journals he edited in China, who wrote a novel in English, *Moment in Pek*ing, while he lived as an expatriate in New York. Lin's attitude to Chinese culture, as evidenced in his many popular books in English, was of course quite different from Rushdie's. As is well known, Lin's sentimental attachment to the aesthetic side of traditional Chinese literati culture won him great popularity in America, whereas Rushdie's literary nostalgia toward his imagined homeland is more ambivalent and ironical. It would be hard to imagine a *Satanic Verses* from Lin Yutang's pen, or from any other Chinese expatriate writer. Why?

I use the examples of these two illustrious writers as a way to raise some questions about my obsessive concern, language, and genre: Would Rushdie be capable of such biting irony if he could still write in his native language? Could he create a *Satanic Verses* in Hindi together with all the puns and language plays intact? Why did Lin **not** choose to write in the English equivalent of the xiaopin wen — the English essay form by drawing some inspiration from Addison and Steele? After all *The Spectator* and *The Tattler* may indeed have been his models for the two journals he established in China: *Renjian shi* (*The Human World*) and *Yuzhou feng* (*Wind of Universe*). Is the essay form in Chinese more immediate and in more present tense, thus less capable of the task of introducing Chinese culture or reclaiming his homeland than fiction? Why is my own "fictional" urge nevertheless re-channeled into essay writing (aside from my poverty of fictional skills)? Do I feel no need, as Rushdie claims he does, to reclaim an imagined homeland of my own? Or perhaps it has something to do with language: publishing my Chinese essays in the trans-Chinese public spheres somehow brings me closer to the **real** homelands on the other shores.

"What does it mean to be 'Indian' outside of India?" Rushdie asks. For an Indian writer outside India, he continues, "this raises immediately the question of whom one is writing for. My own, short answer is that I have never had a reader in mind. I have ideas, people, events, shapes, and I write 'for' those things, and hope that the completed work will be of interest to others."[19] This self-effacing pose nevertheless betrays a high Modernist stance (although the form of his novels is more postmodern). It is a luxury of art I cannot afford. But I would argue that Rushdie's fiction is still, on the whole, a Western construction, for no other reason than the simple fact that he has chosen to write in English. At the risk of immodesty, I must admit that I definitely have my imagined readers in mind, otherwise my Chinese essay-writing would be meaningless. The question, however, remains: for whom one is writing, for what kind of readers?

I realize that I have been working at cross-writing in Chinese in almost the same way that Rushdie struggles with his English: "To conquer English may be to complete the process of making ourselves free."[20] Except that my emancipation is of a different sort: I do not wish to either conquer English or surrender myself to it; I just want to escape from time to time. Nor, for that matter, do I wish to conquer or surrender myself to Chinese. This bilingual stance, stemming from a set of sensibilities I have tried to describe, brings me to a final reflection on the issue of biculturalism. It has to do, in fact, with negotiating my distance from both my homeland ("where you are from") and my adopted country ("where you are now"). To that extent it is also a reflection of "diasporic consciousness." To escape from a professional predicament, such as writing solely in scholarly or theoretical English, by writing in another language (Chinese) and genre (essay) may not be a politically correct thing to do. On the other hand, to stand too close to the American academic institution (where you are now) as the principal site of intellectual activity and existential meaning makes you feel somewhat distanced from the "imagined homeland" where you are from. Sometimes the "tactics of intervention in contemporary cultural studies," to borrow a phrase from Rey Chow, takes more than one site, one language, or one genre. Thus I offer a final and rather personal argument: for anyone who chooses not to belong in a monolingual environment, this form of cross-writing provides a much needed mental space, a "buffer zone" in which one may negotiate the schizophrenic sensibilities of one's own self.

Notes

1. Lao She (1981). "Xiaobo de shengri" (Xiaobo's birthday). In *Lao She wenji (The works of Lao She)*, Vol. 2, pp. 13–15. Beijing: Renmin wenxue chubanshe.
2. Wang Runhua, (WongYoonWah) (1995). "Lao She xiaoshuo xinlun" (*A new view of Lao She's fiction*). Taipei: Dongda, pp. 29–46.
3. Lao She (1981). "Xiaobo de shengri", p. 13.
4. Hu Shi (1953). "Jianshe de wenxue geming lun" (A constructive view of literary revolution). In *Hu Shi wencun (Collected works of Hu Shi)*, Vol. 1, pp. 57–61. Taipei: Yuandong tushu gongsi.
5. Han Shaogong (1997). *Maqiao cidian (A dictionary of Maqiao village)*. Taipei: Xinrenjian.
6. Li Tuo (1990). "Xuebeng hechu" (Where goes the avalanche). In Preface to Yu Hua, *Shibasui chuyuanmen (Going Afar at Age Eighteen)*, p. 12. Taipei: Yuanliu chuban gonsi.
7. Quoted in Huang Jinshu (1998). *Mahua wenxue yu Zhongguo xing (Malaysian-Chinese literature and Chineseness)*. Taipei: Yuanzun wenhua, p. 75.
8. *Ibid.*, pp. 73–78.
9. *Ibid.*, p. 77.
10. Wong Phui Nam (1991). "Out of the stony ... a personal perspective on the writing of verse in English in Malaysia". In *Perceiving Other Worlds*, Edwin Thumboo (ed.), Chapter 17. Singapore: Times Academic Press.
11. Catherine Lim (1991). "The writer as a cultural anomaly". In *Perceiving Other Worlds*, Edwin Thumboo (ed.), Chapter 35. Singapore: Times Academic Press.
12. *Ibid.*
13. Gilles Deleuze and Felix Guattari (1986). *Kafka: Towards a Minor Literature* (cr. Dana Polan). Minneapolis: University of Minnesota Press, p. 16.
14. *Ibid.*, pp. 16–17.
15. *Ibid.*, p. 19.
16. Constantine Boundas (ed.) (1993). *The Deleuze Reader*. New York: Columbia University Press, p. 147.

17. Salman Rushdie (1992). *Imagined Homelands: Essays and Criticism 1981–1991*. New York: Penguin Books, p. 17.
18. *Ibid.*, p. 10.
19. *Ibid.*, p. 19.
20. *Ibid.*, p. 17.

6

ZHENG HE: NAVIGATOR, DISCOVERER, AND DIPLOMAT*

CHIN LING-YEONG

University of Hong Kong

Ban Gu (班固), in his *Han Shu* (汉书), Book 28B, has clearly recorded that Chinese sailors were frequent visitors to the present Indo-China coast, the Malay Peninsula, Indonesia and as far as India.[1] The voyages of Kang Tai (康泰) and Zhu Ying (朱应) to Funan (扶南) in the 3rd century opened a new epoch in China's geographical knowledge of Southeast Asia.[2]

In 399 AD, Fa Xian (法显), a Buddhist monk, left Zhangan (长安) to India with several disciples on a pilgrimage by land and returned to China in 413–414 AD by sea. On his return journey, he visited Sumatra; in his book entitled *A Record of the Buddhist Kingdoms* (佛国记)[3] he gives a detailed account of its geographical position. His experience encouraged other monks to leave for India by sea.[4] As a result of these voyages, the northern coast of the Shandong Peninsula and Guangzhou became key areas for both inbound and outbound maritime activities.

When Sui Yangdi (隋炀帝) ascended the throne in 605 AD, he dispatched Chang Jun (常骏) and Wang Junzheng (王君政) to Chi Tu (赤土) as imperial envoys. They set sail for Southeast Asia from Nanhai prefecture in 607 AD. They were warmly welcomed upon their arrival in Chi Tu.[5]

With the rise of Tang in 618 AD, a new era in China's maritime expansion to Southeast Asia began. Jia Dan (贾耽) and Daxi Tong (达奚通) in their geographical writings, give us a vivid and depictive

---

*This chapter is a reproduction of the Wu Teh Yao memorial lecture given by the author in 2000.

account about countries which had maritime relations with China.⁶ Yijing (义净), a Buddhist monk, set sail for India and Southeast Asia in 671 AD and returned to China in 689 AD. He again left for Shrivijaya with Zhen Gu (贞固) in the same year and returned to Luoyang (洛阳) in 695 AD. Since Yijing had been abroad for more than 20 years, his writing about Southeast Asia and the Indian coast is of the highest geographical and historical value.⁷

Ibn Khordadbeh, the famous Arabian traveler and historian, records in his book that Yangzhou, Quanzhou, and Guangdong were the most important ports for export and import trade during the Tang period. The appointment of Shiposi or superintendent of customs in the early Tang period to levy tax on foreign goods was, in fact, stimulated by the influx of foreign merchants to the coastal regions of China. These foreigners, most of whom were Arabs, stayed in a place outside the city areas assigned by the local authorities. As most of these visitors were skilful sailors, their experience in sailing the high sea helped the Chinese mariners to refine their own techniques in shipbuilding. These contacts played an important role in Tang's maritime expansion.⁸ They were interrupted toward the end of the dynasty when China lapsed into a period of political chaos and disunity.

After China was reunited in 960 AD, Zhao Kuangyin (赵匡胤), and other Song emperors encouraged maritime expansion, and trade by sea flourished again.⁹ From 1280 AD onward, China was under the Mongol rule. The alien conquerors did not interfere with the maritime activities established in previous dynasties. On the contrary, Shi Bi (史弼), and Gao Xing (高兴) were ordered to lead an expedition to conquer Java in 1292 AD. This was not Yuan's first maritime expedition; in 1279 AD, Yang Tingbi (杨庭璧) had traveled to Southeast Asia as an imperial envoy. By the end of the Yuan Dynasty, maritime activities were more widespread, especially among the inhabitants of the coastal region. Many built their own junks, while other merchants used junks built by the government for these activities.¹⁰ Nevertheless, Chinese maritime expansion had to wait until the rise of Zhu Yuanzhang (朱元璋) (1328–1398) in 1368 AD before it reached its peak.

Zhu Yuanzhang, the first emperor of Ming, ruled from 1368 AD to 1398 AD. Immediately after his ascendancy, he sent envoys to Japan and

Southeast Asia to announce his ascent to the throne. The emperor's intention was not to establish close relations with neighboring countries; he hoped that, in case of necessity, he might call on their aid. From the very beginning of his reign, the emperor was afraid that his political enemies might ally themselves with countries in Southeast Asia to challenge his realm. In the 4th year of his reign, he ordered the former crew of Fang Guozhen (方国珍) to retreat from the coastal regions and placed them under his personal garrison.[11] He later issued an edict forbidding his subjects to have private maritime trade with foreigners.[12] The emperor knew that maritime trade could bring prosperity to the country, but he did not want his subjects to be his competitors. He re-established the office of superintendent of customs in Taicang (太仓). It was later moved to Ningbo, Quanzhou, and Guangdong, after it was found that Taicang was unsuitable. The re-establishment of the superintendent of customs was to enforce a monopoly of the import and export trade with foreigners. If tribute envoys from Korea and Palembang brought their local products to China, either as gifts or for trade, they could be exempted from taxation.[13] The attitude of the emperor, of course, was to attract foreigners to China. But he did not encourage people along the coast to have commercial ties with foreigners. The emperor's policy, however, proved to be impracticable, for people of the coastal regions usually enjoyed close relations with the local authorities. Thus, private maritime expeditions to Southeast Asia continued. Moreover, as the tribute envoys found private trade to be more profitable, they ignored the imperial decree as well as the superintendent of customs.[14] Indeed, the office of the superintendent of customs was abolished in the 7th year of Hongwu (1374 AD). At the same time, the emperor issued a decree that foreign countries had to be classified into two categories: the conquerable states and the vassal states. Countries in Southeast Asia and East Asia, such as Korea, Japan, Ryukyu, Annam, Cambodia, Siam, Champa, Java, Palembang, Brunei, and Sumatra, fell into the latter category. Theoretically, these countries had to pay tribute to China at least once in every three to five years. However, the emperor reserved the right to reject their tribute offerings. In the 6th year of Hongwu, he had twice rejected the Siamese tribute without giving an explanation, while in the 13th year of his reign, the emperor detained the Javanese envoy for more than a month, because the king of Java had assassinated a Ming envoy on his way to present a golden seal to the king of Palembang. When he expelled the Javanese envoy from the Chinese territory, the emperor contended that envoys from Java and other countries in Southeast Asia were coming to extend their commercial ties with Chinese merchants and had no intention of showing their loyalty to the Son of Heaven.[15] The emperor realized that smuggling was still active; he probably knew that it was these envoys who were behind it. Moreover, in coming to China, most foreigners concealed the fact that they were tribute envoys. In 1383 AD, Entry Documents were issued to Southeast Asian countries for intending envoys to China. The duplicates of the documents were lodged in the department concerned in Guangdong and Fujian. If the envoys failed to produce these documents or if their identities were doubtful they would be either prohibited from entering China or severely punished. Furthermore, even if they indeed possessed the legal Entry Documents, they would be fined if they brought with them local products for trade. In 1391 AD, through the investigation of Hu Weiyong's (胡惟庸) conspiracy,[16] the emperor discovered that Japan, Mongolia, and Palembang had secretly intrigued with Hu. Since he had always feared that these countries might conspire with his opponents against his regime, he not only forbade his people to go abroad but also prohibited their use of foreign goods such as spices and perfumes.[17] In 1397 AD, the Minister of the Board of Rites presented a memorial to the emperor reporting that most countries in Southeast Asia had not brought tribute to the Imperial Court for a long time and advised the emperor to dispatch warnings to these countries.

Zhu Yuanzhang was fully aware of the situation and he also realized that a new kingdom at Ayuttaya had been established in Siam and supported by a Chinese merchant named U Thong who became a member of the ruling families of Lopburi and Suphanburi through marriages. The emperor then instructed the Minister of Rites the following decree to warn Java and Palembang through Siam to fulfill their duties:

> In the beginning of my reign, envoys from different countries came regularly to pay tribute. These countries numbered thirty, including Annam, Champa, Cambodia, Siam, Java, Ryukyu, Palembang, Brunei and Sumatra. The hostility of Palembang towards China resulted from the discovery of Hu Weiyong's conspiracy. Our envoys were purposely

enticed (by Palembang) to that country. The king of Java, having heard this, sent his men to warn our envoys and escort them back (to China) with great respectfulness. Since that time, commercial ties have been severed, and relations with these countries can hardly be maintained. However, Annam, Champa, Cambodia, Siam and Ryukyu have continued to come to my Court and pay tribute as before. Furthermore, Ryukyu has also sent young men to further their studies (in China). Envoys from foreign countries are all warmly received and well treated. I have never shown any indifference towards them. The policy of these countries (towards China) is beyond our ability to judge. If imperial envoys are to be sent to Java, I am afraid Palembang will stop them on their way (to Java). As Palembang was originally a vassal state of Java, you (the Minister of Rites) now have to convey my views to Siam and it must be communicated to Java that Palembang and other countries in Southeast Asia have to resume their tribute offerings.

Zhu Yuanzhang was fully aware that Java was the real power behind the political activities of the Southeast Asian states. He could not condemn Java even though Palembang was her subordinate. The emperor realized that he had to warn his fellow ruler by some means. So he tactfully and diplomatically asked his ministers to pass on his words to Siam, thereby forcing Siam to act as a bridge between China and Java. Nevertheless, throughout his reign, his policy toward Southeast Asia was comparatively conservative. An active foreign policy which would lead China's maritime expansion to its full height had to wait until the accession of his son, Zhu Di (朱棣) to the throne in 1403 AD (Emperor Chengzu (成祖), commonly referred to by his reign-name Yongle (永乐)).

Yongle indeed brought China's maritime expansion to a new epoch. Immediately after his accession Chinese envoys were sent to Japan, Korea, Ryukyu, and countries in Southeast Asia to announce that he had ascended the throne.[18] In the second year of his reign, he ordered that the offices of the superintendent of customs were to be re-activated in the Guangdong, Fujian, and Zhejiang regions to handle the import and export trade.[19] However, the emperor was very lenient and generous; most of the envoys who came to China for commercial purposes were exempted from taxation. Moreover, maritime trade was very active along the coastal region. After a few years' preparation, the emperor thought it was time for him to send a maritime expedition overseas in order to show that China was rich and strong. Zheng He, a favorite eunuch of the emperor, was ordered to lead the expedition. During his reign, Zheng He led six expeditions to Xiyang (西洋, or "Western Sea") and the seventh expedition was launched during the reign of Xuan Zong (宣宗).

Zheng He was born in 1371 AD at Kunyang (昆阳) in Yunnan province. He was born to a Muslim family. His surname at birth was Ma, a very common surname among Muslims in China.[20] His grandfather's given name was Bayan and his father's was Haji and both of them had made the pilgrimage to Mecca. Zheng He's mother was from the Wan family. She had two sons and four daughters, and Zheng He was the second son of her six children. In 1382 AD, the Ming army, under the leadership of Fu Youde (傅友德) defeated the Mongols in Yunnan. Zheng He was among the captives brought back to the imperial capital where he was made an eunuch and assigned to serve in the palace of the Prince of Yan (燕王), the later Emperor Yongle. Zheng He's ability was soon recognized and he was gradually promoted to the rank of the first eunuch.

When the Prince of Yan usurped the throne in 1403 AD, he suspected that his predecessor, Emperor Jianwen (建文), had taken refuge in Southeast Asia. He wanted to locate him and at the same time to publicize China's maritime supremacy to countries in Southeast Asia and beyond. In 1405 AD, therefore, Zheng He was ordered, along with Wang Jinghong (王景弘), to head the first maritime expedition to Xiyang.[21] Why was early Ming China so confident that the emperor should decide to send envoys to countries in Southeast Asia and beyond? In fact, the first Emperor of Ming was able to unify China because of his experience in commanding the sea and river battles over his rivals. Even Chen Youliang's (陈友谅) louchuan (楼船, fleet or galleons) was unable to win during the Poyang Lake Campaign. More importantly, Zhang Shicheng's (张士诚) collaborators were capable of plying between China waters and Japan without any difficulty.

From 1405 AD to 1433 AD., Zheng He led seven major expeditions to Xiyang.[22] The dates of these expeditions were as follows:

1st expedition 1405–1407
2nd expedition 1407–1409

3rd expedition 1409–1411
4th expedition 1413–1415
5th expedition 1417–1419
6th expedition 1421–1422
7th expedition 1431–1433

On these seven expeditions, Zheng He visited Champa, Cambodia, Siam, Brunei and Java, Kelantan, Pahang, and Malacca in the Malay Peninsula; Palembang, Aru, Sumatra, Battak, and Lambri on the island of Sumatra; Bengal, Negapatam, Quilon, Cochin, Calicut, Cambay, and Ahmedabad in the Indian sub-continent; Ceylon and the Maldives Islands, Hormuz on the Persian Gulf; Djofar on the South Arabian coast; Mogadishu, Brawn, Djobo, Malindi and other places in East Africa which cannot be identified: in all he visited more than 30 "countries."[23]

Most of the time, Zheng He and his companions set off from the Liujia River (刘家河) at Taicang. Ships which Zheng He used for his expedition were mostly built at the Longjiang Shipyard (龙江船厂) Nanjing. The ships, according to *Xiyang Ji* (西洋记), a historical novel by Luo Maodeng (罗懋登), published in 1697, can be classified into five types with their dimensions given[24]:

1. Treasure-ship or baochuan (宝船), 9 masts, 44.4 zhang (丈) long and 18 zhang (丈) broad.
2. Horse-ship or machuan (马船), 8 masts, 37 zhang (丈) long and 15 zhang (丈) broad.
3. Supply-ship or liangchuan (粮船), 7 masts, 28 zhang (丈) long and 12 zhang (丈) broad.
4. Billet-ship or caochuan (漕船), 6 masts, 24 zhang (丈) long and 9.4 zhang (丈) broad.
5. Battle-ship or zhanchuan (战船), 5 masts, 18 zhang (丈) long and 6.8 zhang (丈) broad.[25]

The first expedition began in July 1405. Sixty-three ships were assigned to this mission. Zheng He and Wang Jinghong (王景弘) brought with them 27,800 soldiers. According to *Zheng He Jiapu* (郑和家谱), these "soldiers" included seven imperial eunuchs serving as envoys,

10 proctors as deputy envoys, 10 junior eunuchs, 53 eunuch-chamberlains, two regional military commissioners, 93 guard commanders, 104 battalion commanders, 403 company commanders, one director from the Ministry of Revenue, two officers from the Court of State Ceremonial, two drafters, one instructor, one Yinyang officer and four assistants, 108 medical officers and medical assistants, and 26,803 military officers, chosen officers, strong men, soldiers, cooks, interpreters, and clerks.

They first reached Champa, then proceeded to Java, Palembang, Malacca and sailed as far as Aden.[26] On his return journey, Zheng He had to quell a Chinese pirate nest led by Chen Zuyi (陈祖义), Liang Daoming (梁道明), and Zheng Boke (郑伯可) in Palembang. After fierce battle between Zheng He and the pirates, Zheng He destroyed the pirate nest completely and brought Chen, Liang, and Zheng back to China for execution.[27]

The second expedition left China in 1407 AD. During this expedition, Zheng He and his companions reached as far as Calicut and returned home in 1409. As soon as he reached China, he was immediately commissioned to head the third expedition. Zheng He and his entourage left Liujia River (刘家河) in October 1409 AD. This time he visited Champa, Siam, Java, Malacca, Aru, Sumatra, Lambri, Ceylon, Cail(Z), Quiton, Cochin, Calicut, and Cambay. In this expedition, the king of Ceylon, Alagakkonara, plotted an attack on Zheng He and his fleet, but Zheng maneuvered a strong counter-attack. He had the king captured and brought him and his family to the imperial capital in 1411 AD.[28] Approximately two years later, Zheng He was ordered a fourth time to head an expedition to Xiyang. The fleet left China at the end of 1413 AD, visited most of the countries in Southeast Asia and reached as far as the eastern coast of Africa.[29] When Zheng He and his company reached Sumatra, the legitimate king appealed to Zheng for help claiming that the rebel leader, who is identified in Chinese as Su-kan-la, was attempting to overthrow him. He asked Zheng to suppress Su-kan-la and his rebellious troops. Thereupon, Zheng sent his soldiers to take Su-kan-la prisoner and brought him back to China for execution in 1415 AD.[30]

In 1417 AD, two years after the fourth expedition, Zheng He, now an experienced mariner, led a fifth expedition to Xiyang. According to *Ming Shilu* (明实录), he visited more than 19 "countries". The farthest of these "countries" were Hormuz and Mogadishu.[31] Zheng He returned in 1419 AD.

In 1421 AD, Zheng He set off on the sixth expedition. The purpose of this expedition is unknown. However, we know that Zheng had visited Siam, Sumatra, Djofar, Aden, Mogadishu, and Brawa.[32] He returned in 1423 AD.

In 1425 AD, Emperor Yongle, the patron of these expeditions, died. His son, Emperor Ren Zong (仁宗), was not in favor of the maritime expeditions. He appointed Zheng He to be Grand Commandant at Nanjing. Emperor Ren Zong died in the following year. His successor, Emperor Xuan Zong, followed his father's policy at the beginning of his reign. In the sixth month of 1430 AD, it was discovered that foreign countries had not come to pay tribute for quite a long time. The emperor, therefore, ordered Zheng He to head the seventh expedition to Xiyang.

Zheng He, together with Wang Jinghong (王景弘), Li Xing (李兴), Zhu Liang (朱良), Yang Zhen (杨珍), Hong Bao (洪保), and Gong Zhen (巩珍) set off in 1431 AD. Zhu Yunming (祝允明) (1461–1527), in his work entitled *Qianwen Ji* (前闻记), logs the following[33]:

- January 19, 1431, Zheng He and his companions set sail from Long Wan (龙湾)
- January 23, reached Xu Shan (徐山)
- February 3, reached Liujia River (刘家港)
- April 8, reached Changle River (长乐港)
- December 16, reached Fudou Shan (福斗山)
- January 12, 1432, reached Wuhu Men (五虎门) and left for Champa
- January 27, reached Champa
- February 12, left Champa
- March 7, reached Surabaya in Java
- July 13, left Java
- July 24, reached Palembang
- July 27, left Palembang
- August 3, reached Malacca
- September 2, left Malacca
- September 12, reached Sumatra
- November 2, left Sumatra

- November 28, reached Ceylon
- December 2, left Ceylon
- December 10, reached Calicut
- December 14, left Calicut
- January 17, 1433, reached Hormuz
- March 9, left for China from Hormuz
- March 31, reached Calicut
- April 9, left Calicut
- April 25, reached Sumatra
- May 1, left Sumatra
- May 9, reached Malaeca
- May 27, reached Kunlun Sea (昆仑洋)[34]
- June 9, reached west of Champa
- June 13, reached Champa
- June 17, left Champa
- June 19, reached Wailuo Shan (外罗山)
- June 25, reached Nanao Shan (南澳山)
- June 26, reached WanglanghuiShan (望郎回山)
- June 30, reached Qitou Yang (奇头洋) near Zhejiang (浙江)
- July 1, reached Wandie Island (碗碟屿)
- July 6, passed Daxiao Chi (大小赤)
- July 7, reached Liujia River (刘家港)
- July 22, Zheng He and his companions reached Nanjing.

From the above record, it is obvious that from Long Wan to Wuhu Men, they had to wait for one year and three days before they set sail for Champa. They had to stay in the Fujian waters because of the winter monsoon. They also had to wait the summer monsoon on their voyage home.

Zhu Yunming (祝允明) also records that Zheng He's ships were named as follows: Qinghe (清和), Huikang (惠康), Changning (长宁), Anji (安济), Qingyuan (清远), and others were marked with serial numbers. Moreover, the ships were also classified into big eight-paddles and medium eight-paddles.

On these seven expeditions, Zheng He had made Malacca his depot.[35] As Zheng He could not visit all the countries in Southeast Asia, India, and Africa by himself, he had to deputize his followers to act on his behalf. As a result, the fleet headed by Zheng He was called dazong (大宗, the main fleet) and those led by his followers were called fenzong (分宗, the branch fleets).[36] The fenzong would leave the dazong in Champa, Sumatra, Ceylon, Calicut, and Quilon and set sail directly to its assigned countries.[37] However, all the fenzong had to assemble in Malacca after accomplishing their missions. Malacca was, therefore, strongly fortified. When the fenzong and dazong anchored in Malacca, treasures and precious goods, provisions, and confidential documents would be stowed away. All of them would stay and wait for the summer monsoon to resume their homeward voyage.[38]

The senior eunuchs who accompanied Zheng He to the "Western Sea" were Wang Jinghong, Hou Xian (侯显), Li Xing (李兴), Zhu Liang (朱良), Zhou Meng (周满), Hong Bao (洪保), Yang Chen (杨珍), Zhang Da (张达), Wu Zhong (吴忠). Of all these names, Wang Jinghong and Hou Hsien were particularly important because of their other diplomatic commitments either to the Western Sea or to countries in the present Central Asia.[39]

Wang Jinghong became a subject of dramatization in Luo Maodeng's (罗懋登) historical romance entitled *Sanbao taijian xiyang ji yanyi* (三保太监西洋记演义). Hou Xian, on the other hand, has served as a Ming diplomat and was very active in countries of the present South Asia.[40]

There were three officials who served Zheng He either as interpreters or record-keepers. When they returned to China, each of them wrote a book on their trips. The first one was Ma Huan (马欢), who was from Zhejiang (浙江). Ma accompanied Zheng He to the "Western Sea" in 1413, 1421, and 1431. Upon his return to China, he compiled a book known as *Yengyai shenglan* (瀛涯胜览). Ma carefully described all the countries he had visited in the early 15th century and many of these countries had never been mentioned by Chinese sailors or travellers.[41]

The second person was Fei Xin (费信). In his *Singcha shenglan* (星槎胜览), he disclosed that he has followed Zheng He to the "Western Sea" four times. In the preface of his book, Fei was with Zheng He three times and with a eunuch named Yang once. Fei was a better scholar and his work was beautifully written. However, historians of later generations believed that Fei must have relied very heavily on Wang Dayuan's (汪大渊) *Daoyi zhilue* (岛夷志略).[42]

The last was Gong Zhen (巩珍). He accompanied Zheng He only on the 7th expedition. After his return to China, he wrote the *Xiyang fanguo zhi* (西洋番国志) reporting that he has visited 20 countries and some of his accounts deserve a detailed study.[43]

The above-named eunuchs and officials who went to the "Western Sea" with Zheng He were either experienced sailors or old hands in dealing with affairs of foreign countries. Wang and Hou were Zheng He's close associates and their contributions toward these seven expeditions should not be neglected.

Zheng He's expeditions had complex motives and it is difficult to argue which one should rank top on the list.[44] However, it was these expeditions which stimulated commercial relations between China and countries in Southeast Asia. It was also these expeditions which demonstrated China's maritime superiority over other sea-powers of the 15th century.

Zheng He's voyages brought all countries in Southeast Asia, the Middle East, and as far as East Africa to establish closer and harmonious relations with Ming China. These relations continued to prevail until the end of the 15th century.

Chinese historians of today are of the opinion that it was court politics which had stopped Zheng He's mission after the reign Xuanzong (宣宗). However, Chinese merchants continued to visit and trade with the above-mentioned countries and also played a dominant part, politically, economically, socially, culturally, and ecclesiastically. It is believed that the daughter of Shi Jinqing (施进卿), known as Shi Erjie (施二姐) or Njai Gede Pinatih, has been honored as a religious leader and served as a Shahbandar in Java and was very powerful and influential.[45] This indeed is another important episode about Ming China's maritime trade with overseas in the late 15th and early 16th centuries.

The arrival of the Portuguese and Spanish fleets on the China waters enlarged China's perspectives; it offered Ming China a chance to realize the importance of foreign relations and international trade. I feel I must not indulge myself to go further, for an important topic of this kind needs another occasion for further deliberation.

Notes

1. Ban Gu (1912). *Han Shu* 28B (*Treatise on Geography*) (transl. and annot P Pelliot) in *T'oung Pao*, Vol. XIII, pp. 453–455; Ferrand, G (1919). "Le K'ouen-louen et les anciennes navigations interoceaniques dans les mers du Suds". *Journal Asiatique*, tome XIII, 233–239, 431–492 and tome XIV, 6–68, 201–241; Cf. Ling-yeong, C (1965). "Chinese maritime expansion, 1368–1644". *Journal of the Oriental Society of Australia*, 3(1), 27–47. Paul Wheatley (1980). *The Golden Khersonese*, Chapter 1. Kuala Lumpur: University Malaya Press.
2. Chen Shou (陈寿), *Sanguo zhi* (三国志), 60, *Wuzhi* (吴志) (*Biography of Lu Dai* 吕岱), 15. 9a (baina ben 百衲本): Pelliot, P (1903). "Le Fou-nan". *Bulletin de f"Ecole Francaise d'Extreme-Orient*, 111, 248–330; Coedes, G (1948). *Les etats hindouises d'Indochine et d'Indonesie*, Paris, E. De Boccard, p. 69; Briggs, L (1951). *The Ancient Khmer Empire*. Philadelphia: Transactions of the American Philosophical Society, p. 122, and also my paper, "China's Relations with Funan", *History Annals*, University of Hong Kong, 11, 1962. Paul Wheatley *ibid*., p. 14.
3. Translated by James Legge, Oxford, 1886.
4. Feng Chengjun (冯承钧) (1936). *Zhongguo nanyang jiaotong shi* (中国南洋交通史). Shanghai: Commercial Press, pp. 31–37. Paul Wheatley *Op. cit*., Chapter IV.
5. *Sui Shu* (隋书), Chapter 82; Feng Chengjun *Op. cit*., pp. 38–41; Paul Wheatley *Op. cit*., pp. 26–36.
6. Jia Dan (729–805): Geographical Treatise, appended to the geographical section of the *Xin Tang Shu* (新唐书), 43B. He describes seven routes from China to foreign countries. He gives a detailed description of the route from Southeast China to the Persian Gulf and the mouth of the Euphrates. See also Lo Hsiang-lin (罗香林) "Tunmen yu qi di zi Tang zhi Ming zbi haishang jiaotong" 屯门与其地自唐至明之海上交通. *Hsin Ya hsueh-pao* 新亚学报, 11(2), 271–300; Edwin O. Reischauer (1940). "Notes on T'ang Dynasty sea routes". *Harvard Journal of Asiatic Studies*, V, 142–164. For Daxi Tong, see Wada, H (1950). Todaino Nankai ken-shi. *Toyogakuho*, XXXIII(1), December; Paul Wheatly *Op. cit*., p. 47.
7. Yijing, *qiufa gaoseng chuan* 求法高僧传 (1894). (transl. E Chavannes) *Voyages des Pelerins Bouddhistes*, Paris, pp. 10–26; and Liang Qichao (梁启超) (1989). *Qian wubai nian qian zhi Zhonggun liuxuesheng* (千五百年前之中国留学生) p. 18, in *Yinbingshi quanji* (饮冰室全集), Vol. 9. Peking: Zhonghua Book Co.
8. Jia Dan *Op. cit*.
9. For Song maritime expansion, see the opening section of Rockhill, WW (1941). "Notes on the relations and the trade of China with the Eastern Archipelago the India Ocean during the Fourteenth century". *T'oung Pao*, Ser II, XV, 419–423; Zhou Qufei (周去非), *Lingwai daita* (岭外代答) and *Zhao Rukuo* (赵汝适), *Zhufan zhi* (诸蕃志).
10. Cf. Biography of Luo Shiyung. In *Yuan Shi* (元史), *Yuan wenlei* (元文类), c. 4; Sung Lian (宋濂), *Hanyuan xuji* (汉园续集); Tao Zongyi (陶宗仪), *Chuogeng lu* (辍耕录), c. 23 and 27; and also Zhou Daguan (周达观) *Zhenla fengtu ji* (真腊风土记)

(Memoires sur les countumes du Cambodge de Tcheou Ta-Kouan (transl. P Pelliot) in *Bulletin d'Ecole Francaise d'Extreme-Orient*, II, 1902).

11. Hongwu (洪武), *Ming shilu* (明实录) (hereafter cited *MSL*), c. 7, Reprinted from the manuscript edition in the *Jiangsu guoxue tushu guan* (江苏国学图书馆).
12. *Daminglu* (大明律), c. 8.
13. Hongwu, *MSL*, c. 68:6a.
14. Cf. Sakuma Shigeo (1953). On the prohibition of the overseas trade under the Ming Dynasty. *Tohogaku*, VI.
15. Hongwu, *MSL*, Chapter 134, p. 3a.
16. Biography of Hu Weiyong (胡惟庸), *Ming Shi* (明史), c. 308.
17. Hongwu, *MSL*, c. 231, 26-3a. Tarling, N (ed.) (1992). *Cambridge History of Southeast Asia*, Vol. 1, Cambridge: Cambridge University Press. pp. 170–175.
18. Yongle (永乐) *MSL*, c. 10A. 8c; c. 21, 3a.
19. Yongle, *MSL*, c. 21, 3b-4a.
20. Biography of Zheng He (郑和), *Ming Shi*, c. 304; Li Zhigang (李志刚), *Zheng He jiapu* 郑和家谱: Zhu Xie 朱契, Zheng He, Peking, 1956, pp. 23–27; Xu Yuhu徐玉虎, *Zheng He pingchuan* 郑和评传 Taibei, 1958, pp. 1–6, Miyazaki Masakatsu (宫崎正胜) *Teiwa no Nankai Daiensei*, 郑和南海大远征, 中公新书, Tokyo; Chuo Koronsha, 1997, 东京: 中央公论社 (Chuko Shinsho). Liu Zhie 刘志鹗 *Zheng He* 郑和, Jiangsu (1984). *Levathes, When China Ruled the Sea — The Treasure Fleet of the Dragon Throne, 1405–1433*. Simon & Schuster, 1994.
21. *Xiyang* is an expression used to denote places west of Malacca during the Ming Dynasty. Cf. Yongle, *MSL*, c. 35. 6b.
22. Apart from these seven expeditions, Zheng He had also been sent to Palembang in the 1st month of 1424 as imperial envoy to appoint Shi Jinqing (施进卿) as Xuanweisi (宣慰司). Cf. *Ming Shi*, c. 304. For Zheng He's expedition, see J.J.L. Duyvendak (1949). *China's Discovery of Africa*. London: Arthur Probsthain; Pelliot, P (1933). "Les grands voyages maritimes Chinois au debut du Xve Siecle". *T'oung Pao*, XXX, 237–452; Duyvendak, JJL (1938). "The true dates of the Chinese maritime expeditions in the early Fifteenth century". *T'oung Pao*, XXXI(V), 341–412; W. Willetts (1964). "The maritime adventures of Grand Eunuch Ho". *Journal of Southeast Asian History*, V(2), 25–42. See also my article (1967–1968). "Ji Ming shi Zhongguo zai Dongnanya zhi Shli", 记明时中国人在东南亚之势力, *United Journal*, United College, Chinese University of Hong Kong, Vol. VI, pp. 189–204.
23. Cf. Biography of Zheng He, *Ming Shi*, c. 304.
24. Cf. PaoTsen-peng (包遵彭) (1962). "On the Ships of Cheng Ho", *International Association of Historians of Asia, 2nd Biennial Conf. Proc.*, Taibei, pp. 409–429.
25. One *Zhang* (丈) is equal to ten feet or 3.3 meter.
26. According to *Guoque* (国榷) by Tan Qian (谈迁) of the Ming Dynasty, Zheng He visited Champa, Siam, Java, Palembang, Malacca, Aru, Sumatra, Battak, Lide, Lambri, the Nicobar Islands, Bengal, Ceylon, the Maldive Islands, Quilon Cochin, Calicut, Hormuz, Djofar, Aden, and Mecca on this expedition.

27. Palembang was conquered by Java in or about 1377. At that time, Java was still not a unified country and the Chinese population in Java was very powerful. Java could not do anything except appoint a Shahbandar to levy taxes upon exports and imports. It was believed that some of the Chinese in Palembang had closed relations with Hu Weiyong. The leaders of the Palembang Chinese were Liang Worming, Zheng poke, Chen Zuyi, and Shi Jinqing. In 1407, when Zheng He's maritime expedition returned from other countries in Southeast Asia and anchored at Palembang, Chen and others maneuvered to attack Zheng He. Shi seized this opportunity and disclosed Chen's conspiracy to Zheng He. Zheng, therefore, planned a counter-attack and made Chen Zuyi and others prisoners. They were brought back to the imperial capital for execution. Shi was later appointed to the rank of *Xuanwei si*. In this battle, Zheng He killed nearly 5,000 of Zuyi supporters. Ten of Chen's ships were either destroyed or capsized. Seven were captured. Two copper seals bearing Chen's authority were ordered to be burned. Cf. Yongle, *MSL*, c. 33, 5ab; c. 39. 4a; c. 52. 1a 5b-6a.
28. Willetts, W *Op. cit.*, pp. 31–36; Feng Chengjun *Op. cit.*, pp. 94–95; Yongle, *MSL*, c. 116.
29. Yongle, *MSL*, c. 134 records that Zheng He had visited Champa, Kelantan, Pahang, Java, Malacca, Aru, Sumatra, Lambri, the Maldives Islands, Cail, Cochin, Calicut, Hormuz, Brawa, and Sun-la (probably in East Africa, identity uncertain) on this expedition.
30. *Ming Shil*, c. 325; Ma Huan (马欢), *Yingyai shenglan*.
31. Yongle, *MSL*, c. 183 records the following 19 "countries" visited by Zheng He: Champa, Pahang, Java, Palembang, Malacca, Sumatra, Lambri, Vizagapatinam, Ceylon, the Maldives Islands, Malabar, Cochin, Calicut, Hormuz, Aden, Mogadishu, Brawa, Malindi, and the uncertain La-sa.
32. Cf. Pelloit, P *Les grands voyages*, *op. cit.*
33. V. Xiang Da (向达) (ed.) (1961). *Xiyang fanguo zhi* 西洋番国志 Appendix 2. Peking: Zhonghua Book Co.
34. K'un-lun (昆仑) is in the eastern waters of Indo-china, Cf. G. Ferrand, *Op. cit.*
35. Xiang Da, *Op. cit.*, pp. 14–16.
36. The character zong has been widely discussed by Mayers, "Chinese Exploration of the Indian Ocean During the Fifteenth Century", *China Review*, No. 3, 1874–1875; Rockhill (1913–1915). "Notes on the relations and trade of China with Eastern Archipelago and the coast of the Indian Ocean during the Fourteenth century". *T'oung Pao*, tome XIV., 473–476, tome XV, 419–447, and tome XVI, 61–159, 236–271, 374–392, 435–467, 604–626; Duyvendak, *Ma Huan Re-exarnined*; and Pelliot, "Les grand voyages." However, none of them has come to a definite conclusion. Pao Tsenpeng, in his article entitled "On the ships of Cheng Ho", says that the character zong means "ships of various sizes and of a more or less fixed number, grouped together into a fleet". Pao also quotes from *Ming Shi*, c. 91 to support his argument.
37. There were about five fenzong in Zheng He's expedition. The first one was from Champa to Borneo, Siam and via Karimata and Billiton to Surabaya. The second

one was from Sumatra to Bengal and Ceylon. The third one was from Ceylon to the Maldives Islands and Quilon. The fourth one was from Quilon to Cochin and Mogadishu. The last one was from Calicut to Hormuz, Djofar, and Aden. Cf. Fang Hao (方豪) (1955). *Zhongxi jiaotongshi* 中西交通史, Vol. 3. pp. 200–201. Taibei.

38. XiangDa, *Op. cit.*
39. Lo Hsiang-lin *Op. cit.*
40. Chan Hok-lam (1991). "The career of Wang Ching-hung: A neglected commander-in-chief of the early Ming maritime expansion" 明王景弘下西洋史事钩沉. *Hanxue yanjin* 汉学研究, IX(2), Taipei.
41. Mill, JVG and Ma Huan (1970). *Yingyai shenglan* (The Overall Survey of the Ocean's Shores, 1433). Cambridge: Cambridge University Press. Wheatley, *op. cit.*, pp. 321–324.
42. Wheatley, *Op. cit.*, pp. 111–113 and pp. 323–325.
43. Cf. Xiang Da (ed.) (1961). *Xiyang fanguo ji*, Appendix 2. Peking: Zhonghua Book Co.
44. See my article (1992). "Lun Zheng He shouci sin xiyang zhi yuanyin" 论郑和首次下西洋之原因, *The Proceeding of the 2nd International Conference on Sino-foreign Relations*, Taipei, Tam Kang University 第二届中外关系史国际学术研讨会论文集, 台北, 淡江大学历史系, 1992, pp. 227–233.
45. Shahbandar is a word of Persian origin, see Chin Ling-yeong *Op. cit.*; Cf. G. Ferrand, (1924). "L' element persan dans les testes nautiques arabes des Xve et XVIe siècles." *Journal Asiatigue*, 239; P. Purbatjaraka (1961). "Shahbandars in the Archipelago." *Journal of Southeast Asian History*, II(2), 1–10; J. Hageman "Jortan Wedergevonden", *Tijdschrift voor Indische Taal-Landen Voilkenkunde*, Batavia, XVII, p. 368; Cf. Lai Yung hsiang (1962). "Li-tai pao-on 历代宝案 a collection of Documents on Foreign Relations of the Ryukyu Islands," *International Association of Historians of Asia, Second Biennial Conference Proceedings*, Taibei, pp. 301–318.

∞ 7 ∞

PLURALITY OF CULTURES IN THE CONTEXT OF GLOBALIZATION AND A NEW PERSPECTIVE OF COMPARATIVE LITERATURE*

YUE DAIYUN

Peking University, China

In today's world where national economies are becoming more and more integrated into a larger whole, we are faced with the question of what is going to happen to the cultural aspects of our life such as philosophy, religion, ethics, literature, art, etc. Are they also going to be gradually homogenized or is there a need and possibility to maintain the multiplicity of these cultural forms? This topic is discussed in the following six sections.

7.1. Significance of Plurality of Culture

Cultural plurality is a historical fact. For over 3000 years, the Greek, Chinese, Hebrew, Arabian, and African cultural traditions have taken deep roots in human societies in different ways. Historically speaking, the development of a culture depends upon humans' ability to learn and pass on their knowledge to future generations. In that long process, each generation adds something new to their culture, and the new elements include their own inventions as well as those they borrow from other cultures.

---

* This chapter is a reproduction of the Wu Teh Yao memorial lecture given by the author in 2001.

This means that culture is the product of historical inheritance as well as horizontal expansion across borders. The former tends to "conform" to the cultural mainstream, whereas the latter tends to "depart" from it, but both are necessary. With respect to an academic discipline, horizontal expansion means acceptance of influence from foreign cultures, appropriation of knowledge from other fields, and exploration into hitherto neglected marginal areas of culture. All these factors take place at the same time and they modify the direction of historical evolution.

Of the three factors mentioned above, the most important and most complex is the influx and influence of foreign cultures. It is quite obvious that differences among cultures can provide a cultural repertoire from which people draw inspirations to enrich their native cultures.

Take contemporary Western culture, for example. Wherever we go in Europe and America, we see and hear influences of African music and sculpture, Japanese wood engravings and architecture as well as the decorative art of ancient Chinese gardening. The most illustrative case, of course, is the excavation in the 1920s of the tombs of Tutankhamun (approx. 1343–1325 BC). The event set off an Egyptian vogue both in Europe and America, which swept over various fields of art such as Jazz music composition, stage decoration, and jewelry design. Egyptian pyramids even inspired the design of the famous Las Vegas plaza in 1990s.

In 1922, English philosopher Bertrand Russell pointed out in one of his papers written in China when he taught in Peking University at 1921 titled *The Comparison of Chinese and Western Cultures*:

> Exchanges between cultures have been proven many times in the past to be the landmarks in the evolution of human civilization. Greece learned from Egypt; Rome borrowed from Greece; Arabs imitated the Roman Empire; the Europe of the Middle Age followed the example of Arabs; and the Europe of Renaissance saw the Byzantine Empire as its model.

It is no exaggeration to say that the vitality of Western culture lies in learning and borrowing from other cultures, which has made it richer and fresher. Likewise, Chinese culture has been absorbing various foreign cultures in its development. Buddhism, for example, came from India and injected new blood into Chinese philosophy, religion, literature, and art. And in that process the religion itself has been greatly expanded, even more than in its birthplace. It blended with different aspects of Chinese culture and developed into various sects such as Tiantai, Hua Yan, and Zen (Chan Zhong). These Buddhist sects played an important role in the formation of Neo-Confucianism in the Song and Ming dynasties and were later transported into Korea and Japan and in turn influenced the cultures there. It is quite obvious that differences among cultures can provide a cultural repertoire from which people draw inspirations to enrich their own native cultures. If we do not have different cultures in various forms, human civilization could never be so colorful and so full of life.

7.2. Relationship Between Globalization and Cultural Plurality

Although cultures have always existed in various forms, "cultural pluralization" as a concept and as practice has come up only recently due to globalization. Globalization means worldwide integration of economy and standardization of scientific technology, especially in the highly developed system of communication, which has turned the world into a "global village." It also helps spread "dominant" cultures around the globe, assimilating and submerging "dominated" cultures along the way. Thus, for many people, globalization seems to work against the plurality of cultures. Yet this is only part of the story, for it is exactly globalization, which makes cultural plurality an issue.

First of all, globalization has hastened the disintegration of colonialism and brought in the Postcolonial era. When the old colonies gained their political independence, the immediate task they face is to locate their national identities, hence the importance of adhering to their unique cultures. After World War II, Malaysians have been insisting on using their native tongue as national language in order to assert their ethnic identity; in Israel, Hebrew was liberated from its limited use in religious ceremonies and given a new role as the language of everyday life; there are also oriental state leaders and scholars *who* felt the need to stress "Asian values" as their own hallmarks. From these examples we can see that economic integration and technological standardization have *not* homogenized cultures *but*, on the contrary, have pointed to the need of cultural plurality. In this sense, postcolonialism has laid down a basis for the pluralization of cultures.

Second, economic globalization and postcolonialism have brought Western society into a new phase of development. Postmodernism has brought about a disintegration of "centers." Being one part of a larger *whole*, every corner of the world legitimizes its existence in its own way. The all-binding "universal laws" and "grand narratives" are being challenged, and people are no longer interested in intangible, timeless "pure" and "ideal" forms, *but* are concerned about the tangible "body" which breathes, *acts*, and experiences pain and pleasure. This constitutes a great liberating force for the pluralization of cultures. With this profound change in our epistemology, such issues as the search for "*the* other" have been brought up. Many people have come to realize that we cannot well understand ourselves inside our own angle, we do need a perspective, from outside, i.e., from "*the* other." This is an understanding of so-called reciprocal cognition, or knowledge produced from interactivity (互动认知).

In order to achieve this, we need to broaden our horizon and become familiar with other ways of thinking and behavior patterns. A French scholar, Francois Jullien has recently made a very good point in his *Why We Westerners cannot Avoid China in Our Study of Philosophy?*

> When we choose to start, we actually choose to depart so that we could have a broader view for our meditation. In the remotest corners of the exotic world, such activities are carried out all the time. We pass through China because we want to know Greece better. Despite some gaps in our knowledge, we are still too close to and familiar with the Greek thought which is part of our own heritage. In order to understand it and make new discoveries, we have to cut ourselves off from this familiarity so that we could form a fresh perspective from the outside.

As a matter of fact, to observe oneself from an outside angle has long been a dream for human being. In one of his poems, Robert Bums (1759–1796), a Scottish poet once longed for a gift bestowed by God that could illuminate himself in the eyes of somebody else. Shu Shi (1037–1101), a Chinese poet, had also sighed over the inability to gain an outside standpoint:

> "It's a range viewed in face
> And peaks viewed from the side,
> Assuming different shapes viewed from far and wide.

Of mountain Lu we cannot make out the true face,
For we are lost in the heart of the very place."

横看成岭侧成峰,远近高低各不同。
不识庐山真面目,只缘身在此山中。

What he wanted to convey is that the appearance of mountain changes constantly because of the observer's different standpoints and perspectives. The only possibility of gaining a comprehensive view of the true Mountain Lu lies in adopting a vantage point from outside the mountain. That means, in order to understand yourself better, you not only need to study yourself from the view of your own but also pay attention to the opinions that other people hold about you. Very often, you start to notice something only when "others" remind you of it.

Sometimes, you and "the other" are not in direct contact, but are situated in a common realm, which constitutes a "cultural field." You and "the other" form a comparison and sometimes a contrast to each other so that each shows its characteristics, which would not be noticed otherwise. Such a contrast, whether you are aware of it or not, puts the two parties in a relationship of potential effect. For instance, as an ancient Chinese philosopher Wang Yangming pointed out, we can say that tortoises have no hair and rabbits have no horns only because there exist things that have hair and horns. Otherwise, the definition does not make sense. In making such references, our aim is not to expect tortoises with hair or rabbits with horns of course, but to know more about hairless and hornless animals through potential comparisons. This ancient Chinese wisdom has existed for a long time, but it is only under the "postmodern" and postcolonial circumstances that we realize their importance and relevance.

Last but not the least, it is pertinent to mention that the economic development brought about by globalization has also made it possible for people in those undeveloped areas to develop their own cultures. With economic and technological development, human contacts have become more frequent than ever before. The growth of tourist industry brings people to every corner of the world, which prompts the development of the minority cultures in many isolated areas. Although we detect a certain amount of formalism and mannerism in these activities, they attract people's attention to those cultures which otherwise would have been neglected. Therefore, Globalization may not suppress the plurality of culture but make it possible to promote a multiculturalism with which people can construct a more harmonious and tolerant mode of life.

7.3. Contradiction Between Maintaining Purity and Conducting Exchanges

In the discussion of homogenization and departure, we come across a paradox: On the one hand, we want to maintain the multiplicity of cultures. In this occasion, the purer and more "authentic" cultures are the better. On the other hand, different cultures are bound to penetrate one another so that they can draw nutrition for new growth. Does such interpenetration work against the uniqueness of individual cultures? Will it continue to reduce the difference among cultures, and at last make the special characteristics of different cultures disappear altogether? To answer this question, first, let us consider the matter in relation to our historical experience. The assimilation of foreign cultures has always been carried out within one's own cultural framework, and there have been very few cases in which another slavishly copies one culture. When Buddhism was introduced to China, some of its tenets on the ultimate source of knowledge, although very popular in India, contradicted the traditional Chinese way of thinking and were consequently eliminated. As Chen Yinke pointed out, "the part on human sexuality in Buddhist teachings is incompatible with the ethical tradition of China," and was therefore unacceptable to the Chinese followers" who "remain mostly silent on the issue," and the Buddhist story about a mother and her daughter loving the same man at the same time never spread in China for the same reason. The same can be said of the influence of French Symbolist Movement of the 1930s on modern Chinese poetry. The works of a large number of French Symbolic poets were translated into Chinese, but Mallarme, the most prominent representative of French Symbolist poetry, was barely known in China. All these point to the existence of a selective mechanism operating in cultural contacts.

Second, the migration of cultural elements from one system into another is not static. When they enter the new system, these elements no longer follow their old orbit of movement but blend with local elements, which can bear even more magnificent fruits. As the old Chinese saying: The orange trees grow upon the Huai river, when it was moved to the other side, its fruits changed to be persimmons ("淮桔成柿").

As we can see, Greek culture was first imported into Arab, but it was not further enriched till it became the foundation of European culture. Indian Buddhism was imported to China, but there it mixed with the various elements of the local culture, giving rise to Chinese versions of Buddhism such as Tiantai, Hua Yan, and Zen. These branches of Buddhism later served as a driving force for the development of Neo-Confucianism in the Song and Ming dynasties. What these examples point out is that the interaction between cultures is more an "assimilation" or "integration": it is also a process, in which new things emerge in different cultural environments. As the ancient Chinese philosopher said: "co-existence of differences generates new things while similarity puts an end to development" (和实生物, 同则不继). Things growing up in a new environment certainly cannot retain their original "purity," but on the other hand they are not the same with the local things because of the unique inheritance possessed by their own before.

There are many more examples of the expansion of culture in foreign lands in history, and they tell us that new things are born out of complementary differences. If all things were alike, there would be no development. Because they are products of different social and historical situations, cultures certainly lose their purity when they are mingled with others. On the other hand, they grow out of their own unique traditions and therefore will not be homogenized.

From what we have discussed, we can draw a conclusion that in the foreseeable future, different cultures, especially those cultures that have exerted great influences on others in the development of human civilization, are going to stay active for a long time to come. This does not mean that cultures last forever. History tells us that some cultures emerge and survive, while others decline and disappear. Of the existing cultures in the world, we could say that a small number may eventually decline and die in the process of globalization, but most will develop and flourish in the mainstream of multicultures. It is our responsibility to save certain cultures from dying just as we try to save some of the natural species from extinction so that the world remains in a balanced and harmonious state. We should protect the ecology of culture as we protect the ecology of nature and devote ourselves to save the rare and declining cultures.

7.4. Cultural Isolationism: A Danger in the Process of Pluralization

Having been suppressed for quite a long period, some nations desperately strive to defend themselves by adhering to the principle of cultural relativism which overemphasizes the importance of preserving their native culture in an unchangeable way, hence the danger of "cultural isolationism" or "cultural tribalism."

According to cultural relativism, every culture may produce its own value system, that is, people's belief and code of conducts (rules of behavior) are determined by certain social environment. Every cultural phenomenon such as beliefs and customs can only be assessed within its own value system. It implies that an ultimate value that can be shared by all societies does not exist at all; it is even worse to evaluate other cultures in the perspective of once own value. Considering all these, cultural relativism not only makes a point of respecting cultural difference and the value of different modes of living, stresses the importance of seeking mutual understanding and harmonious coexistence but also proposes to avoid making rash value judgment on or even destroying those which are incompatible with its own culture, and insists that only when it has been tested in various cultures.

In comparison with cultural conquest (cultural assimilation or destruction) and cultural plunder, cultural relativism is undoubtedly a great progress that has been playing a positive role. However, cultural relativism also displays some intrinsic contradictions and defects. For example, by narcissistically foregrounding the superiority of its native culture, cultural relativism may overlook the potential blindness of it by stressing the "purity" of its own culture and opposing to communicating with other cultures; it may adopt a policy of cultural segregation or isolation, and by emphasizing the "unity" of its own culture and resisting any form of any development, it may desperately try to silence the voices for positive changes and innovations from within, resulting into self-smugness and hysteric exclusivism and consequently stagnating the development of its own culture. In addition, to totally accept the doctrines of cultural relativism means to negate consensus shared by all human races, and this may quite naturally lead us to draw an absurd conclusion that some negative cultural phenomenon that has brought great sufferings to mankind has to be tolerated altogether (for instance, the Japanese Militarism, and German Nazism were once widespread and accepted at a certain place as cultural phenomena). In fact, it is impossible to completely deny the basic needs demanded by human uniformity (such as the need of food, clothes, sheltering, and a sense of security, etc). Besides, physiologically, human cerebra are structured in the same way and have almost the same capacity across all races; history has long proved that mutual understanding, interpenetration, and interaction across different cultures are not only possible but also indispensable. Last but not least, social groups or individuals may have different interpretations of things even if they are from the same cultural environment, for people's cognizance is always related to their living situations. It is obviously a fallacy to emphasize the so-called purity of one culture alone while turning a blind eye to such differences within that very culture. On the whole, cultural relativism constitutes a theoretical foundation for the development of multiculturalism; however, its intrinsic defects unavoidably make it a hindrance for pluralization of cultures.

As a matter of fact, those nations, which have gained their independence and are anxious to develop their national cultures face the danger of isolationism. Having experienced various obstacles and setbacks in cultural encounters, some people are pessimistic about the future of their native cultures. Sometimes they are so worried that their national cultures would be submerged or simply disappear that they strive to preserve their cultures at any cost. This, of course, is beneficial to preserve the different cultures, but with the trend also comes the regressive theory of cultural isolationism, which ignores the long history of international and cross-cultural exchanges, and calls for a return to the so-called authentic native culture that has never been "polluted" by outside influences. However, the notion of a "pure" native culture is only a fallacy. Besides those "dead," changeless objects such as bronze vessels and ancient architecture, all we can see in human civilization are the results of cultural developments, which have been affected by foreign elements and gone through selection, preservation, and renovation in history. If we discard all these to search for the so-called root, our efforts will surely go to no avail.

Cultural isolationism often occurs in the study of cultural identities as part of postcolonialist theories, but these two are in fact totally different. The latter seeks national and cultural identity in the context of multiculturalism, while the former wants to retreat from the real historical context of cultural interaction to a closed system looking for a nonexistent "authentic" culture, obviously, it could lead to the exclusion of other cultures, stressing the importance of its native culture to the extent of neglecting any of its cultural disadvantages. In order to retain the "purity" of its culture, cultural isolationism refuses to communicate and exchange with other cultures so that its native culture would not be polluted. If we suppress differences and communications to seek uniformity, we could only bring our cultures to self-suffocation and decline.

7.5. Cultural Hegemony: A Danger in the Process of Globalization

On the other hand, we must also be aware of the existence of "cultural hegemony" where a certain ideology is imposed upon another by dint of greater economic, political, and military power. Cultural hegemony not only exists in the West but also in the East, where the old Japanese dream of "the East Asian Belt of Common prosperity" (大东亚共荣圈) which cause the Japanese invasion is still alive. There is a long way for us to go before West or East centrism is eliminated from people's mind. Professor Armando Gnisci, an Italian comparatist, points out in his extremely insightful article entitled *Comparative Literature as a Discipline of Decolonization*:

> If comparative literature represents a way of understanding, studying, and realizing decolonization for countries who have gained their independence from their Western colonizers, it stands for a mode of thinking, self criticizing, and learning or emancipation from the colonization of the self for us European scholars. This will not be empty words granted that we admit to the fact that we belong to a post-colonial world where ex-colonizers and ex-colonized live the same way and coexist. The "discipline" I am talking about is related to self-criticism as well as educating and reforming others.

Contrary to this, there are politicians, theorist, and scholars, who openly advocate imposition of their own ideology on others and claim on totality and universality. As a matter of fact, with the rapid global boom of economic and scientific unification and media popularization, the ideology of universalism also develops greatly. For the Universalists, all the nations or races must conform to certain specific social and political patterns, which they think are best. Like the Jacobins during the French revolution, they do not hesitate to take every political or even military measure to "speak for all human beings." They impose their own moral tenets on others in order to carry out their self-approved beliefs. Such a moral tyranny also pays the price: that is the sacrifice of the will and lives of millions of people.

Slightly different from universalism, neo-conservatism emphasizes the fact that beautiful things and moral tenets created together by human beings over thousands of years remain unvarnished with the development of history and will appear repeatedly in different historical stages. The "universality," therefore, should be respected by every race all the times. Theoretically, there is nothing wrong, but the problem is the thought that these "universal values" and "virtues" which have nothing to do with specific time and space are not only changeless over time but also universally applicable. They extol the abstract universality at the expense of the particularity formed over the long course of history and in different geopolitical conditions. More important, the "universal values" they advocate are mainly Western oriented and barely take values of other civilizations into consideration. When met with resistance when imposing their values on others, they will gradually become New Jacobins, resorting to violence and developing a new cultural hegemony.

Generally speaking, I am not against totality and universality in any situation, it is very true that there are very precious universal heritage created by human being in the long history. What I resist is to force people into doing things they do not want to do, no matter how good and attractive their ideas seem. Take French revolution as an example, the idea of liberty, equality, and fraternity is absolutely good, but this is not the reason for the Jacobins to kill so many people who were not in complete agreement with it. In China, the same thing happened many times and gave terrible lessons to all Chinese people. It is enough to make us see that we have a long way to go in our efforts to overcome all kinds of New Jacobinism, disguised hegemonism "centrism" and to achieve cultural pluralism.

In short, we need to be alert, on the one hand, to the danger of being submerged or assimilated by other dominant cultures, and on the other hand, to the danger of falling into cultural isolationism which leaves us behind the cultural development of today's world. All nations should have a global consciousness while we develop our individual cultures. That means that we should also be concerned with the common problems faced by the world as a whole and try to find out the best possible solutions utilizing the cultural resources of all nations.

7.6. The New Perspective of Comparative Literature

In my viewpoint, the key of resolving these problems mentioned above is to increase communication and understanding among different cultures and to enlarge the living space for negotiation, toleration, and coexistence.

Comparative literature will be inevitably standing in the front position to fulfill this mission, if it is defined as "inter-cultural and inter-disciplinary study on literature." According to this definition, the basic aim of comparative literature is to promote the communication and understanding among different cultures and different disciplines. It will accelerate cultural exchange, avert the disastrous cultural conflict, and improve the plurality of culture. Another word, the main task of comparative literature is to arouse the mutual understanding, mutual confirmation, and mutual complement among different literatures in different cultural traditions.

First, the mutual understanding is discussed. Prof. Earl Miner points out in his book *Comparative Poetics*, that the need for mutual understanding is the mother of comparative literature. Comparative literature starts from the wish to understand the other literary tradition. This need usually takes the look of curiosity. The following is a quotation from Prof. Miner:

> "We are fully justified to feed our own herd and smoke tobacco with some farmer friends; however, some other people would trudge a long way to a farther place, which is also compatible with human nature. And there what people find are not sheep but camels, fish and dragon, which

we will bring to local ranch and make us try to find a way to let the camels, fish and sheep get along well with each other and explain this to the friends on the ranch."

Let us take the different attitude toward the moon as an example. In Chinese poetic tradition, the moon always symbolizes eternity and solitude, and reflects the earthly sorrows and the ephemeral life. Li Po (701–702) in *A question for the Moon Drinking* is considered a perfect representative. The following are few lines from this famous poem:

> Contemporaries cannot see the ancient moon,
> Whilst the present-day moon once shone upon the ancients.
> The ancients and the contemporaries are like the flowing water, looking at the same moon.
> I wish in my lonely drinking and singing, upon the golden cup the moon eternally shining.

> "今人不见古时月,今月曾经照古人。
> 今人古人若流水,共看明月皆如此。"

This poem expresses the melancholy feeling of mortal human in front of the immortal moon. On the other hand, the poem reminds us of the poets in different periods who had been under the same moon. It is this same unavoidable distress and helplessness that unite the ancestors together with the successors through the moon — the eternal medium.

There are a lot of descriptions about the moon in Japanese literature. Instead of symbol of eternity, the moon is usually regarded by Japanese as their intimate companion. For example, Myoe Shonin 明惠上人 (1173–1232) wrote a lot of poems about the moon. One of them is *In company with the Winter Moon* ("冬月相伴随"), where he wrote:

> I went forward to meet the setting moon from the top of the mountain.
> And I wish I could spent every night sleeping with you.
> ....
> A cloudless heart shines so bright, even the moon takes me to be the lunar light.[1]

As the winner of the Nobel Prize, Kawabata Yasunari (川端康成) gave a further analysis of this poem in his award speech: "He regarded the moon as his lover rather than a companion. The moon was becoming "I" and the "I" was becoming the moon. Here the poet is harmoniously merging into the "nature." Myoe Shonin's poem and Kawabata Yasunari's analysis give us another perspective and situation to perceive the moon.

And there is more earthly flavor in the Western poetry of the moon. Let us take a look at Baudelaire's *Sadness of the Moon-Goddess*:

> Tonight the Moon dreams with the increased weariness,
> Like a beauty stretched forth on a downy heap
> Of rugs, while her languorous fingers caress
> The contour of her breasts, before falling to sleep.
>
> On the satin back of the avalanche soft,
> She falls into lingering swoons, as she dies,
> While she lifteth her eyes to white visions aloft,
> Which like efflorescence float up to the skies.
>
> When at times, in her languor, down on to this sphere,
> She slyly lets trickle a furtive tear,
> A poet, desiring a slumber to shun,
>
> Takes up this pale tear in the palm of his hand
> (The colors of which like an old opal blend),
> And buries it far from the eyes of the sun.[2]

Such description is a little bit blasphemous for the oriental people. As different from Li Po's metaphysical feelings and Myoe Shonin's intimate harmony, the moon in Baudelaire's poem is an independent object. It sheds its tears onto the earth and also into the heart of the poet who is an independent subject meditating under the moon.

These three poets, in different time, culture, and mode, give us an equally perfect aesthetical enjoyment. We cannot acquire the aesthetical enjoyment without any of these different perceiving alternatives. From the above example, we realize that the idea of identification in comparative literature is aimed at mutual understanding and appreciation of the literature in different traditional context.

Second, the mutual confirmation means to seek the various answers to the same problem in the different literary traditions and thereafter to reach a further consensus through dialogue. There are a lot of similar literary topics in different traditions. The life forms of human being are always the same: male and female, older and younger, father and son, man and nature, man and fate, and so on, and people always experience the same feeling: joy and sorrow, separation and reunion, hope and despair, love and hatred, life and death, etc. Apparently, there must be many similar aspects in literature which aims at the description of human life and feeling, such as the consciousness of death, the problem of ecology, the eschatological expectation, the utopian thirst and the idea of recluse, etc. All these problems are answered by different people from different cultural traditions according to their own ways of living and thinking. These answers are echoing back the voice of history; meanwhile, they are re-interpreted by the contemporaries in their contemporary context.

Third, mutual complement, that means the mutual absorption between different cultures, which does not injure the self-identity of either part but makes them richer. There are a lot of such facts in the literary history. For instance, the influence of Walter Whitman upon modern Chinese romanticism and E. Pound's misreading of Li Po's poetry lead to the creation of American imagism; besides, it also signifies the new development of a particular text in a totally different context. For instance, Ibsen, the Norwegian play writer acquired his new appearance from Lu Xun's creative interpretation in Chinese social context. He raises the question: where is Nana to go after her leaving? ("娜拉走后怎样")? And the figure of Nana are emerged and recreated in Lu Xun, Hu Shi, and Mao Dun's works. This entire literary phenomenon illuminates how different cultures had been enriched by the communication and exchange with the other.

Lastly, comparative literature will play a big role in the reciprocal cognition (or interactive knowledge), which is in hot discussion recently.

It is for this consideration that Chinese culture, which has a rather long history and abundant cultural heritage and which had developed in a relatively enclosed context a different "other" in sharp contrast with

Western culture or a frame of reference through which the West can reflect itself from another perspective. This is clearly expressed by Francois Jullien:

> "The Chinese language, which is outside the enormous Indo-European language system, explored another possibility of writing. The Chinese civilization is the one that has the longest history and that had evolved independently without being influenced by the European culture .... All in all, China is an ideal image contrasted with which we will be able to free ourselves from some preconceived ideas and gaze at our own thoughts from the outside."

In fact, quite a number of works full of insightful ideas aiming at reflecting Western culture from the frame of reference of Chinese culture have come up in recent years. As the most suitable "other," more and more theorists are attending to China. Three books written in collaboration by Roger Ames and David Hall caused quite a sensation. The first one, *Thinking through Confucius* makes a reflection upon Western through Confucian thoughts; the second one *Anticipating China: Thinking through the Narratives of Chinese and Western Culture* and the third *Thinking from the Han: Self, Truth and Transcendence* all focus on different modes of thinking in perspective of reciprocal cognition. The most important contribution made in those works is the conventional analytic pattern of binary opposition which treats either China or the West as a tangible object independent from the observing subject is discarded: neither Chinese culture nor Western culture is immutable, on the contrary, they assume different shapes in the observations of different subjects. So the process of understanding must be that of a reciprocal cognition. As we can see, the Eastern culture is going to integrate with the Western philosophy and within the main stream of Western culture.

In conclusion, it may be said that if we want to avert conflict, violence, and war, and want to increase communication and understanding among different cultures and to enlarge the living space for negotiation, tolerance, and coexistence, dialogue between different race, class, gender, and different political and religious groups is most important. In this circumstance, comparative literature is not to shrink or decline, but play a more important role.

Notes

1. Quoted from the speech of Kawabata Yasunari at the ceremony where he was conferred the 1968 Nobel Prize.
2. Charles Baudelaire (1909). *The Flowers of Evil* (trans. Cyril Scott). London: Elkin Mathews, Ltd, p. 45.

THE SCIENTIFIC MERIT OF EDUCATIONAL STUDIES*

CHO-YEE TO

University of Michigan, USA

8.1. Introduction

Despite flourishing as academic disciplines, educational studies are far from scientific. The continuing trend of uncritical adherence to "big-name" theories and the popularity of "methodology" run against its scientific legitimization. Do educational researchers really want to see their "sciences" evolve into other type of "science" which have abandoned their original chosen model for that of the rational, objective, and experimental form of inquiry demonstrated by the natural sciences? If this is going to be the future of education studies, then new definitions for the term research and related concepts will have to be created. A different expectation of what education studies can accomplish will have to be formulated. No doubt, the laxity of some scientific requirements and the freedom and variety of approaches will promote many imaginative and colorful investigations, which may manifest wisdom and insight, but without the ability to verify results, these studies will remain inconclusive.

Our goal is to transform education inquiry into scientific research by providing it with an empirical basis and experimental methods. The problem confronting education researchers is how to redirect efforts toward their becoming a stronger scientific inquiry. However, before this topic can be considered, it is necessary to answer a series of crucial questions: Do

---

*This chapter is a reproduction of the Wu Teh Yao memorial lecture given by the author in 2002.

education studies possess the potentiality to become an exact science? In other words, can they fulfil the necessary criteria, as research in the natural sciences for being truly scientific? Will education studies be able to generate research that will assist in the recognition of important systems operating in the education environment? Can they design research that can recognize the regular patterns of human behavior at work in these systems or that will assist in the identification of important human and social and educational variables and parameters within these systems? In other words: will education researchers be able to recognize the exact relationships that exist among these variables and parameters and their relations to entities outside the systems? More importantly, will education researchers be able to identify the constant properties and invariant dynamics at work in these systems? This assumes their willingness and ability of the researchers to overcome the cultural relativity of current education studies.[1]

Whether education studies can become an objective science like the natural sciences depends on whether researchers can identify, locate, and study the invariance in human traits and activities. This comes down to two fundamental questions, as Ernest Gellner puts them: Is there but one kind of man, or are there many? Is there but one world, or are there many?[2]

The answer to one of these questions does not presuppose the answer to the other. Evidence obtained from scientific inquiries into the physical universe has led to the conclusion that there can be but one physical world and one truth about it, and not many. However, the "oneness" of mankind is a separate question. The existence of various cultural traditions and the exhibition of different individual aptitudes have led to the belief that there are indeed many different kinds of human beings, and even to give *out* that some are superior and some inferior, inhabiting "different worlds." Errors in the perception of human phenomena, because of their elusiveness, have complicated the problem further.

If there are different kinds of human beings (other than men and women) and if they are fundamentally different from one another, then difficulty will be encountered when trying to come up with comprehensive and accurate theories about human behavior and societies. However, when studying differences between people, it is also possible to notice similarities. Human beings everywhere share identical molecular structure; all have the same neural system and that makes up their cerebral structure; and all grow in experience in the same way. These common features which set limits to physical and mental behavior are derived from a common human genetic makeup. While each individual differ from another as each possesses unique genetic material, the processes that determine how that genetic material functions are one and the same. Even though each individual accumulates different life experiences, the fundamental physical interpretive faculties for understanding these experiences (i.e., the brain and how it functions) are essentially the same for everyone. Human beings are both different and at the same time similar to one another. The differences are superficial and are largely developed through generations of accommodation and adaptation to the environment; the similarities are more fundamental, being the characteristics of a common human nature. In this sense, all human beings may be said to belong to one family and there is only one human species designated by that name. While the many strains of that same species may exhibit differences, the basic building blocks are identical.

These similarities did not stop controversy from developing after results were obtained from 10 tests conducted on persons of different races. Hereditary factors were exaggerated by some education researchers who claimed the existence of a genetically different human intelligence differing by race.[3] Particularly dangerous were the uncontrolled and incomplete observations of human achievement by social anthropologist philosophers, such as Houston Stewart Chamberlain. Based on developments in the 19th century, Chamberlain concluded that race influenced human personality and behavior. Beyond membership of a social class to racial origins, Chamberlain's work led to claims of racial superiority and incitement to racial hatred by the Nazi ideologue, Alfred Rosenberg, in *Der My thus des 20. Jahrhunderts* in a significant reference to the 20th century in the title of his book.

Diamonds and charcoal are both composed of carbon, but they have many distinct properties. The study of education observes the behavior of human beings both as individuals and collectively. These collective phenomena can be very different, because of the numerous aspects they can assume, from individual ones.

The implications are that human traits and behavior, and perhaps even human thought, may eventually be studied scientifically, particularly through the collaboration of biological and education research. An optimist would predict that if the genetic makeup of individuals were fully understood, scientists could assess the risk of disease years before the first symptoms appeared, identify a criminal from a single hair, and uncover the mysteries of how we think, grow, heal, and age.[4] Successful decoding of the 30,000–40,000 human genes[5] will enable researchers to develop drugs and other treatments tailored to an individual specific genetic profile. As the well-known Genome Project, which has been pursuing an exhaustive investigation of the genetic makeup of the human race, moves along, scientists may have reason to be cautiously optimistic.[6]

The transformation of education research into a fully developed exact science will be an exciting process. It is time to start working toward that goal by removing the three obstacles which delay it. These are the uncritical attachment to and use of popular theories, what may be called guru worship, the entrapment of methodology, and the purposive procedures used by less cautious social researchers who abandon the scientific approach in their investigations. The following nine measures, which adhere to the generally accepted principles of scientific inquiry, are considered essential to promote the scientific advancement of education studies, making them more like natural sciences while retaining their distinctive areas of concern and methodology.

8.2. Clarification of Terms and Terminology

An agreed, common vocabulary, as in the natural sciences, is absolutely essential if there is to be any advance in education studies. They must free themselves from ambiguity and confusion. The misunderstanding of Platonic and Aristotelian terms has dogged the West. The concept behind the Confucian principle of "Rectification of Names" is the key. To quote Confucius, "If names are not rectified, then language will not be in accord with truth. If language is not in accord with truth, then progress will not occur?"[7] Economics, particularly in its post-Marshallian form, is in danger of losing its credibility as a result of the ambiguity and loose nature of its preferred terminology. The deliberate vagueness of much educational theory gives credence to the complaints of practising education researchers that looseness in the use of words indicates a looseness in thought. The overused words "free market," "multicultural," and "intercultural education" are examples.

Certain key terms in education research, such as the term "theory," also "model," and "principle," have not only been defined differently from their use in the natural sciences but it is also a fact that different reference sources in the education studies may define identical terms quite differently.[8] A mechanism, such as an editorial board, consisting of researchers from different areas of education studies, established to work on standardization of nomenclature sponsored by relevant academic bodies would develop general guidelines for the adoption, modification, and change of terms for the various divisions of the education studies and related social sciences as well as for the field as a whole.[9] With unambiguous definitions, superfluous jargon could be eliminated, questionable ideas could be weeded out, allowing education researchers to gradually develop a more consistent, concise, and precise communication system. This is the first prerequisite for any serious scientific inquiry.

8.3. Systematic Investigation and Assessment of Important and Popular Theories in the Education Studies

In the process of constructing a theoretical framework, theories require intense review and scrutiny prior to adoption and application. A comprehensive analysis of the origin, development, research design, generalization and claim of universality, evaluation, and application, and influence of individual theories is needed. A sample scheme has already been developed and has proved effective in such an endeavor.[10]

The scheme was designed by the author at the University of Michigan as an instrument for guiding his graduate students in conducting background investigation of education, social, and behavioural science theories. This was a prerequisite for the interpretation, use and adaptation of any theory in their research. This scheme of investigation consists of nine parts:

(1) identifying the theory founder's biological and intellectual background;

(2) locating the founder's academic works and related writings;
(3) examining works written about the founder of the theory;
(4) assessing the influence of the theory during the founder's lifetime;
(5) studying the approach and processes leading to the formation and establishment of the theory;
(6) investigating the educational, social, and cultural environment in which the theory was developed;
(7) determining whether the founder ever claimed universal validity of the theory, which many theory adherents take for granted;
(8) checking whether the theory has ever been empirically tested by the theory founder or by others; and
(9) finding out how theory founder or others intended for the theory to be used or tested.

This comprehensive scheme represents a serious approach to critically understand an education theory.

8.4. Comparison and Confrontation of Theories Bearing on the Same Theme or Problem

With terms clarified and communication barriers largely removed, individual theories reviewed and their strengths and weaknesses understood, theories which have contributed to accepted relevant topics can be selected, matched, and compared. A "confrontation" of "theories" can allow educators and researchers of different schools of thought to meet, discuss, argue, debate, study with one another, and escape from the confines of their own theoretical traditions. In this way the necessary conditions for productive scientific communication can be established. Relevant research findings obtained through different approaches and interpreted from different perspectives can be freed from misrepresentation, allowing the theoretical counterparts to object with reason or to assent with understanding. Conflicting theories may find points of mutual agreement, which in turn may become the loci for collaborative, further investigations of the topic. Indeed, carefully and intelligently designed comparison and challenge of education research may not only lead to the formation of a new basis for theoretical development but may also foster the arrival of a genuine community of education researchers, in which participants can involve themselves in the pursuit of scientific excellence free from academic biases and ideological and political influences. The crucial question is who decides on the criteria.

The study of the role of the first language (mother tongue) in the acquisition of a second or foreign language can be given as another example of the problems associated with the establishment of psycho-social theory in view of the shifting data which becomes available as the study unfolds and the changing focus of emphasis.

If we take Michael Clyne's widely received 1960s view of the process of language transfer and its effect as the starting point then this has been significantly modified so as to leave the role of the transfer or interference much reduced.[12] It is now accepted to being responsible for learners using certain constructions in the second language which are "incorrect" in that language and which affect the formal properties in language learning. Transfer is absent in language development which is activated with the use of communicative skills and language behavior. This takes place independently in all language systems. Indeed, Pit Corder suggests that no firm conclusion for language teaching can arise from a better understanding of the role of the mother tongue in second language learning since the processes of language use are neither conscious nor available to introspection.

In other words, while the learning process itself can be influenced by the use of some mother tongue structures in the second language, as the latter becomes more fluent it develops independently from the former and can resort to deliberate borrowings from it or indeed from another language altogether.

The acceptance of one or an other transfer theory thus hinges on the emphasis given to the cognitive (learning) or the communicative fluency (behavior) study of the process of second language acquisition.[13] Including the affective dimension in the process which can determine its speed, what with learners actually wanting to or not wanting to learn another language, would make the setting up of another education "certainty" more problematic. Empirical evidence is controversial because of the fact that second language knowledge stems from three sources: language universals as well as mother tongue and the target (second) language.

8.5. Extensive Survey of the Range and Scope of Human Problems to Obtain a Vision of the Whole Picture Enabling a Comprehensive Agenda for Inquiry to be Designed, and Solutions Reviewed and Adjusted Periodically

The interconnectedness of various problems, issues, and topics has to be understood so as to make it possible to identify the appropriate, specific items for investigation. While the topics chosen for the study should be small enough to be controllable, the study itself should be substantial enough to be significant to accommodate understanding the topic itself as well as to allow planning the investigation of a larger area on the agenda. The eventual goal of education research is to work toward achieving as complete and accurate knowledge as is possible of people and their societies, while allowing for the fact that they may be different in detail and that education research procedures are liable to be tested at any time. This will require individual education researchers to appreciate the importance of communication and cooperation among fellow workers on a long-term basis; a daunting task judging from past experience. Through the continuous efforts of both involved individuals and groups, information, insights, procedural techniques, and skills will gradually accumulate and be refined, enabling a scientific understanding of human society to emerge.

The role played by memory in the development of human learning and the impact of information stimuli have been differently evaluated regarding the role assigned to television on children's learning. The James Bulger murder committed in November 1993 in Bootle, England, by two 11-year-old boys was compared with the more recent Luk Chi case in 1998 Hong Kong involving a gang of adolescents four years older than the victim. In both cases the viewing of television gangster programs by the juvenile perpetrators of the murders was quoted by some as a contributory factor inciting the crimes committed. The court in Hong Kong heard that one of the convicted gang member inflicted blows on Luk while reading a poem inspired by the program "Teddy Boy," a view supported by the academic evidence provided by professor in journalism and communication. The psychological opinions of the causal relationship quoted were divided. The judge in the British case preferred not to bring in the factor of the impact of television viewing into his judgment, while, "violence in the media" was brought in by the defence in the Hong Kong trial. The "confusion between fact and fiction presented as entertainment" makes it difficult to apply moral standards.

8.6. Developing Translation, Transformation, and Unified Theories in the Social Sciences

This insight evolved while studying the development of quantum theory in modern physics. Paul Dirac developed a mathematical proof that Erwin Schrodinger's wave mechanics identical to the matrix mechanics of Heisenberg, that is, developed a transformation theory that showed these two mechanics to be equivalent interpretations of the same nonrelativistic quantum mechanics. In education studies, many "theories" revolve around a certain topic, with all the researchers trying to approach it with their own methods and with their own language. Thus Piaget, Skinner, and Kohlberg, and all contemporaries, investigated how human beings learn. However, each studied learning, starting from a unique approach: Piaget used clinical observations of children in developing his stage theory of mental development;[14] Skinner examined laboratory animals in developing his notion of contingencies of reinforcement and then applied these ideas to the learning environment, that is, learning as occurring through the formation of complex contingencies of reinforcement for children;[15] Kohlberg used interview procedures with socially privileged boys as the foundation for developing his stages of moral education.[16] Each of these theorists may be correct within the confines of his separate approach. However, education research requires a mechanism for bringing together the results of the three perspectives and others like them into a comprehensive theory or framework. For such a mechanism to evolve researchers must be able to effectively communicate with and understand one another across their different approaches.

Since a phenomenon may be investigated using multiple approaches, and from various perspectives within each approach, and since several theories may emerge from these approaches, a preliminary mechanism for effective communication among the diverse approaches is essential. As part of theory development in education studies, researchers could formulate "translation theories" that permit them to understand one another despite using different approaches and theories with similar and differing meanings of terms.

A developed translation theory functions like a specialized dictionary where each term has only one meaning and terms which appear to have the same meaning are identified as to their precise meanings. Wherever required, translation theory would translate terms in one theory into terms in another theory. If more than one theory used the same term, it should be possible to determine whether in the context of each theory or approach the term does represent the same empirical or theoretical entity. If the term has an identical meaning or represents the same entity within each theory, the term should be standardized. If the meaning of the term differs within each theory, it will be necessary to distinguish between the different meanings within each theory and to reveal the differences by revising the term's meaning and creating new, more appropriate terms. If a theory claims to use a unique term, it would be possible to determine whether what the term represents has an alternative term used in other theories. If several terms are being used to represent the same empirical or theoretical entity, then after careful comparison one of the terms or a new term should be chosen as standard. If different terms represent unique entities, each term should become standard for what it represents.[17]

The assumption that different theories about the same phenomenon have discovered unique aspects of that phenomenon can serve as a major stimulus for new research within the separate approaches to confirm the existence of the unique elements claimed. For instance, different terms may be used to refer to different degrees of specificity about an object or process requiring the identification of the different degrees to make it possible to differentiate between the terms used. Terms revealed as just different names for the same entity would be eliminated. Unambiguous and commensurable communication among scholars is a prerequisite for advancement in scientific research. To be sure, the description of this process makes it seem more straightforward than it will turn out in practice, the immediate problem being the selection of samples.

After the translation theory has been adopted, it will be necessary to proceed to formulate transformation theories. To understand the specification of a transformation theory, let us suppose that there are two theories about the same phenomenon, Theory X and Theory Y. The transformation theory turns the theoretical entities and processes and, to the extent that models are concerned, the empirical entities and processes of Theory X, into the relevant entities and processes of Theory Y. It would be desirable that every entity and process of Theory X coincided with one and only one entity or process of Theory Y and conversely that each entity or process of Theory Y had an entity or process in Theory X that coincided with it (an isomorphism). A one-to-one relation-preserving match (i.e., a homomorphism) would probably be sufficient.

Naturally, two such ideal types of matching will occur infrequently since conceptual entities in one theory may have many manifestations in another. However, as a result of the transformation theory not only could researchers communicate using the same language but they could also transform their theory into another theory that may be more appropriate for the particular situation being researched. If we confine ourselves to the disciplines quoted earlier, an investigation of the educational implications of intelligence development under certain conditions would take comparative account of the differences actually measured.[18]

Once the transformation theory has been developed, the procedures that have evolved will enable researchers to formulate a single unified theory about the phenomenon which the different individual theories attempted to explain. The individual theories should not be dismissed, for within particular, smaller area applications they may give simpler, yet adequate, approximations of the system. Analogous to the continued use of Newtonian mechanics, education studies that have been supplanted by a more accurate approximation to the system will still be useful within the approach and environment in which they were originally formulated. These theories would refer the single theory as a foundation. Although education researchers may argue about just how to formulate translation, transformation, and unified theories, they must be able to agree that conducting such research and its subsequent success will significantly strengthen the knowledge base in the social sciences.

8.7. Sorting Out and Clearing the Traps of Method

Education researchers often consider "scientific" research to be determined by the particular method employed in conducting it. No exclusive set of rules, or "scientific method," exists to tell scientists exactly how or where to conduct their individual research. This individually initiated research depends entirely on the creativity of the researcher to devise the means for discovering or testing consistent patterns in a system. An informal process exists, however, requiring the rigorous establishment of results before acceptance by the scientific community. Adherence of most natural scientists to the same world view, that is, agreement on which important field advancing topics to investigate and how to investigate them, assists in this informal process.

Education researchers lack an agreed world view and as a consequence, a weak informal process for deciding when supportive evidence legitimates acceptance of new results. The following paragraphs discuss some aspects of the dynamics of research, namely, data collection, data analysis, and model and theory development. They also suggest some improvements that may help make education research results more valid. A proviso for this discussion is that education researchers can recognize what is researchable and what is not within current limitations and strive toward that which can be accomplished.[19]

Before discussing these aspects of research, a brief introductory description of the "research dynamic" may be helpful. The most important part of research is the collection of relevant data. However, data collection is partially dependent on the identification of the important and relevant parameters and variables in a system. This identification in turn partially relies on the analysis of the limited area from which the data is collected, even with an incomplete identification of parameters and variables. The analysis of the data may assist in specifying a more complete list of parameters and variables requiring the collection of additional data. Hence, as simplistic as this description may be, it is possible to begin to see how research progresses by constant reference to the data and to prior information. Despite possible unidentified and misidentified parameters and variables, the attempted research can progress, based on the data analyses, to develop models and theories about the system. At this point, researchers have the incentive to make the models and theories more accurate through the collection and analysis of additional data relevant to this objective.

This brief description reveals that research is not a linear process directed toward a single climatic objective. Rather, research is a complex recursive network containing many feedback loops the function of which is to reassess prior information in light of current achievements. The dynamic elements of data collection, data analysis, and model and theory development with respect to education research will now be examined.

Data collection in the education research faces some unique obstacles. Most unfortunate is the absence of mechanisms for identifying important and relevant parameters and variables in education and related systems. This difficulty is linked to another obstacle, the heterogeneity of the subject matter of the education studies. Unlike electrons where every electron has the same characteristics as every other electron, human beings and the groups that they form do not possess homogeneous sets of characteristics. As a result, subjects that are enlisted for experiments generate data collected under conditions that can never be fully replicated, using a process of sampling from some total group, or population. It is accepted that the most desirable sample is a random sample, a sample drawn from a population in such a way that every element of the population has an equal chance of being selected.

Given an adequate sample size, a true random sample is accepted as typically representative of the population which permits researchers to make inferences about the general population based on analyses of the sample. However, rarely do education researchers ever obtain true random samples unless the area investigated is small enough to be fully covered by the samples made. Even so, education researchers are prone to produce inferences about the population investigated although the sample is representative only of some subgroup of the total. As mentioned earlier, Piaget studied only European children but claimed his results were representative of all children. Now, unless Piaget was investigating a basic universal characteristic of child growth, which would require a substantiation he did not provide, his inference was inappropriate. This example demonstrates the limitations of such investigations.

The inability of education researchers to collect data from an appropriate sample is largely influenced by factors external to the research proper, such as funding, access, and time. Data collection is usually the most costly part of an education research project, which causes many education researchers to reduce data collection to the minimum required. Education researchers may have access to only a limited segment of the population of interest (due to geographic proximity, or subject availability) while time constraints placed on the researcher may function to further degrade the data collection phase of research. As a result, researchers have often turned to a variety of readily available sources of data to use in their studies. These alternative sources include large government data sources! (such as census data, tax data, and others), private data collection agencies, and the findings of other researchers. The large-scale use of secondary data sources limits the researcher's freedom and control over deciding what data are important to collect and how to collect them. Hence, as a surrogate for the desired data, researchers must utilize the best approximations from the available data set. To the effect that analysis techniques and models and theories advance only as the level of detail and sophistication of the available data improves, this need of substitution has implications for the research enterprise and the accuracy of results that can be expected. As the most important phase of the research dynamics, data collection is well worth the expense and time required to collect representative samples.

Since responsibility for defraying the expenses of a research project is affected by its perceived usefulness to the sponsor, the cost of sampling is a further factor in abandoning education research projects, or labeling them as less scientific before trying them out. Unlike in the field of education, moral value judgments are not essential in the physical sciences, as argued by Scriven.[20] Conversely massive and indiscriminate data collection, where the aims decide the priorities of the inquiry, will not enable researchers to generate meaningful and valid results.

Another aspect of data collection has to do with the procedures used to acquire data. Traditional methods of collecting data in the field of education include surveys, interviews, observations, ethnographic study, and testing. Once a preliminary target sample has been determined, one of these procedures or possibly a number of them will be used to solicit information from subjects in the sample. Discussion of the strengths and weaknesses of these data-collecting procedures for specific types of projects is beyond the scope of this study. Suffice it to say that the effective size and representativeness of the sample which a procedure can draw on, the depth and detail of the obtainable data and the variety of analyses that can be performed on the data, constrain the appropriate use of each procedure.

Issues of calibration of data collection instruments are rarely deliberated in the education studies. When a new or more accurate instrument is introduced, it must be brought into agreement with established knowledge by repeating past experiments with it. Adjustments may have to be made to the new instrument to make it agree closely with the experiments that produced the previous results. When the instrument cannot be calibrated, the natural scientists face a dilemma because they cannot readily decide whether the failure is the result of a bad instrument or whether the new instrument has revealed some flaw in previous theory. Education studies have no mechanism for calibrating new instruments with past theories. This deficiency may in part be due to the lack of a reliable knowledge base upon which to base the calibration process. However, a more significant reason is that in education research, data collection instruments are often situationally designed, that is, education researchers design data collection instruments relative to the topic they are investigating and to the environment in which the study is being conducted. This lack of continuity and consistency in the data record creates a major obstacle for the development of sound, reliable education theories. The ability to calibrate research instrument would help alleviate this deficiency.

Analysis of collected data represents another research dynamic. For the types of data collected, education research analysis procedures are not necessarily wrong. Often, however, the claims and conclusions drawn by education researchers are inappropriate for what the results can actually demonstrate. For instance, many statistical analyses are correlational. Correlation only specifies that a relationship exists between two entities without specifying its precise nature. However, some analysts, basing themselves on a correlational analysis, claim confirmation of a causal relationship. Causal relation between two entities is always the result of an interpretation made by the researcher based on observation of the system, speculation, or experience. Analyses do not locate a relation, nor do they confirm that the relation is causal. Most analyses do not even identify a relation but only test what the researcher believes to be a relationship present in a system. In this sense, most analysis procedures used in education research are exploratory. This property is desirable because education researchers wish to base models and theories on empirical data. However, through exploratory studies one could recognize and differentiate significant parameters and variables and the relations among them. Hence, the challenge for education researchers is to improve their ability to recognize patterns.[21]

An important phase of the research dynamic is the development of abstract models and theories based upon what has been learned from the data analyses. Unfortunately, in the absence of hard empirical evidence, education research often begins with conceptualizing a model or theory of how education phenomena function. Such philosophizing interferes with data collection and analysis processes because empirical data becomes secondary to and supportive of the theory rather than providing the impetus for the discovery of theory. Education researchers tend to prescribe theories for the phenomena that they study. Regardless of whether the prescribed theory accurately represents a phenomenon, human beings can modify their behavior in response to a theory, rendering that theory no longer useful.

Clearly, education theory has a number of obstacles that must be overcome. A way in which these difficulties can be overcome is by developing theories based firmly on empirical research, and once the theory has been established, re-evaluating and improving the data collected and analyses conducted to arrive at the theory. If theories become obsolete because people change their behavior in response to their predictions, then education researchers should learn from these experiences and return to the data to locate parameters, variables, and relations basic enough that they will be invariant to the purposive behavior of people. It must be stressed that theory is not the end of education research. Rather, theory is a new beginning, for certainly the first attempt at theory will not be the most accurate representation of the education problem studied.

8.8. Recognizing that Education Studies are Culturally Bound and Studying the Significance of Cultural Factors in the Selection, Application, and Assessment of Education Theories and Knowledge

Existing education theories were largely constructed upon fashionable and superficial situations current at the time. By no means are they nonspatial, nontemporal, and transcultural. When applying them cross-culturally, unexpected effects and side effects will likely be produced. Arbitrary adoption and application of social theories, economic, educational, political, or other, may lead to less than optimal results, as happened in the Soviet Union, China, North Korea, and Cuba, when they embraced Marxism as their prescriptive theory for society building. Indeed, the transfer, transplanting, or borrowing education and social theories and practices should be made a systematic field for serious investigation. Further research is necessary to test to what extent the application has in fact kept to the original model.

8.9. Use of Education Theories as a Test of Their Function and Power

At this stage of development of the education studies, it will be hard to verify an education theory in a strictly experimental and controlled way. The solution is to select "promising" education theories in teaching, learning, curricular design, policy, or administration; apply them carefully; and evaluate the consequences. Through practise and testing, the public will also become scientifically enlightened and informed, while through application, the education studies will renew and revitalize themselves. Awareness of the power of a theory to predict might assist in the process of testing a theory in education. The problems of using prediction as a validating test are, nevertheless, considerable, even in the natural sciences. How could it be applied, for example, to the science of cosmology, with a time scale of millions of years hence? Indeed, what of the inability of Darwinian theory to predict even in general terms the future course of evolution? Michael Scriven, in his essay, "Explanation and prediction in evolutionary theory,"[22] comments that Darwin has demonstrated that a science can give a satisfactory explanation of the past even when prediction of the future is impossible.

8.10. Bringing New and Substantiated Knowledge Found in Natural Sciences to the Education Studies

It is necessary to establish systematic, two-way, academic channels to provide a constant flow of new knowledge between education research and the natural sciences. This flow of knowledge will strengthen the scientific foundation of the former and create new areas of research for both. An example is the Human Genome Project, which has created a wealth of possibilities for education and social research, as well as cooperative cross-disciplinary inquiries.

In biotechnology research, it is envisioned that revolutionary advancement will generate vital new products that would change the modes of production and consumption as well as the economy and civilization as a whole in the 21st century. For instance, harnessing the conversion of methane into carbon dioxide, sugar, and protein would certainly affect agriculture and thus the nutrition and physical and mental growth of children.

In computer science, it is predicted that in the foreseeable future, satellite computers will guide the operation of agriculture and forestry equipment. These computers will be able to sense the nutrient and water requirement for each individual plant and command the delivery of such. Satellite computers may be used to conduct accurate and speedy research in the social sciences and related fields, such as geology, geography, history, politics, population studies, community development, and school site planning. Another rapidly advancing field is cosmological research. By 2004, it will enable scientists to answer the question as to where mass comes from. And it is predicted that by 2008, a Mars lander will return to Earth with soil samples. If a strand of DNA is found there, then the most challenging question since the Darwinian evolution will arise: What is man's position in the Universe? As a result of new discoveries in natural sciences, educators, along with social scientists, will have to review their inquiries in order to reinterpret their significance.

An early attempt to bring psychological studies and neurological research together was found in the efforts of Donald O. Hebb some 45 years ago. Cross-fertilization of knowledge would allow education researchers to gain not only new insights but also new expertise in the scientific adventure.[23]

It is tempting to consider specifically not only "the idea of science" but also the whole problem of what is acceptable as the "scientific explanation." A philosopher of science, Carl Hempel addresses it in his central thesis,[24] which can be seen as relevant to the "new approach" to education research suggested in this study. His thesis hinges on the nature of the two parts of the "scientific explanation": a statement of the event to be explained (the *explanandum*) and the statement which constitutes the explanation itself (the *explanans*). The *explanans* has to be a general law which has universal application to the class of events of which the *explanandum* is an example. It must be possible to deduce, in a logical fashion, the *explanandum* from the *explanans* which must be, in every sense, true. Following a statement of antecedent conditions, the entire content of the *explanandum* must be empirical, the *explanandum* seen as logically required by the *explanans*. With his advocacy of the use of teleological analysis in the study of purposive behavior, an area of particular significance in the social sciences, Hempel disagrees with the assertion that "a causal type of explanation is inadequate in fields other than physics and chemistry."

It could be to the advantage of learning theory if some universally accepted framework of adequacy of explanation were adopted, in relation to Piaget's stages of intellectual development theory or Skinner's reinforcement hypotheses. Though, because of the stance taken on what exactly is the nature of education studies, some of the literature quoted in this chapter does not see the need, the measures recommended above signify a re-direction of the development of the education research in *general* from superficiality to profundity, from triviality to comprehensiveness, from dispersive to cumulative, and from empirical to scientific inquiry. Progress would be slow in the beginning, but it is bound to accelerate, forming a strong and vital component, an ongoing enterprise in human civilization.

APPENDIX

A Research Instrument for Analysing Social Science
Theorists, their Theories and Influences

This research instrument was used by the author's graduate students at the University of Michigan in their reports on the evolution of the three social science theory constructions dealt with in detail in the book:

Trevor J. Leutscher (Skinner)
Mary Jo May (Piaget)
Helen M.Marks (Kohlberg)

Formation of a Theory: Piaget, Skinner, and Kohlberg
The Theorist and the Theory — Analysis and Assessment Data Review Instrument

1. Describe the theorist's biographical and intellectual background:
    1.1 Give the theorist's full-name, birthplace, dates of birth and death, nationality and ethnicity.
        1.1.1 Provide biographical information (parent's educational levels, occupations, sibling's ages, social/economic status.)
        1.1.2 What influenced the theorist in his early life?
    1.2 Describe the theorist's primary/secondary education — (geographical region, school type):
        1.2.1 List the theorist's colleges and qualifications obtained (where, majors/minors, degrees/awards.)
        1.2.2 What were the theorist's early occupations (if any) ?
        1.2.3 Describe the theorist's graduate studies — university, field of research, advisors, the theorist's dissertation.
        1.2.4 What positions did the theorist hold early in his career?
        1.2.5 What other fields interested the theorist?

2. Survey some of the theorist's works:
   2.1 Name the theorist's major works: books, journals articles, others (reviews etc.).
   2.2 Provide a comprehensive bibliography of the theorist.
   2.3 Describe the theorist's scholarly productivity.
      2.3.1 Identity the theorist's early writing.
      2.3.2 Identity the theorist's most creative, productive stage.
      2.3.3 What works were written later in life?
3. Survey works written about the theorist:
   3.1 Identity the major works about the theorist and his theory/theories:
      3.1.1 Books
      3.1.2 Journal articles
      3.1.3 Other materials
   3.2 What are the major contributions of the theorist's theory/theories?
   3.3 Identity the major criticisms of the theorist's theory/theories and their nature.
   3.4 How did the theorist respond to these criticisms?
4. How influential were the theorist's major theories during the theorist's lifetime, and how influential are they now?
   4.1 How influential was the theorist at the height of his career?
      4.1.1 What was the theorist's influence in learned associations and societies concerned with the field of study (any positions held by the theorist)?
      4.1.2 What new programs about the theory/theories were started at universities or research institutions?
      4.1.3 What research/dissertations were done on the theorist's theory/theories by others?
      4.1.4 Were versions of the ideas discussed in popular journals?
   4.2 How did political, geographical factors affect the influence of the theory/theories?
      4.2.1 What did the theorist's own countrymen think of the theory/theories?

- 4.2.2 How did those outside the theorist's own country regard the theory/theories?
- 4.2.3 Were the domestic and international judgments similar, identical, or different?

4.3 Was/were the theorist's theory/theories controversial? In what ways?

4.4 Can one find non-rational, emotional basis for the popularity of the theory/theories?

4.5 What is the theorist's influence on his field/fields now?

5. How did the theorist develop his theory/theories?

    5.1 What were the theorist's major objectives?

    5.2 What was the cultural/social setting in which the theorist developed his theory/theories?

      - 5.2.1 Describe the tradition in which the theorist worked.
      - 5.2.2 What were the primary and secondary influences upon the theorist's work?
      - 5.2.3 What are the major theory/theories the theorist claims to refute?

    5.3 What was the theorist's rationale?

      - 5.3.1 What was the theorist's subject matter and substantive interest?
      - 5.3.2 Describe the types of theory/theories: taxonomic, axiomatic, discursive.
      - 5.3.3 What major metaphors were used by the theorist?

    5.4 What are the theorist's own views of his limitations?

    5.5 Was/were the theory/theories revised? If so, how?

6. Describe and characterize the intellectual environment in which the theorist developed his theory/theories.

7. Did the theorist confidently claim university for his theory/theories?

    7.1 Cite the statements made by the theorist and/or by others.

    7.2 Did his claims ever get qualified later?

    7.3 Who were the audiences for whom this was done (identify some meetings of academic associations, etc.)

8. Have the theory/ theories ever been tested empirically by the theorist or others? If so, what were the results?
   8.1 Explain the tests conducted by the theorist, if any.
       8.1.1 Describe the methods.
       8.1.2 How were the generalizations attained?
       8.1.3 What results were produced?
       8.1.4 How were the findings presented?
   8.2 Describe the tests replicated by others, if any.
       8.2.1 Describe the methods.
       8.2.2 What results were produced?
       8.2.3 Give information on research reports: availability, records, raw data, replication of research.
9. Locate any evidence showing the importance and influence of the theorist's major theory/theories.
   9.1 What schools/programs were modeled upon the theorist's theory/ theories?
   9.2 What curriculum designs did the theorist inspire?
   9.3 Describe the experiments based on the theory/theories
   9.4 Did students of the subject subscribe to this theory/ theories on the basis of opinion or evidence?
10. Did the theorist or others give suggestions about how the theory/ theories might be used?
    10.1 What did the theorist say about how the theory/theories might be applied?
        10.1.1 What kind of guidelines on the application of the theory/ theories did the theorist give?
        10.1.2 What parts constitute expected requirements?
    10.2 What precautions did the theorist consider necessary in applying the theory/theories?
    10.3 What precautions have others suggested?
    10.4 What did the theorist think could be expected from application of the theory/ theories?
    10.5 What current projects are based partly or completely on the theory/theories?

Notes

1. In his *Making Science: Between Nature and Society*. Cambridge, MA: Harvard University Press, Stephen Cole (1992) does not make a distinction between the validity of the social and natural sciences, while Harold Kincaid (1996) in his stimulating *Philosophical Foundations of the Social Sciences: Analysing Controversies in Social Research*. Cambridge: Cambridge University Press, argues that social science research, which include education, can be a "good" science.
2. Ernest Gellner (1985). *Relativism and the Social Sciences*. Cambridge and New York: Cambridge University Press, pp. 83–85.
3. The chapters by James Flynn "Race and IQ: Jensen's case refuted" and Arthur Jensen's "Differential psychology: Towards consensus" in the volume *Arthur Jensen Consensus and Controversy* edited by Sohan Modgil and Celia Modgil (1987). New York, London: The Falmer Press, give good arguments for the opposing views on the IQ tests. See also: Richard J. Herrnstein and Charles Murray (1994). *The Bell Curve: Intelligence and Class Structure in American Life*. New York: Free Press. More details of the racist implications can be found in J Phillippe Rushton (1994). *Race Evolution and Behaviour. A Life History Perspective*. New Brunswick, NJ: Transaction.
4. A cover statement from Robert Shapiro's (1991). *The Human Blueprint: The Race to Unlock the Secrets of Our Genetic Code*. New York: Bantam Books.
5. Initial sequencing and analysis of the human genome (February 15, 2001). *Nature*, 409, pp. 860–921.
6. An internet search on the Human Genome Project in January 1999 turned up many pages of information. A brief introduction is as follows: Begun in 1990, the Human Genome *Project* is a 15-year effort coordinated by the US Department of Energy and the National Institute of Health to (1) identify all the estimated 30,000 genes in human DNA, and (2) determine the sequences of the 3 billion chemical bases that make up human DNA, store this information in databases, and develop tools for a data analysis. To help achieve these goals, researchers *are* also studying the genetic makeup of several nonhuman organisms. These include the common human gut bacterium *Escherichia coli*, the fruit fly, and the laboratory mouse. A unique aspect of the US Human Genome *Project* is that it is the first large scientific undertaking to address the ethical, legal, and social issues (ELSI) that may arise from the *project*. (Ref.: URL: www.ornLgov/hgmis)
7. The quotation comes from *A Source Book* in *Chinese Philosophy* (p. 40), translated and compiled by Wing-Tsit Chan (1969). Princeton NJ: Princeton University *Press*.
8. For instance, although references from natural sciences and the social sciences and education research express similar characteristics for "theory," the definitions differ in regard to what kinds of entities a theory should explain. See also: Robert K. Barnhart (1986). *The American Heritage Dictionary of Science*. Boston, MA: Houghton Mifflin Company.
9. As the division between natural science and social science, which include education research, begins to blur, it would also be necessary to include natural scientists among

the members of this editorial board so as to not isolate the social sciences and education studies from the broader scientific community. This editorial board should be comprised of scholars in all fields of science, supported by the professional organizations to which they belong. It certainly should not be a government *project*.

10. This is the 10-point analysis model used for the study of Piaget, Skinner, and Kohlberg. See Appendix on page 164.
11. Academic conferences in the social sciences *are* gatherings of interest *groups or* collections of unrelated, eclectic presentations. If the idea of "theory challenge" recommended in this chapter is adopted, the routine convention could become a vital event for acknowledging research advancement (other than presentation) for education studies and the social sciences. See also: C. Wade Savage (1990). *Scientific Theories: Minnesota Studies in the Philosophy of Science*, Vol. XIV. Minneapolis: University of Minnesota Press.
12. Michael G. Clyne (1972). "Perception of code-switching by bilinguals: An experiment". *ITL, Review of Applied Linguistics*, 16, 45–48.
13. See S. Pit Corder (1991). "A role for the mother tongue". In *Language Transfer in Language Learning*, SM Gass and L Selinker (eds.). Amsterdam and Philadelphia: John Benjamins Publishing Company; see also Robert Politzer (1974). "Developmental sentence scoring as a method". In *Modern Language Journal* 58 and Helmut Zobl (1984). "Cross-generalisations and the contrastive dimension of the interlanguage Hypothesis". In Alan Davis, Clive Criper and A.P.R. Howatt (eds.). *Interlanguage*, Edinburgh: Edinburgh University Press.
14. See, e.g., Piaget's (1974–1980) *Genetic Epistemology* (E. Duckworth, Transl.), New York: Columbia; *The Development of Thought: Equilibration of Cognitive Structures* (A. Rosin, Transl.), New York: Viking Press; and *Adaptation and Intelligence: Organic Selection and Phenocopy* (S. Eames, Transl.), Chicago: University of Chicago Press.
15. See, for instance, Skinner's (1954–1986) "The science of learning and the art of teaching". *Harvard Education Review*, 24, pp. 86–97; "Why we need teaching machines". *Harvard Education Review*, 31, pp. 377–398; "Reflections on a decade of teaching Machines". *Teachers College Record*, 65, pp. 168–177; "Contingency management in the classroom". *Education*, 90, pp. 93–100; *The Technology of teaching*, New York: Appleton-Century-Croft; and "Programmed instruction revisited". *Phi delta Kappan*, 68(2), pp. 103–110.
16. See, e.g., Kohlberg's (1984–1987) *Essays in Moral, Development*, Vol. II. *The Psychology of Moral Development*. San Francisco: Harper and Row and *Child Psychology and Childhood Education: A Cognitive-developmental View*. New York: Longmans.
17. See also Barnhart's *The American Heritage Dictionary of Science* (1986) quoted above. John Coates' (1996) *The claims of Common Sense: Moore, Wittgenstein, Keynes and the Social Sciences*. Cambridge: Cambridge University Press, examines the "vague" terminology used by the three social scientists discussed.
18. See also Lous Heshusius and Keith Ballard (ed.) (1997). *From Positivism to Interpretivism and Beyond: Tales of Transformation in Educational and Social research (The Mind–Body Connection)*. New York: Teachers Colleges Press.

19. See Steve Joshua Heims (1993). *Constructing a Social Science for Postwar America: The Cybernetics Group*, 1946–1953. Cambridge, MA: The MIT Press.
20. Michael Scriven (1967). "The contribution of philosophy of the social sciences to educational development". In *Philosophy and Educational Development*, HD Aiken, W Kaufman and M Scriven (eds.). London: G.H. Harrap Ltd.
21. See Paul Humphreys (1989). *The Chances of Explanation: Causal Explanation in the Social, Medical, and Physical Sciences*. Princeton, NJ: Princeton University Press.
22. Michael Scriven (1959). "Explanation and prediction in evolutionary theory". *Science*, 130, pp. 477–482.
23. Peter M. Milner (1993). "The mind and Donald O. Hebb". *Scientific American*, 274(1), pp. 124–129. See also Patricia Smith Churchland (1986). *Neurophilosophy: Toward a Unified Science of the Mind-Brain*. Cambridge, MA: The MIT Press. In 2000, a three-year, cross-disciplinary study on neuro-cognitive science and language acquisition was established in Hong Kong with joint sponsorship from the local government and four universities. Neuro-science Technology is employed along with conventional test and measurement in classroom setting. For further information, please contact Professor Cho-Yee To or Principal TF Kwan, 249 Sino Building, The Chinese University of Hong Kong, Hong Kong.
24. Carl G. Hempel (1965). *Aspects of Scientific Explanation and Other Essays in the Philosophy of Science*. New York: The Free Press and London: Collier-Macmillan Ltd. Steven C. Ward (1996). *Reconfiguring Truth: Post-modernism, Science Studies, and the Search for a New Model of Knowledge*. Lanham, MD: Rowan and Littlefield.

IN THE BEGINNING: SEARCHING FOR CHILDHOOD IN CHINESE HISTORY AND PHILOSOPHY*

HSIUNG PING-CHEN

Chinese University of Hong Kong

9.1. Children and Childhood in Traditional China

9.1.1. *Historical studies of children*

Historical studies of children and childhood have not attracted major attention. The small number of scholars who venture into the field, with scattered efforts and seemingly random results, nevertheless labor with certain convictions. To them, history concerning children, or viewing the world from the vantage point of youth, is by no means a trivial matter. It is necessary, valuable, and imperative.

Among them, a certain necessity appeared the earliest, the challenge of the question of "the discovery of childhood in history." The artful and provocative work of Philippe Ariés took readers, historians, and others, by surprise with his novel idea that the notion of childhood in Western history was only a recent invention.[1] A number of industrious scholars, Europeanists especially, have since challenged this thesis, coming forth with evidence of early concepts of childhood as well as the evolving experience of children in history.[2] However, the premises that prompted historians of mentality, like Ariés, in their quest for a history of childhood

---

This chapter is a reproduction of the Wu Teh Yao memorial lecture given by the author in 2003.

in the first place, remain valid, that is, a better understanding of people's ideas and treatments of children must constitute an important part of the overall appraisal of that era. In fact, in Ariés case, it took the center stage as a means to access the core values of any given society. However, followers of the idea or the method remain few. For although manners and mentalities have drawn increasing attention from historians in the wake of the influence of the *Annales School* with their refreshing look at the humble and the obscure, the lives of infants and children have never claimed the mainstream interest of historians. Even though Ariés and his critics show together that children and childhood not only did have a history but also that the subject carries unique value unlike any other kind of history. For their works judiciously demonstrate that the handling of the young was never a fixed matter in time. Since any society's understanding of their youngest and most vulnerable members changes with time, this in itself becomes a story worth knowing and telling. Since in treating children, society is often exposed, the urgent and intimate nature of the task should rid people of their usual pretensions. Partly due to the vital nature of the endeavor, there has never been a lack of information, or of views, for the purpose of a historian, although the disconcerting abundance of such may catch the conventional historical methodology quite unprepared.

Once investigators of the history of mentality first tackled the concept of childhood, family historians felt compelled to look into the conditions of children in the past. Though not the sole focus, information pertaining to the experiences of the very young became an important part of their narrative. The history of infants and children, for them, may not cast unique light on the study of families, yet it is "necessary" to the familial story of society. A quantity of fine research in American and European history in the 1970s demonstrated the benefits that such a study of childhood could contribute to the general understanding of family and community. Philip Greven Jr., in his captivating reconstruction of four generations of family life in Colonial Andover, shows how an appreciation for the experience of the young is needed to arrive at a better understanding of successive generations. He devotes particular discussion to the search for independence that developed out of the traditional mode of dependence among children of families in mid-18th century Massachusetts.[3] Readers, thus, start recognizing better the inter-dependence of all generations in their formulation of individuality as well as daily familial operations. The same year, John Demos published his work on family life in Plymouth colony entitled *A Little Commonwealth*. His study also shows that parent–child relations, as well as infant and childhood experiences, have become a regular concern for family historians.[4] Recognizing the "everyday routine" of "average people" in the fields of family and social history led scholars to the discovery of children and childhood. By the time Lawrence Stone produced his exhaustive observations on family, sex, and marriage in early modern England, therefore, adult–child relations constituted one of the cornerstones in his theory.[5]

In addition to monographic studies on specific communities and social groups, general works on long-term changes in family history have also incorporated information on children and young people as legitimate and valuable contents. Steven Ozment's treatment of family life in reformation Europe,[6] Michael Mitteraner and Reinhard Sieder's explanation of the evolving function of families in central and western Europe,[7] Beatrice Cottlieb's analysis of the family in the West from the Black Death to the industrial age,[8] and Ralph Houlbrooke's investigation of the English family from the mid-15th to the late 17th centuries,[9] all devote extensive attention to the questions of procreation, child-rearing, parent–child relations, and the physical, social, and emotional conditions of children. Studies of women's history and motherhood have also increased people's awareness of domestic conditions related to early-childhood experience.[10] Pooled together, both the historical concept and the daily experience of the very young become much more recognizable than they were a mere few decades ago. In fact from the late 1970s and the early 1980s onward, discussions of children's lives have become part and parcel of standard Western family history,[11] as parent–child experiences received special attention[12] and unexpected discoveries were regularly unearthed.[13]

It is at this juncture that, from a different angle, scholars interested in changing prejudices and social welfare also turned their attention to issues regarding children, on such topics as infanticide, child desertion, and child labor. Selective elimination or active killing of newborn infants or young children, whether as habitual customs or as a way to limit family size, and deemed barbaric, were thought to be found only in ancient and Asian societies. More recently, scholars have been prepared to consider their existence in the history of Western societies.[14] In addition to patterns and statistics, studies of infanticide in pre-modern times help bring to light the socioeconomic circumstances for its occurrence. Since, in such considerations, the social and legal definitions of the "infant" were often broader than that of the neonatal, these studies invariably question human motivations as well as the cultural and historical environment in which the very young lived or perished.[15]

Desertion and neglect of children, a lasting and fairly widespread phenomenon, whether perceived from the viewpoint of the deserters or the deserted, have also been examined accordingly. Historical studies focusing on the fate of unwanted children in different eras and in various places have added to our understanding of the functioning or ill-functioning of the social fabric.[16] Whatever the focus or concern, such studies yield a picture of children's abandonment, adoption and foster-care that had long been missing not only regarding the fate of a significant section of the population, but also regarding a vital aspect of social and institutional history.[17] The sudden surge of these studies in the 1980s and their shared outlook suggest, therefore, a new intellectual consciousness. The picture they present collectively extends beyond the discoveries of mere details in the lives of children to a wide host of issues on popular attitudes, social practices, family life, community networks, politics, urban and rural relations, economic developments and demographic realities — a good example of the kind of larger relevance and greater ramifications children's history can produce for our general knowledge of the past. That a society had been habitually "disposing" of at least a quarter of its newborns, or witnessing three-fourths of its children perish before reaching their fifth year, obviously tells us a great deal about its inner workings and daily circumstances.

Child labor and the policy and laws it generates, like infanticide and desertion, is another area which has received recent historical attention. Along with scholars in other fields, social and demographic historians became increasingly aware of the fact that work was as much a part of children's routine experience as play. For a large number of children in pre-modern times, it represented a more significant activity than education or schooling. Although still lacking systematic analyses, historians of ancient Rome, early modern England, and colonial America have ingeniously pieced together data to show us the working life of youngsters.[18] Those who study child labor in the early modern and modern era also unavoidably encounter the question of children's "rights and protection," as concepts which led the reforms toward social legislation and welfare policies as they surfaced, at the same time that proto-industrialization presented new opportunities for employment of children, albeit under harsh conditions.[19] Just as infanticide and desertion bring up the question of calculated cruelty and neglect, on the one hand, and fostering and philanthropy on the other, the world of laboring children touches upon communal reliance, pauperism, and self-help. Scholars looking into the foundling hospitals, the poor laws, or workhouses, often focused first on the administration of welfare. Inevitably, these discussions concern the development of civil liberty, social legislation, and state intervention, not just the lives of children. Similar was the issue of early education. Though not directly related to social welfare, it was concerned with the same kind of institutional construction of childhood as those mentioned in economic production and the labor force, or foster-homes and adoption procedures. For with varying degrees of success, employing different methods and teaching materials, and under all kinds of circumstances, an ever-increasing number of young children began to have access to pedagogical instruction in the early modern era. Historians of early education, though not necessarily with a sole interest in children, have uncovered much about the literary experience and the intellectual process that different learning activities involved.[20] A number of these studies contain information about vocational training, including that for nonelite children, even specific educational initiative for girls, providing important glimpses into another significant, though previously blank, area.[21] Together, these studies demonstrate that for a fair understanding of any social change, a historical account that omits the experiences of the very young seems "incomplete at best and distorted at worst."

Besides historians of mentality, the family and social institutions, all of whom are recognizing in various ways the importance of including children in history, a third group showing interest in children are the historical demographers.[22] For them coming to terms with the fate of the youngest group in the population is indispensable to a responsible grasp of their subject in the aggregate. Though mostly working with quantitative data and statistical models, the kind of questions they pose and the findings they manage to pull together are of vital value to historical studies of children. Because historical demography not only directs people's attention, for example, to infanticide, but also to the social implications of birth, death, average life expectancy, migration, and marriage. It thus creates new possibilities for structuring our understanding of children's lives as they move through time, space, and changing circumstances.[23] We become aware of some of the fundamental forces under which the young coexist with the adults. The many discoveries in demographic history, minute or grand, often shatter old impressions or establish startling new assumptions in overall historical understanding. Furthermore, its emphasis on life cycles and the interconnections among personal time, group (or family) time, and historical time help to address the relations between individual lives and collective involvement, which suggests a linkage between micro-studies and macro-history, a link that all historical observation needs. Historians of children and childhood everywhere, therefore, have a duty to make clear how such insights may relate their seemingly "insignificant" and marginal subject to the broader field of history or the study of children in other disciplines.[24]

This brief overview of recent inquiries into childhood history gives us a sense of the kind of direction and categories which may be pursued, whether from the angle of history of mentality, family, welfare, education, or demography. Many other important and potentially fruitful questions could, of course, be added to the list. Toward the end of which this study of childhood history and historical understanding of children, as those on women, lower classes, ethnic or religious minorities, social misfits, and other overlooked subjects can become legitimate intellectual pursuits. As a historical investigation, it begins by focusing on the historical experience of the youngest section of the human population, but soon presents its own agenda as it mingles with those of the "mainstream," just as past observations of children's experiences, whether from the angle of the social, cultural, intellectual, economic, political, or institutional uncovered important information not simply pertaining to their specific area of interest. Together they also suggest the kind of intellectual curiosity and academic outlook such inquiries entail and further stimulate. One distinct sociocultural position, for modern researchers to contemplate, both in the West and elsewhere, is the very modern definition of a child and childhood, based primarily on biophysical understandings and the Freudian psychological scheme, as the bottom line for all child studies, which is rarely treated as a hypothesis with specific cultural historical contexts.[25] In addition to the Enlightenment and its faith in rationality and linear progression often found at the root of most studies on children and the history of childhood, modern investigations in psychology, cognitive development, and education remain powerful positivist forces behind most interests in children, including research into the childhood experience of the past.[26]

9.1.2. *The case of China*

In the light of the above, what we may learn about, or wish to make of, the history of children and childhood in China? First, interest in children and childhood, thus far, claims even less attention among historians of China than among those elsewhere. The history of mentality, the field that first spurred the history of childhood, has yet to attract any serious pursuit by historians of China. The "discovery of the concept of children and childhood" has hardly been a question in Chinese history, as the main forces in modern Chinese historiography have thus far been preoccupied with quite different set of problems. Any preliminary examination on children and childhood in Chinese history will also make clear the kind of specific context which might give rise to special information that may promise intellectual reflections at variance from similar undertakings thus far developed in the Western intellectual environment. The broad overview attempted in this chapter, other than providing a general context for what follows, also shows the many uncharted fields and thus exciting possibilities that a comparison of the two may subsequently present.

In the midst of this general oblivion, two works have recently dealt with the Chinese case at length. One is Jon Saari's study of the transitional nature of the lives of schoolboys growing up in the late-19th and early 20th centuries, called *Legacies of Childhood* (1990),[27] and the other is Anne Behnke Kinney's edited volume examining *Chinese Views of Childhood* (1995).[28] Of the two, Saari's book appeared first, and remains the only monographic treatment on childhood experience in Chinese history. As its title and many chapter headings suggest, Saari gives much of his attention to the problem of "growing up Chinese," especially to the particularities of that experience "in a time of crisis," meaning in this case encountering the modern era. A richly nuanced study, it is a pioneering endeavor, shouldering many tasks, answering or raising a wide array of questions. Its primary purpose, however, is to show how a particular generation of elite schoolboys shaped their own views and self-management during social and political upheaval, applying Freudian and Ericksonian theses on character formation and personality development. The author succeeds in this to an appreciable degree. This mostly elite group of Chinese youths growing up at the very end of the Ch'ing dynasty and the beginning of the Republic reveals to us the sociopsychological theories of socialization, identify formation, and personal crisis which lend themselves to being conveniently useful, though perhaps ultimately, limiting intellectual tools. For the most part, Saari's sources are school-age youths (*t'ung nien*) 7 to 14 or even 15 to early-20's, rather than young children (*êrh t'ung*). The questions he raises concerning the Chinese way of "learning to become human (*hsüeh tso jên*)" are therefore only partially resolved as an explanatory story picked up halfway. The vital differences between infants, children, and young people with regard to the problem of growing-up hardly receive adequate treatment. Even so, the work stands as a valuable groundbreaker.

Kinney's symposium volume, as its title suggests, is an overview of expressed "views of childhood" throughout China's long history. It provides an initial look at the childhood question from a variety of angles (literature, art history, history, medicine, philosophy, and so forth) from early China to the 20th century. Though not "a rounded history of childhood in China," as John Sommervill succinctly pointed out, the book focuses on "cultural and ideological aspects," presenting a good collective survey at an early stage in anticipation of "a social history of children."[29] Read closely, each essay contains a merit of its own. Kinney's review of the philosophical, popular-mythical and hagiographic origins of ideas related to children,[30] and Wu Hung's piece on the engraving of child images in early Chinese art are useful explorations inviting further elaboration.[31] For the later imperial period, Wu Pei-yi's fascinating introduction to the evolving parent–child bond brings a wealth of information. Within the context of the inner world of Chinese familial relations and emotional life, the essay opens up numerous questions regarding the conditions of young children. It demonstrates a wealth of the necrological literature (poems and burial inscriptions) for gaining access to the experiential aspects of childhood and the construction of emotional bonds in the formation of adult–child relations. Wu Pei-yi also points out that a general trend toward including children and focusing attention on them occurred from pre-Sung (roughly 10th century) times to the 18th century, with special help from the philosophy of the Wang Yang-ming school and the beginning of "the cult of the child." Wu's depiction of loving father–daughter ties and a potentially positive bias toward young girls, at least among educated Chinese families, also demands further examination of these, thus far, little understood subjects.[32]

A few other essays in the volume discuss issues related to the lives of infants and children in the late-imperial period. Charlotte Furth's analysis of the concept of the beginning of life and its origins in biomedial sources familiarizes the reader with basic terminology and notions regarding birth, growth, and development.[33] Ann Waltner's provocative contemplation of the possible gender linkage between female infanticide, the dowry system and the competitive marriage market in Ming society is a bold and imaginative attempt, begging deeper probing into the world of the "gendered status of children" to be connected with our larger understanding of the political, economic, social, and cultural circumstances of this era.[34] Angela Liang contrasts the new features of relief institutions for children in 19th century China with their counterparts from earlier times, as well as with those in the West. The emerging view of the child as a social being belonging to the community, she asserts, contrasts with the increasingly less protective treatment children were receiving from the state.[35]

As a whole, most essays in Kinney's edited anthology provide valuable clues to long-neglected topics in Chinese studies. Many of the findings, in part due to the preliminary nature of the field, require further clarification and systematic investigation. These merits not withstanding, this first fully fledged attempt to examine views of Chinese childhood fails higher expectations on a few important accounts. First, the conceptualization and treatment of the concept of children and childhood are far too loose and imprecise. As the first work of its kind, it may be quite understandable to include essays about gestation (Furth) as well as about the adolescent in Hong-lou Mêng (Miller), or rebellious youths in the PRC (Lupher).[36] Some working definition taking into account traditional Chinese and/or general modern concepts of the stages of life, including infancy, childhood (early childhood, later childhood), on the one hand, and adolescent and youth on the other, is desperately needed in order to prevent overly vague conclusions. Second, a clearer intellectual framework needs to be established before a more systematic and better balanced analysis may flow from these, at times, sparse, random, and seemingly anecdotal observations across massive periods of time and widely varying regions.

In addition to a better definition of "the child" and "childhood" in the Chinese historical context, the very "Chinese-ness" of these cases, and their changing characters in time, are some other areas in need of explanation. For assorted views of children and childhood throughout Chinese history can leave readers with an unresolved curiosity about the familiar problem of "generality" versus "particularity" or theoretical concepts as opposed to everyday practice. Nor can the readers be certain as to the basic character of the kind of historical changes taking place around these views or the comparative significance of Chinese notions of childhoods in the past. Tentatively, can we say whether the survey has whetted our appetite to know Chinese views on childhood? Does it tempt us to discover whether Chinese children's experience itself has changed and, if so, for better or for worse over these thousands of years? More importantly still, whose views or which children's childhood did such changes represent, during what period, in which places, under what circumstances, through what process and for what reasons? Until such basic questions are confronted, our observations and concerns about things related to children and childhood will remain superficial, even superfluous, to the structural intellect.

To investigate some of these issues in part, there do exist other related studies: Ann Waltner's investigation of the practice of adoption[37] and Hui-chen Wang Liu's and Charlotte Furth's analyses of clan rules and family instructions[38] address key questions in Chinese family history. Angela Leung's study of relief agencies for orphans sheds significant light on the institutions and cultural environment in which the young lived, as her work on early education in the Ch'ing reveals the extra-familial forces impacting on "handling" of children.[39] The pioneering works by Liu Ts'ui-jung and James Lee and their associates in Chinese historical demography, furthermore, provide vital statistical data and answer key questions regarding the birth, death, and treatment of infants and children.[40] Even works in intellectual history and moral philosophy, rooted in the culture's peculiar approach to the ethics of neonatal life, can have much to say regarding historical "attitudes" toward or "management" of "the child." Joanna Handlin's insights into the concerns and labors of the 16th century gentry-scholar Lü K'un provide a good example.[41] These cry out for a more structured comprehension of the lives of children, one rooted in a substantiated conceptual framework.

Against this background, the chapters in this study, represent a collection of essays and lectures prepared under varying circumstances, not a preconceived and comprehensively executed monographic treatment. As such, they could hardly meet the requirement of an introduction to, or an organized presentation of children and childhood in late imperial Chinese history. Yet, the work-in-progress behind it all, when examined in parallel with its intellectual siblings in Chinese academia, does suggest a set of thoughts and systematic inquiry more persistent than immediately apparent. What this book offers falls short, therefore, of any expectation of a thorough treatment on the subject. What we have, in its stead, is a many-faceted, multidocumented narrative on a few topics related to the subject of children and childhood in Chinese history. They are presented to ask broad historical questions, even though the answers may not be readily forthcoming.[42]

For instance, regarding the historical evolution of Chinese childhood, have the lives of young children in China changed much? If so, in what ways, at what points of time, and how so? As the rest of the population moved through China's long history, did children fare better, or worse, or both in different terms? Broadly and roughly speaking, between the establishment of a classical mode in pre-Han times and the massive transformation after the mid-19th century, two periods are suggested as time markers for our subject: the Southern Sung and the mid-Ming, as both ushered in mixed blessings for China's younger population. During the Southern Sung, or between the 11th and 12th centuries, powerful social and cultural forces changed the lives of children in significant ways. Paramount among these were the maturing of Neo-Confucian philosophy and the establishment of pediatric medicine.[43] The former attempted to chart social, moral, and behavioral codes and to define the emotional and educational experiences of the young,[44] which influenced domestic life, and clan organizations at the social level and character formation and daily attitudes on the individual level. The Ch'êng-Chu school's stress on the values of quietness (*ching*), respect (*ching*), and sincerity (*ch'êng*) redefined Chinese childrearing culture and early-education training within families and in communal schools.⁴⁵ A certain emphasis on acquiescence, quietude, control in expression, and bodily gestures crept into the everyday experience of infants and children. Infants were more carefully bundled up and at times overly protected. Pets, outdoor boisterousness, and physical games (such as ball playing) became forbidden. Tacit, timid, inactive, shy and "girl-like" boys were openly praised and widely adored. Whether in the form of tightened family rules, or community reform efforts by such moralists as Lü K'un (1536–1618) and his father Lü Tê-shêng with indoctrinating literature like the *Words for Little Children* (*Hsiao-êrh yü*) and *Words for Little Girls* (*Nü Hsiao-êrh yü*),⁴⁶ or the trickling down of popular religious tracts and itinerant theater, the Neo-Confucian perspective formed a new baseline for mainstream concepts in human conduct, thus of childhood environment during the second millennium of imperial China. On the other hand, pediatrics brought "professional" care and "specialized" attention to this social group, resulting in a wide array of physical, material, and cultural re-orientation. Furthermore, the artistic representation of young children in Sung paintings and other art work points to a society in which many embraced an engagingly "focused" attitude toward younger lives. The provision of schooling and teaching materials is another important indication of renewed collective concern and cultural interest in children.⁴⁷ In the present work the essays in section one and some in section two allude to the dawning of this era in Chinese social and cultural history, including considerations from the angle of the children who lived through it.

Mid-Ming was another pivotal time of alteration and redirection in the lives of children and childhood in fundamental ways. First, physical and health-related evidence suggests that pediatric medicine, which first established a foothold five centuries previously in the Sung, continued to mature and proliferate. So that by the mid-16th century, pre-modern China came close to a society that provided special health care to a large number of the young. Better childbearing practices, too, with pharmaceutical recipes and emergency self-aid procedures were permeating into different regions, trickling down the social ladder, going from urban centers to towns and villages, following trade networks and other travel routes. As a result of the popularizing efforts by the elite, a booming printing industry, and the bustling commercialization of Ming society, the clinical work of pediatricians grew and debates occurred among them, helped by the relatively "open-ended" character of their knowledge, inescapably mingled with the suspicious conservatism of the society and endless gossip. Second, in the area of philosophy and education, the appearance of Wang Yang-ming and his followers, and their optimistic view of human nature endowed with a peculiarly "liberating" air toward socialization and early education, marked another turning point. As a direct response to the Ch'êng-Chu school of thought, Wang Yang-ming's *hsin-hsüeh* teaching brought forth an alternative view on humanity and early education as well as a revisionist view on the question of children's hearts (*t'ung-hsin*). It advocated some sort of a naturalist outlook, a more sympathetic attitude, and an overtly child-oriented emphasis. Wang, and his radical followers like Li Chih, spoke and wrote fervently on children's education and the innocent nature of the child, directing satirical criticism on the rigid discipline cooked up by what were to them polluting and hypocritical adults. This "emancipating" and iconoclastic spirit posed a subversive challenge to the old Ch'êng-Chu orthodoxy in child training and education. It also served as a major social and intellectual dialectic in late-imperial Chinese discourse about children and childhood. It provided a vital inspiration from which later reform-minded educationalists and enlightened thinkers continued to draw for centuries in debate and re-negotiation. How well either the restrictive Ch'êng-Chu or the liberal Yang-ming schools, or both, fared in formulating actual childhood experiences for different social groups and cultural–geographic regions is a subject pleading further investigation.[48] Third, in the hardly touched field of children's entertainment and literature in this period, unmistakable signposts recommend themselves for further elucidation. Although literary productions for all sorts of pedagogical purposes had existed long before this, and occasional mention has been made of special street entertainers catering to the amusement of young urban customers in Sung times, it was not until the late 16th-and 17th-century that we have direct evidence of the commercial "outpouring" of collections of stories explicitly intended for children, which surely marks the ever-evolving world of the young in important ways.[49]

This crude "periodization" of Chinese children's history demands further substantiation, articulation, and revision. Both micro-level assessments and theoretical considerations on Chinese childhood and children's lives are needed. For example, in observing that improvements in the provision of children's health and health management seems to have been continuously on the rise since the Sung, though not without periodic setbacks or regional and class differentiation. Are we seeing a case where the longstanding culture of ancestor worship and patriarchal clan organization finally coalesced with a philosophical emphasis on the beginning of humanity, and growing trends in commercialization and urbanization to provide a timely last push for a scientific–technological breakthrough in medical specialization? Material provisions for the young based on daily accounts, biographies, and local history records appear to have improved for much of late-imperial history. Opportunities for education and the enjoyment of literature especially prepared for the young also grew phenomenally after the mid-16th century.[50] Yet ironically, the downside of childhood and children's history in this period is that it can be seen as not contrasting to or separated from, but in fact closely associated with, these very positive aspects abovementioned. Neo-Confucianism's intense interest in human nature and its "nourishment" and "cultivation" represented one such preeminent force behind people's concern and control of young children. Increased activities in early education, like the more elaborate ideas on the well being of the very young, in the likes of family instruction and clan rules, marked not just intensified care but also greatly strengthened manipulation and refinement. The depictions of "children at play" in Sung paintings is the juncture where the physically more carefree and indulgent older mode of childhood made its last public appearance before being "taken over" and "obliterated" from the social history scene. In its place came a child's life much reduced in scale, in clarity, and in centrality (compare, for instance, the size and the place of the few Ming paintings with children's themes to their Sung and Yûan predecessors).[51] Outdoor fun and physical activities were temporarily under siege until picked up and boosted again by the Yang-ming school, after which came not any definitive turn-about but a protracted debate, both in people's minds and in social practices. The aftermath of this debate carries us right down to the modern era in the late 19th and early 20th centuries.

A general "downturn" in the lives of children occurred when China's moral philosophy and social ethics developed a special ambivalence about their interests and control of children and people's formative years. The population over the last half-millennium, not unlike what had happened elsewhere or in other places, show that improved care, increased concern, enhanced management, and strengthened indoctrination were often merely different manifestations of exactly the same set of social and cultural forces.[52] Both positive and negative results regarding developments in compulsive schooling for increasingly younger children in Ming-Ch'ing China serve as a somewhat awkward concurrence to scholars like Ariés's pronouncements on the ambivalent implications of similar phenomena in European developments.[53]

From Sung onward, the age for teaching basic knowledge and skills in small children appears to have decreased one year or so for every one or one-and-a-half centuries. That is, whereas a highly privileged child in the 11th century did not start learning arithmetic and writing until he (or very occasionally she) reached nine or ten, as recommended by Ssû-ma Kuang (1019–1086), some 100 years later we see eight-year-olds given such instructions. The onset of primary education continued to lower until during the Ming, children at the average age of four or five were made to learn things that children double their age would not have managed a few centuries before. Significantly, this trend in training and the emphasis on early intelligence (*tsao hui*) and child prodigies, though stressing cognitive abilities, was never limited to the social elites or confined to intellectual subjects.[54] Sketchy but discernible evidence from peasant, merchant, and artisan families indicates a similarly competitive parenting and early-start mode in apprenticeship for the middle and lower echelons of late-imperial Chinese society. On the one hand, an increasing number of parents in farming, crafts, and various trades were anxious to send their children for a "functional literary" education. On the other, there were also signs that vocational initiation was being moved down to an ever younger age group as time passed. Under such factors as the entrenched civil service examination and the growing commercialization in agriculture and industry, a certain wakening up to the marketability of human capital helped to create the desire for ever younger members of society to be made to join the work units. As a traditionally utilitarian society was given increasing and increased opportunities in profit-making, a clear "re-orientation" in values and everyday actions emerged quickly in social institutions. The nurturing of a "daughter indulgence" culture in a primarily "son-favoring" society, as we will be discussing, shows one instance in a formation of great inner complexity.

These lead us to two further questions: First, what have we to gain from a history that includes children, and second, how differently our intellectual terrain may appear once childhood is added on, patched up, or put into proper perspective? For the former, the case of Chinese history in the late-imperial period may serve as a good point of reference. The benefit of such an endeavor may need a little explanation: to finally restore the experience of one-third to one-half of the population (an estimated portion of the young in any demographically pre-transitional society) seems but a belated makeup for an inexcusable negligence and a horrific void. The common inattentiveness in this regard becomes less bearable as other categorical neglect such as ethnicity, class, and gender begin to make their appearance in society and academia. Some sort of grappling with the experience of the young thus fills a vital and basic vacuum in our collective knowledge of the neglected history, even if only to scratch the mere surface of these issues as they were related to family structure, material life, health, medicine, education, social network, economic development, politics, and philosophy. The effect this kind of intellectual exploration, including a systematic consideration of the factor of age and phases of life may produce is a further understanding in a number of organizational concepts (e.g., the achievement-measured and functional-oriented outlook in history) and operational methods (e.g., less reliance on textual evidence and more educated employment of informing objects) in research on the past.

Finally, this quest for a history of children and childhood rewards challenges us in two fundamental ways. One, it reminds us that history and human existence are not only made both of the collective and the individual but each individual's life journey is made up of many different phases. A person's station and standing in any one of these various periods entails conditions and experiences that are not just culturally or historically specific but are also defined by his/her particular age in that society. The other side of the same coin is that those living through the same period of time, in the same sections of population (in terms of region, class, and gender), constituted an "age group" whose historical dimension is hardly clear. This wrestling with a history of children and childhood thus raises conceptual and methodological questions unlike historical exercises of the familiar kind. For with children and childhood we are confronted with a social category that is both biologically and socially "transitory," and subjectively and objectively "tentative" in nature. This metamorphosizing character of children and their social identity sets this question in stark difference to other sociocultural categories such as ethnicity, regionality, class, or gender, which, granted degrees of fluidity, hybridity, and multiplicity, assume a mostly fixed and constant character. In looking at children and childhood, however, historians have to take on lives in the form of social caterpillars or tadpoles, to determine whether their particular state and stage in existence may generate interest or information of a lasting or mutating kind. This engages historical studies in ways potentially at odds with the older framework of social, political, economic, and cultural history, studied according to people's seemingly more lasting roles and statuses.

More than other "new frontiers" in the field of the humanities, the subject of infants' and children's lives asks that we move beyond conventional intellectual tools and training methods, to try to employ (or simply to imagine) ways that will perceive the basic picture in alternate fashions. Plenty of examples in the past have demonstrated that random studies introduced for the purpose of supplying additional information in a compensating or supplementary manner may turn out to herald the birth of entirely novel ideas, eventually leading to a new intellectual impasse. The study of children's and childhood history, if usefully exercised, requires a fundamental re-examination of historical outlook that will not only take the experience of the younger population into new consideration in a "mechanical," or "static" sense but will also identify social change and historical development by taking into account the interaction of generations of constantly evolving historical characters and social circumstances. Coming to terms with this need requires freshly conceived ideas and investigations. The question of whether or how to allow for a subjective participation of young children and to elucidate "the voices" of infants at a nonverbal stage demands that we mine hitherto unexplored sources, get underneath or beyond accustomed ways of deciphering traces filtered through the literature of the adults. In the unpacking of these nonverbal messages regarding body movement and physical gestures, the sights and sounds of weeping, kicking, smiling, screaming or simply a restful sleep need to be included as meaningful information for contextualization and systematic decoding. Toward this end, this chapter has attempted a first step. To produce a better grasp of this subject, however, far more committed engagements are called for. In the end, we may discover that, with vigor and concern, the acts of the feeble and the sounds of the dumb will not remain elusive or insignificant, but powerful workings of life, much like the meanings of silence in music or linguistics or of empty space in a painting or architectural form. In history, as in the arts, the ability to take note of hidden existences and elusive presences is a vital move, because this is, from inception, woven into the original composition and in fact created in the first phase of construction.[55]

9.1.3. *Sources*

Since "children" refers to the young section of a population, whereas "childhood" points to the experience of people and the philosophical, cultural, and social understandings of that phase of the human life cycle, the source materials which are pertinent in an investigation of the two subjects are related, though not identical. From a historical perspective, both the conceptual and experiential aspects appear mostly a social and cultural construct.[56] For China, as elsewhere, people's understanding and handling of both children and childhood in the past not only were derived from words and ideas but were also revealed in deeds and gestures, as preserved, reflected, or suggested through textual and other evidence.

By explaining the various genres of primary sources, the multiplicity of the concepts of children and childhood as well as plausible interpretations to account for it in Chinese history become apparent. In the end, therefore, questions other than development and changes over time cannot but be evoked, along with the significance and potential challenge such rediscovery may carry for modern notions on these two subjects in society or the academic understanding on them in humanities, social sciences, and science.

Materials in some way pertaining to the lives of children or a certain notion or treatment of childhood are scattered, though abundant, in Chinese history. Typologically, they belong to several categories. First is what may be called "prescriptive and didactic works." Among these one finds standard ritual texts, such as *The Book of Rites* (*Li-chi*)[57] and the many family rituals (*chia-li*),⁵⁸ which in their effort to codify social customs and daily behavior present us with passages devoted to child care and child education, usually from a normative perspective. Philosophical treatises on ethics and education can also be viewed as a subsection under this category, as were discussions of human nature (*jên-hsing*), human heart (*jên-hsin*), rules for individual or group conduct, and materials for primary education. Different intellectual schools and changing times produced concepts and rules at a greater or lesser variance from one another. The differences often reflect larger philosophical, social, and political concerns. From these children- or childhood-related theories and opinions on education to the Neo-Confucian arguments on the "child's heart," we witness cultural forces large or small interplaying with social practices at the micro- or macro-level.⁵⁹ Although never strictly or solely focused on children's issues, such forces were nevertheless part of factors that shaped the world of the young conceptually and in everyday living.

Closely related to this last group of ritual texts and philosophical treatises were the numerous "family instructions (*chia-hsün*) and children's primers (*yu-mêng*)," produced with an aim toward molding the social character and intellectual development of the young. In terms of historical context, these two *genres* of literature did not come from the same background and thus should not be taken as representing the same discourse. But in terms of social function and for historical considerations here, they were both formulated to produce properly minded, well-behaved offspring. Family instructions did so by telling parents and elders what to do. An example is the famous *Yen Family Instructions* (*Yen-shih chia-hsün*) from the 6th century, or *Shih-lin Family Instructions* (*Shih-lin chia hsün*) from the Sung dynasty.⁶⁰ Numerous Ming-Ch'ing writings of lesser status followed in terms of format and in spirit; directly or indirectly they influenced people's treatment of children and the domestic experience of childhood, as borne out by large amounts of biographical data. Children's primers, on the other hand, appeared as a mirror reflection of family instruction. Instead of instructing the parents and elders with ways of handling the young they went directly to work on the youngsters' minds with well-prepared "soul food" for correct training. For over 1000 years, such popular items as *San-pai-ch'ien*, namely *The Three-character Classic* (*San-tzû-ching*), *A Hundred Surnames* (*Pai-chia-hsing*), and *A Thousand-character Classic* (*Ch'ien-tzû-wên*), and other such things poured out, supplying children with their first characters and initiating them in basic knowledge of numerals, geography, history, and social norms. Other rhymed verses or illustrated manuals, such as *Words for Little Children* (*Hsiao-êrh yü*) and *A Collection of Valuable Stories for Elementary Learning* (*Yu-hsüeh ku-shih ch'iung-lin*), also flooded the "children's market" in the late-imperial period.[61] Ample evidence, therefore, of children and childhood can be derived from examining these instructive family tomes advising adults as carers and supervisors and the children's primers for the behavioral package they took since very young.

Individual descriptive and confessional voices, carefully elucidated, form a useful counterpoint to this formalistic general background. Biographical accounts like *nien-p'u* (chronological biography), autobiographical records like *tzû-shu* (self-narration) or *tzû-ting* (self-compiled) *nien-p'u*, give events of a child's or a group of children's earliest years, with details of activities, incidents, and experiences encountered in a particular context.[62] Personal diaries, private notes, intimate letters, and poems exchanged among families and close friends yield records, through both flimsy memories and lucid accounts, of one's own or somebody else's childhood years. Recollections of joy or pain in the daily existence of youth memorial essays and poems remembering one's own children, by late-imperial times, were no longer rare in the world of China's educated. Such genres form a valuable base to check against normative records and to illustrate a certain kind of "children's culture" or "juvenile mentality," when properly unpacked. Family records, such as genealogies, *chia-p'u* or *tzu-p'u*, often containing meticulous household rules to be applied to the young, can reveal cases of specific children who were chastened or praised. For the study of children and childhood in Chinese history, in other words, the problem is not a lack of source materials but how to approach, understand, and represent the wide array of this disjointed collection of materials which often bypasses or contradicts itself.

In contrast to the prescriptive and descriptive materials, there existed after the 11th century what may be called technical or empirical data on children's physical conditions and people's notions of childhood in the context of people's knowledge and management about the young human body. Prominent in this category are the voluminous pediatric texts, a medical sub-specialty that came increasingly into its own after the Sung period. Professional discussions on prevalent health problems (*i-lun*), therapeutic prescriptions enlisted for their improvement (*i-fang*), and clinical case records (*i-an*) reveal not only disease and health patterns but also the material conditions children lived through. Views on children and childhood and practices of childbearing are also found slipping through these notes, presenting both the "expert's ideas" on the nature of human physiology and child care, as well as actual strategies in ordinary familial handling of their young. Owing to the pragmatic and mundane nature of these sources, and owing to the large amount preserved, these medical records fill a vacuum in our appraisal of the material and physical aspects of Chinese children's experience. Any report on conceptions or treatment of children and childhood from this era cannot be complete without properly consulting these voluminous records in detail.[63] The pediatrician's understanding of the living child and infancy or childhood in the abstract is also of value to intellectual or cultural history as it constituted a particular historical force that, together with the more familiar social and cultural conventions, formed a varied and composite environment for the child. The qualitative details and the quantitative character of this pediatric archive, moreover, may be tabbed to respond to typological questions such as the regional and class differences, or the material conditions of this particular history.[64]

In a less substantial, but still significant way, late-imperial Chinese legal documents bear traces of people's recognition of the young. The act of granting amnesty demonstrates a certain appreciation for the special character of children as a legal entity. Records of prosecutions of actual lawsuits involving children (there were at least three homicide cases involving young children from Ch'ing legal documents) give concrete cases in which statutory regulations met with social reality on the question of young lives.

Other policies, institutions, codes, and regulations should also be sifted to gain a better idea of the conditions of children and childhood in politics and the public arena. Stipulations on taxation and conscription age, as well as actual child-soldiers participating in combat can all be made to start a meaningful discussion on this little understood area.

Economic history materials too ought to be looked at to bring out information related to children as an economic entity and to consider the childhood phase in regards to labor and productivity. To begin with, procreation could be a well calculated as well as a natural fact in family life. The various fertility manipulation techniques and infanticide that we are aware of reveal but the tip of the iceberg in the reproductive strategies of historical China.[65] Child labor doubtlessly existed in its agrarian, commercial, and handicraft sectors, representing the connection of childhood from reproduction to production both in fact and in the abstract. A contextualized understanding for this connection and the contrast between the need and welfare of living children and the understanding and changing notions of childhood is obviously demanded. In any event, medical texts, legal documents, political and economic sources, aspects of children's lives, and the changing conceptions of childhood in China's past and present, mean there is, at the start, more than enough for anybody's taste.

Prescriptive, descriptive, and technical representations aside, artistic or imaginative works depicting children constitute yet an additional angle of appreciation and analysis. Illustrations of children at play (*ying-hsi-t'u*), of traveling toy venders (*huo-lang t'u*) and other auspicious social scenes centered around child-like activities (such as the symbolic *pai-tzŭ t'u*, the humorous *nao-hsüeh-t'u* the various joyful market scenes in *ch'un-shih t'u*, or idealized depictions of rural life in *keng-chih t'u*) flourished as special genres from the Sung on. Similar children's themes appear in other traditional Chinese art works, such as porcelain, lacquer ware, bamboo and woodcarving, wood-block printing and paper cutting. With such bountiful presentations of happy life and communal prosperity there are obviously overt as well as hidden messages, not necessarily serious, or realistic caricatures of children.[66] This notwithstanding, meaningful changes through time in the various "images" of children or childhood as depicted in, or reflected through, artistic means still invite educated interpretation. Whether they suggest any gradual evolution in the collective sentiment in attitude toward domestic life or young lives or simply a separate artistic realm of expression, are the kinds of question worth exploring.

In this regard, two other kinds of material should be mentioned. One has to do with the various literary works created for, about, or by children, the other with the myriad of material objects surrounding the physical environments under which children lived. The former include stories produced directly or indirectly for the enjoyment of young audiences, and often developed around child protagonists, as well as the countless songs, rhymes and verses accompanying children's everyday activities in bathing, playing, quarrelling, or simple distress. Together these works of "children's literature" provide another window for us to gaze at the worlds related to childhood in different corners in the later imperial period.[67] Evidence of food and clothing, snacks and toys, furniture and architecture, used by or designed for children, each in its own way, also tells much about the specific material conditions and physical makeup under which youthful days were spent and perceived by youngsters in different stations of life.

9.1.4. *Childhood: a multiplicity of views*

The above survey of the more obvious source materials will bring home to scholars a complexity and multiplicity of the subject that is at once exhilarating and bewildering. Clearly, even in the same historical period, different concepts of children and childhood existed in different quarters and form different angles, each representing a wide array of complementary or conflicting forces at work. Reorientation and debates abound from the very beginning, arising from different sectors, aiming at different goals.

Contemporary studies in sociology, psychology, and education dealing with children and childhood that pose differentiation between the adult-oriented and the child-centered position represent another set of polemics from which historians formulate their investigations. The association with a cultural attitude or value system that is considered "authoritative, disciplinary and oppressive" as opposed to "sympathetic, permissive, or indulgent" represents familiar rhetoric cast in the "modern" intonation. That previous examinations of European and American family histories, including attitudes toward children, equated traditional society with the former set of values, whereas the modern era as a time when people gradually moved closer to the latter set of norms could be an interpretation skewed toward this peculiar "modern" persuasion.[68] Evidence from late-imperial China, on the other hand, seemingly harder to fit into this posterior system of explanation, may bring forth examples when both strands of thought or practices existed side-by-side, involved negotiation and intermingling over centuries of social life and cultural exercises, thus helping us to view critically any "evolutionary" or "enlightening" assumptions that deem society to be moving from the "authoritative" to the "sympathetic," or oscillating between the two. Whereas didactic and prescriptive materials in ritual texts and primers might be identified as adult-oriented and carrying heavy disciplinary and oppressive weight, the sources of personal reflection and biographical information, or the artistic and imaginative depictions, may be thought as relatively indulgent and child-centered. Technical records, such as the pediatric texts, belong to yet another category of sources: that could be argued as both firmly "progressive" and hopelessly "old-fashioned." Though not without their own cultural constraints, due to pragmatic and vocational concerns, practicing physicians did not merely operate from within the normative moral culture; they had to see, feel, and understand the situation from their young clients' positions. Although this may not be the same thing as "child-centeredness" or "permissiveness," it does provide concrete examples and tangible evidence for the possibility of grasping views other than the authoritative versus child-sensitive mode from the pre-modern context. Artistic and literary depictions can suggest a similar outlook; even private letters and memorials may be analyzed to show sentiments varying from mainstream presumptions and authoritative "adult" views of the child. But these are not the same as the child-centered or childlike representations that somehow satisfy the modern inclination. All these traces related to children and childhood, as a matter of fact, coexisted and interacted with one another in the everyday life of the young and old in imperial China. While furnishing a complex of the concepts of children and childhood in the past, it is clear that it cannot be captured under any monolithic mode of explanation. It certainly diminishes the usefulness of any usual binary approach — the old "child versus adult," or, "positive versus negative," "progressive versus traditional" mode — whereby the concept of a continuous social evolution or linear progression in history surfaces. Elements of both not only coexisted for a long while but probably also shared some kind of a working relationship to form a world with views of the young that are neither entirely "adult oppressive" nor "child indulgent." For those investigators looking carefully and skeptically into the social, cultural, and conceptual history of the child, reconstruction and guided tours of the past cast in terms of the binary approach make clear nothing but the very domineering and almost inescapable character of historical studies, primarily grown out of, nurtured, then developed and executed under the peculiarly "modern mentality" long in the making in the mostly European–American cultural context (whose history is too complicated to be reviewed here, though whose implication is by no means insignificant to our present concern).

9.1.5. *The child: three related meanings*

Examining the multitude of sources, we will also realize that linguistically and conceptually the subject of the child (*tzû* or *t'ung* or *yu*) has meaning at three different levels, the first being the "social child" focusing on the "junior (*pei-yu*)" position it has vis-à-vis the senior (*tsun-chang*). Since this terminology and its compounds are used flexibly and interchangeably, it is important for us to denote their semantic implications so as not to misread or over-interpret them, while at the same time learning to appreciate the sociocultural interconnectedness of their various connotations. Broadly speaking, this notion of "child," a *tzû*, is understood here mostly as a social status relative to his or her elders. It denotes the subordinate, humble, and inferior status of a child in a subservient role to that of his or her elders, ancestors, and others in a hierarchically superior position. Thus it implies an identity that, though it often relates to youth, is not necessarily tied to it. In this sense, as long as one's parents were alive, or whenever speaking or acting vis-à-vis the elders in the house, any offspring at whatever age always assumes the position of a *tzû*. This was the "child" that most Chinese ritual texts, such as *Li-chi*, referred to when mentioning the word. It is also the meaning most of China's philosophical references, family instructions, and legal documents adopt in consideration. Socially speaking, that is how *tzû* was meant to be read in such important contexts as the *Twenty-four Filial Stories* (*Êrh-shih-ssû hsiao*). The broad, social meaning of *tzû* as a relative status gave it a role with clear obligations and definite rules, regardless of age, a key point in the concept of the "child" in its pre-modern context. It is in this social, culturally immature, secondary, and legally unaccountable position that we see societies, including historical China, relate other nonkin categories of inferior people such as slaves, servants, and foreigners in the inferior, dependant (at times legally or institutionally defined) status of a child. Most modern societies can also understand the notion of an "adult child," though this aspect had hardly been elucidated by historians of children or childhood as an issue closely associated with their subject.

A second layer of meaning in the Chinese notion of child *tzû*, or *t'ung*, or *yu*, is one closer to the common modern understanding. It is perceived as a phase in a person's lifespan, the early period of a human existence before adulthood. This narrower, more mechanical and biophysically defined, notion of the *tzû* is seen not only in such technical literature as traditional Chinese pediatric texts but also in such areas as early education (*Mêng-hsün*), or biographical and autobiographical writings. By the Ming period, interestingly, important thinkers like Wang Yang-ming (1472–1528) and Li Chih (1527–1602) adopted this more specific meaning of *t'ung-tzû*, a young child in the narrower sense, to combat the more general, social-status type definition of the child, to create and allow for a fresh, more liberating attitude toward children and child education.[69]

Finally, a third and more abstract meaning of the word child takes place when *t'ung* and *tzû* are used philosophically and aesthetically to highlight certain specific traits or qualities as a state in human nature, to refer to qualities as an existentially "childlike" characteristics. Especially in discussing art and literature, but also in other cultural settings, people can speak of some inclination, artistic styles or ethical values as representing or appearing close to "the spirit of a child." Many a Chinese proverb uses *t'ung* and *tzû* and their associated adjectives to stress this cultural appreciation of "child" as a state of mind: to describe a person as remaining "innocent (*t'ien chen*)," to admire poets and painters as having "the sentiment and fun of a young child (*chih ch'ing chih ch'ü*)" in their artistic expressions, to praise a functional adult as someone who has "not lost his or her child's heart (*t'ung hsin wei min*)," or even to marvel at a person (usually a man) whose hair is "like the (old) crane's yet with the appearance of a child (*ho fa t'ung yen*)." These are the innocence, heart, sentiment, fun, and physique of a child that anyone may embody regardless of age or status. This enlarged, intellectualized, philosophically contemplative meaning of the child is seen operating actively in the Taoist philosophy and religion. In their convictions, pursuits, and practices, it represented cultivation of a physical and mental state approaching that of an "eternal child," picturing "innate innocence" as something akin to immortality. This concept of a child in spirit and in body also exerted a powerful influence on Chinese medicine and health culture in its search for the healing exhibited by the body's natural ability to rejuvenate and regenerate. It is important to our appreciation of the concept of childhood, because it brings out a typical feature in the broad discourse about the child in China's multifaceted and interrelated contexts for which there is ample material as well as cultural evidence.

The relatively autonomous yet mutually communicative character of these notions of a "child" in three different domains ensured that though a certain understanding of "childhood" may be the operating force when it comes to specific areas of activity or concern (e.g. regarding problems in health, domestic life, or philosophical exercise), yet no singular view dominates the overall conception or treatment of children or childhood. In their interconnectedness, we recognize that, first, the prevalent social value which sees children as indispensable junior members of the family obeying and serving the needs of their elders as well as transmitting and carrying on the familial line was a most powerful force that prompted the birth, kept the need for, and maintained the growth of the old pediatric medicine. Whereas, second, this technical understanding of infants and children as humans in their biophysical initial and younger stage of life helped to protect and preserve the survival of people's offspring and thus rendered possible the practice of the social ethics required of the junior status of the young. On the other hand, this evolving biophysical appreciation of the human body in its constantly evolving state accepted, fed into, and also revised people's changing consideration of innocence, naiveté, and youth, an area deserving separate treatment that is too complicated to deal with here. Third, the philosophical, religious, and aesthetic search for a permanent infantile child in the abstract as representing the nondegenerative, permanently elevating quality of one's "childlike nature" provided a much needed contrast and counterbalance to both the limitation of the biophysical law physicians recognized and the rigidly suffocating subservient status that younger and junior members were assigned in the late-imperial Confucian social order. The liberating, rebellious, and subversive character of this philosophical, existential child as an eternal possibility at all stages of people's lives regardless of the familial roles or worldly obligations expected of them created a timely crack and precious breathing space in Ming-Ch'ing social hierarchy and politics. It also promised or suggested a spiritual transcendence outside of or beyond the visible and physical existence of humanity.

A good look at the world of children and childhood in Chinese history, therefore, has more to offer than an opportunity to patch up lost chapters in human experience. It opens up new windows to appreciate the power of such categorical factors as age and biosocial phases at play in the organization and operation of human society. As an analytical tool, it also reminds people of the illumination history can bring to bear on the culturally specific character of many social sciences in examination of questions pertaining to the "intrinsic state" of humanity. For, as samples of a particular historical population, it is conceivable that results from studies of social problems like children and childhood can be conceptually limited by the very "modern" outlook of disciplines like social psychology, early education, or sociology and demography on the one hand, and, on the other, these academic perceptions as products of modern sociocultural forces themselves have been powerful influences informing and formulating the attitudes and experiences of the subjects they are supposed to investigate and learn from. Historical evidence coming from a different era constructed under different forces, by contrast, alerts people to common social science theoretical models as potentially self-fulfilling prophesies based on data their ideas in part helped to create. By the same token, evolutionary psychology appears too sweeping to satisfy our curiosity about the daily operation of different societies, whereas evolutionary biology when applied to human society is too crude an inspiration to illuminate the changing practices and circumstances of human customs.

The concept of *tz'ǔ-hang*,[70] originated in Chinese Buddhism and later slipping into Ming pediatric literature (known as the journey of compassion and loosely rendered here as tender voyage), reminds us of the existence of an outlook toward infants and children borne out of a different phase in human history. In its slightly twisted English incarnation,[71] it means to reintroduce a sociocultural ecology whereby life at its early stage or not, is much more interconnected than a separated domain for "pitying down" or "studying up" as history has indulged their residents and the reflective minds from a later era. The modern "discovery" of children and childhood, by society or scholars, therefore entails more than a recovery of the biophysical, material, socioemotional conditions under which the survival of infants, and the growing-up process, or denial of growing-up became possible. It certainly cannot be an indicator or measurement of the linear progression of the collective, as once suggested and still circulating. Its presence in late imperial Chinese history points out that this very experience and its representation have never been, and thus should hardly become, traces of either particularity or universality. With it the ever-changing multiplicity, in time, regionality, gender, ethnicity, and class, of this history of children and childhood has only begun to see the light. What we have learned so far alerts us to the generic, constant, biophysically defined, children or childhood often (though not always) implied in such modern disciplines as pediatrics, early education, child psychology, which together with sociology and demography can now finally benefit from some of the complications afforded by time and space.

The lives of young children and the experience of early childhood are projected here as a tender voyage in Chinese history,[72] as this earliest phase in a long arduous journey through the human lifespan which exemplifies the frailty of human existence, sustainable only with compassion. Though in late imperial China the roughly 100 million infants and young children who existed at any given time represented different things to different people, and certainly lived differently in different locations, the temporary, vulnerable, yet enchanting quality of that existence invites and requires attention, the significance of which goes beyond the Chinese political or cultural border. In the considerably altered material and cultural environment of modern times, much of the context to that struggling existence has been shifted, along with its accompanying economic, philosophical, and physical conditions. A perusing of this passage of time in not so distant a past rewards the viewers not only with retrospective understanding but also with fresh perspectives at the present intersection of the tender voyage to interconnect the travelers. For an intellectual voyager, then, this present attempt hopes to inspire further understanding in the journeys ahead.

9.2. Meetings of Different Minds

9.2.1. *The perspective of children and childhood in history*

Much of what we learn (or try to unlearn) from contemporary research on infants and children, e.g., early education, child psychology, or pediatrics, is based on the notion of, and belief in, the "modern, scientific child" — a certain universal, standardized quality in the abstract — which is historically specific, yet whose particular complexity in cultural terms is yet to be confronted. We realize this as we read back and forth between modern theories and past records on children. More critically minded scholars in developmental psychology, cognitive studies, autistic children's centers, or children's courts also recognize this when they reflect on the peculiarity of the situations children are in, thus demonstrating the particularity or temporality of their own expertise and the intellectual validity they represent.

Being confronted with or in confronting such questions, unfortunately, past research by historians on children and childhood has scarcely offered any creative dialogue or independent assessment to close this gap, widened by one-sided admiration and uncritical reference. The complex substance and profound ambivalence represented by Chinese source materials, partly disclosed above, promises an intriguing set of both counter-arguments and comparative insights of an unusual kind. Debates on children and childhood based on Chu Hsi's or Wang Yang-ming's views from this perspective may be just as relevant and revealing as any theses or surveys modeled after the moral philosophy of, say, David Hume.

While ample evidence of one-sided and arbitrary, "modern views" now present themselves as the "common outlook" based on "objective" studies of children and continue to dominate both the academic and popular worlds, any visit to the subject in recent or distant history brings back forgotten pockets in comparative discussion casting doubts and raising fundamental questions.

The pioneering works produced by Western historians of children and childhood have failed as intellectual mediation between modern, scientific understanding and other unstreamlined experiences. Most have shown themselves to be committed followers of contemporary children's studies at a time when modern disciplines such as developmental psychology, early education, sociology, and demography appear to have held a certain "common" analysis in matters related to human development on life course or age factors. These offer numerous "theoretical frameworks" and serious evaluation of messier human records and seemingly odd examples from the distant past got lost in the shuffle. Investigations into medieval European or early modern French childrearing practices were mostly done to document the anticipated historical developments leading up to "the rise of the egalitarian family," the "discovery of the (modern) notion of childhood" as they corresponded to expected patterns in historical developments and manifested themselves under the sway of linear progression. The humanities could hardly, then, turn the table around and begin to query the applicability of much of these 19th or 20th century assumptions, less still engage in any serious conversation, any deeper negotiation, with contemporary pediatricians, child psychologists, or children's court judges regarding potentially alternative views on childhood or human existence at large.

Some of the material presented above, in the case of Chinese history of children and the child, should make it clear that the prevailing modern stance on children and the life course inherits many striking characteristics of modernity that beg for re-assessment. The assumption that, for instance, human existence is understood much like the movement of history or as a process, as biophysically fixed stages in an mechanically irreversible journey toward some common endpoint in the long run (be it physical fatality or spiritual salvation) remains an uncontested homily and received truth that attracts rare questioning and little suspicion. Any progression or "advances" in this journey, in other words phases in the life course, are thus conceived as objective, standard movements in common areas of humanity whether individually or collectively. These different sections in a human life (infancy, childhood, adolescence, adulthood, and old age) are then taken, without a blink, to be biophysically, therefore "scientifically," founded (be it socioculturally constructed and personally lived). With these inherently modern notions of human existence, a "child" could not but be identified as the dialectic opposite of the "adult." Infancy and childhood becomes an irrecoverable sweet memory or a nightmare in a person's past. One's hypothetical ability to experience or behold the child-state and adult-character simultaneously as Taoist philosophy assumed, or classical Chinese aesthetics advocated, can only become a logical nonsense. Social and cultural conditions in the later imperial period in China, as yet unacquainted with the European enlightenment, were lived out on some of these older premises as they could hardly even dream of the sociohistorical transformation they were just about to experience in this regard. The old Taoist idea that a human life is existentially a cyclical procession, or some fluid state with no definite end or any fixed later phase in sight, carried the potential to allow people to return to their first, innate, original infantile innocence and had a curious revival under joint state sponsorship, Neo-Confucian reification, and popular religious movements in post-Ming China. The Confucian conviction of interconnected generational relations and the Mencian belief in the inherent "maturity" or "cultivatable goodness" innate to any newborn, on the other hand, formed a central theme in the Neo-Confucian social and cultural ethos. In Ming philosophical eclecticism, or the Ch'ing development of clan organizations later, one witnesses the manifestation of these abstract notions as concrete social dynamics, combined with the growth of material consumption and a market economy (in children's goods and ritual commodities). As sociocultural forces the idea of the basic distinction between a child and an adult, of a child as carrying something innately "completable" and on its way to "adult-like" maturing qualities continued to operate in the daily practices of late imperial China. The Chinese term commonly taken to mean adult, "*ch'êng-jên*," literally points at a complete person, emphasizing the "mature" and "fulfilled" nature of a human being, rather than some assumed mechanical advancement in the physical phases of ageing. Similarly, thereby, any adult may still be granted the possibility to be in a childlike state maintaining within him or her, all along, the natural attributes usually present at the beginnings of human life as desirable and pursuable expressions of physical, social, and spiritual endowments, qualities moral, conservative or social conventions may deem annoying or comical, but which philosophical idealists or Taoist followers admired and cultivated. A sage, in this light, could be someone who managed never to have lost his childlike purity to worldly decadence, in the rough and tumble of harsh reality. Physically, it was imagined that if a body continued to be exercised and cultivated properly to retain, regain, or rejuvenate this infantile energy and vitality, a condition approaching natural immortality in the material and spiritual sense could be thinkable. Bearing this in mind, the difference between children and adults could hardly be a fixed one, as neither is identified as an objective fixture embedded in the yet-to-come universal "scientific" understanding of humanity.

9.2.2. *The question of memory and representation*

Re-evoking views of childhood, of one aspect or place in human life, in the past, in a distant land, inevitably presses upon the person questions of memory and representation. To begin with, since infants and children under the age of six are unable to speak or express themselves coherently or articulately through the usual means of communication, they are often rendered "voiceless" and their ability to bear direct witness or account for the occurrences in their daily lives becomes blatantly problematic. Although people habitually recall and tell of things happening to them at earlier points in their lives, often in ways suggesting a "historical present tense," consciously observing and recording those experiences contemporaneously, such as customary "memory counting," "sentiment recollecting," and story producing, can hardly be taken at face value. Tso Tsung-t'ang tells us time and again, as related earlier, of the days his mother used to chew rice to feed him when he was a six-month nursling. Mo Tê-hui wanted everybody to know that the nickname he later gave himself was chosen to commemorate the red willow tree under which his mother breastfed him. In searching and researching traces of life in this earliest blurred stage, searching for "evidence" of infancy and childhood, one is constantly confronted with the ambiguity through which the creation, transmission, recording, preservation, and circulation of memories occur. There remains undoubtedly much to learn and be questioned regarding the occurrence, preservation, presentation and representation of these sources of information as a perilous process taking place among the actual interplay of living and experiencing "in history." With the rapid development in cognitive studies and neural sciences, a historian is compelled to look at both the data and the thinking behind the old humanist's methodological questions, while wondering about newly informed ways of deciphering these increasingly "classical-" looking codes and traces. As the past retreats from us in physical time, moreover, this double-edged task threatens to be more and more unattainable and alluring at the same time.

Here, in fact, the rediscovery and mapping out of the history of Chinese infants and children may help us to dwell upon a few stimulating thoughts. First, in its historical and sociocultural configuration, which varies substantially from the familiar modern Western norm, the nature of human existence is not necessarily manifested to us as a single unity or as any progressive procession in a first place. One of the implications this may carry for us, then, is to consider the usefulness in seeing that an individual self may be endowed with a certain "multiplicity" from the beginning to the end. The Chinese notion of a person's life as carrying both a "self" in the limited, individualistic sense, (called the "small self"; *hsiao-wo*) as opposed to some existential state with its broader, extended character (called the "larger self"; *ta-wo*) provides one interesting example in question. Second, in a similar vein, time in a personal manner or on the abstract physical level, does not have to move on single track either. In other words, before modern standardized "physical time" came to dominate and impinge on the comprehension and management of personal lives, there was a myriad of sociocultural timetables conceived and consummated, some of which allowed for a grasping and experiencing of multiple tracks of time via human existence simultaneously, even as certain forms of reversible "fluidity." Third, the long Chinese tradition of compassion (*tz'û*) and filiality (*hsiao*), when erected upon these conceptual premises, created a particular kind of continuous interplay of human existence in ways seemingly both bewilderingly "modern" and hopelessly "traditional."[73] In stressing intergenerational connectedness, it bred its youths to anticipate, and play up to, the peculiar character of the old order, while the seniors in society were allowed to rejuvenate and return to "infancy" within their own worldly journey. This was even possible, for deceased ancestors in their thinking, when at the sacrificial altar. Both parents and children then, in the "cultural allowances" or social resources of life, each of pre-modern Chinese making, could be living out a historical existence that moved with multiple constructions whereby more than one human time track was imagined and executed.

When one contrasts the modern notion of "progression" or life course within this context, different socially orchestrated compositions with multiple leitmotifs begin to play. The question of memory and subjectivity in cultural historical representation (such as the biographies and autobiographies that we view as source materials) becomes both a problem and a convenient though unsatisfying answer interwoven into the construction of the problem. Further investigation into questions like cultural rupture versus historical continuity may identify them as being associated rather than opposites on the same temporal level. What appear to a modern mind as pretentiously old fashioned sentiments or expressions (e.g., the assumption that a young child can hardly "comprehend," live in the same world as the old, or identify herself/himself with the family tradition, or the habits that a person should be made to remember in his infancy) could be "genuine" ambiguities construed under different lights as a different sociopsychological formation.

9.2.3. *Listening to silence and seeing the void*

When approaching conditions of infancy and early childhood in the past, a certain conceptual and methodological reconsideration calls for an intention, if not an ability, to decipher silence, both real and metaphorical, in human existence. This need or possibility is suggested in the context of Chinese children's history on at least three levels: First, the documentation of nonverbal expression as recorded in conventional historical sources demands a more serious and systematic elucidation. The facial expressions, vocal sounds, bodily gestures, physical motion, daily activities and even motionless inactivity carry complex social, political, cultural, and psychological messages that plead for elucidation. We should overlook this other side while continuing to focus on textual representations solely as the habitual information of analysis in our intellectual investigation into this "vulnerable" or seemingly ordinary subject.

Second, nontextual evidence of human existence requires, as a result, vigorous thoughtful deciphering: what anthropologists call objects of material culture, e.g., food, clothing, furniture, architecture, toys, the arranging of plants, the handling of animals, and the viewing of rocks and trees, together with other traces of ordinary interaction could reveal powerful messages about the outlook, attitudes, strengths, and vulnerability of individuals and their social environments, about which young lives were but among the less familiar examples. The implications these may unearth however are far from insignificant.[74] Much more still awaits exploration in this direction, and not simply for the intellectual justice of representing the frail and neglected in the past.

Third, in a fundamental way, we must recognize that what is missing, both literally and figuratively, gives meaning to what turns out to be present. The ability to imagine, articulate, reconstruct, and make sense of what has been absent (lives lost in infanticide for instance) provides key information to a less arbitrary and particularly exclusive understanding of what is familiarly present or has been crudely and cruelly excluded.

Such conceptual and methodological questions relate to the question of historical subjectivity and agency. For if infants and children were to be accorded any subjectivity in history and if there is to be any serious discussion over their historical presence, the manner of determining "participation" in history would be immediately called into question, and also the various ways historical understanding continues to be anticipated and consumed. Because many people have always been missing from the usual historical records, and the exercise of historiography, infants and children could be the most blatant, intellectually innocent, and professionally overlooked, among the unrepresented (some would say unrepresentable). Their nonappearance and ambiguity hangs heavily on the conscience of the intellect of the collective. The kind of silence or absence that we are left with and have learned to live by becomes increasingly difficult to be reckoned as some hopeless, thus "natural," sort of absence as liberalization and democratization spread from the body politic to the intellect and back again. In this regard, high infant and child mortality in the past, which used to rob many young lives of their physical being before they had a chance to leave other traces behind, can hardly grant a continuous excuse for omission of attention or discussion. The frail and silent character of this earliest phase in humanity, the pre-verbal and pre-literary condition that such lives were in, admittedly deprived them of much opportunity to produce on their own much recording of significance in the conventional fashion, as written accounts by those close to them, inscribed on behalf of the incapable and less important. The deprivation that such leaves us in the world of understanding and knowledge, of any direct access to that world of the young, was however only partially predetermined, while the elusive subjectivity concealed within, or hiding behind, indirect representation points out some glaring characteristics of modern academic orientations that can hardly go without increasing questioning. Other factors contributing to the silencing and absence of children in history also bear much witness to the "artificial" human-made environment of history (e.g., infanticide denying the unwanted the rights to live, neglect, and prejudice differentiating the chance of survival according to socioeconomic status, and selective historical consciousness arbitrating the visibility or the nonvisibility of infants and young children in people's, observation and awareness). And in these, infants and children do not stand alone in their buried state and "forgettability" in time, or in the industry of knowledge production.

Granted that a fraction of this picture can be altered when different notions are pushed for in history and in the intellect, if one were to dig up and sort out the background of these "silencing" and "vacating" effects, the voice of silence becomes all of a sudden "audible" and evocative, its significance in sounding out overwhelming absence would be such that many would listen and pay attention with a stirred-up and gradually altering conscience and consciousness. Just like appreciating music or conducting research in linguistics, the occurrence, occupying presence, duration, and peculiar characteristics of the "silent" moments, the empty spots, carry powerful significance and profound meaning that no one can afford to ignore or run away from. Similarly, inactivity has always been a natural and indispensable part of activity for humanity. Thus far, that which has been relegated to the "unknowing," the "unrecoverable" of, say, an infant's and small child's world has been represented as less a limitation in expressive vehicles as a glaring intellectual ineptitude and collective conceptual oversight. Acknowledging these preconceived barriers and vocational baggage as part of a broader, social, prejudice, and human inadequacy that has contributed to the unbalanced and "incomplete" picture of the experience of the very young and the very old in the first place, we may begin to appreciate an overall significance when a certain awareness and restoration of what has been missing gradually or suddenly surfaces. Since the other side of the same forces that produced the presence of the strong and powerful also dictated the nonexistence, the historical vacancy, of the rest of the sociopolitical order, what becomes evident in the re-appraisal of the known, as much as the uncovering of the yet-to-be-identified, is a self-critical assessment of modern academic activities of a general rather than a sporadic, particular, kind. History and human society, most would concede, have always been made of both those present and those purposefully or nonpurposefully missing, both the living and the dead, the loud and the voiceless. As any architect, sculptor, or art historian can testify, what, or how empty, the space constructed in their own works, or the works they are viewing, has as much to do with the deeper meaning of the entire composition as what obviously exists superficially. The fundamental flaw in the contemporary humanities is that modern men and women of letters compromise the intellectual value of the less functionally sensible. At times unexplainable and obviously untidy complications in the world of lives represented causes them to act as over-zealous followers of the normative and positivist mentality of social and natural science which makes for a grave loss.

In the case of the lives of infants and small children in late imperial China, the moment leading up to their birth, or as some back then would argue their very "consent to descend," marked already an undeniable participation in the world of humanity, until then made up of their parents and ancestors, a communal existence consisting in addition to the seniors and adults, plants and animals, rocks and stars, gods and ghosts. The very likelihood of this physical world, made of the possibility to inherit any form of life, philosophically also presented a picture for contemporary members of society that was constantly negotiable and alterable, with the addition and subtraction of any elements related to the cosmos. One of the best examples of this view is the transforming power that pregnancy and childbirth had on Chinese women, allowing them the prospect of elevating themselves from the humbling status of a wife to the ultimate achievement of the mother. The same may be said of men in the predicament of a bachelor or in barrenness. As to most other normal couples, they prayed with vehement hope for offspring, presenting eternal gratitude and offerings for those safely born and healthily grown. The actions or inaction of any infant and child thereby were acts of socioecological empowerment in this never-ending human chain, in that larger circle of life. In this sense, the hows and whys of approaching a better representation in history of children and childhood become one, which speaks volumes for the physical and material conditions of the environment as well as the attitude and values which gave rise to it.

9.2.4. *Further thoughts/meetings of different minds*

A few reflections on the "Ariés thesis" are also in order. For with regard to, or despite, its initial stimulation, much has been produced in the way of scholarship to argue with or revise his observation that the notion of children and the awareness of childhood is a relatively "modern" phenomenon. Studies on children and childhood in medieval, even ancient, history have since revealed to us what may be learned of the lives of the very young before the "dawning" of the recent past, which reminds us all of the important difference one ought to maintain between "ignorance" and "absence," as opposed to the missing of commendable, or commendably "modern" attributes (attitudes, conditions) in history. Ancient historians show that parents in Greece and Rome were not without feelings toward their young.[75] Passionate bonds, it was demonstrated, existed between individual adults and their offspring.[76] Information with regard to medieval attitudes, and practice toward children were in fact so abundant that a leading scholar was prompted to comment on the matter. Still this revisionist literature is not as widely read or broadly influential as Ariés's bold pronouncement, especially in fields outside history, especially now that Ariés the intellectual along with his various compositions themselves have become objects of cultural analysis.[77] Against its first thrust and its remaining effect, in social studies and psychology related to the family and child development in particular, a belated response from Chinese history affords both a useful intellectual distance and a needed cultural complexity.

Intellectually, the "discovery of childhood" by pioneers like Phillip Ariés, the attentiveness to the young by his predecessor and kindred spirit Hu Shih (who preceded him in raising the May Fourth critique on people's attitude toward children as the key measurement for the progression of civilization) represented a conscious and constructive effort by enlightened and enlightening modern minds in recognizing and addressing what was perceived as a collective debt to some of society's most vulnerable and neglected. Family historians, demographers, researchers on social welfare, education systems, and children's mental and physical health represent but different work forces which in this broader historical context could be considered as similar agents of modernity. Pressed harder, some may even be willing to identify the birth and development of Chinese pediatric medicine, the evolving characters of Chinese family life, and the spread of early education from the Sung through the Ming and the Ch'ing era, as certain familiar characteristics of a twisted and complicated manifestation of the "progress" of history which may lead all logically to this modernizing and civilizing process, in the long *dureé*.[78]

First, the previous sections reveal that ample materials existed for people to learn about the history of young lives, including changing mentalities toward them, in pre-modern China. The references, despite the many glaring inadequacies of this present work also make clear the numerous areas that await exploration. The value of such endeavors in intellectual archeology, furthermore, does not have to lay with a confirmation of a separate, independent, autonomous, subjective world of children, though the latter may be validated to a surprising degree in the case of late imperial China. Nor should the history of children be yet another latecomer in the seemingly endless string of historical puzzles, another overlooked category or missing piece to make up for the total composition of the history of humanity. Granted that adding the factor of age or life course to the historical perspective, like the category of ethnicity, class, and gender before it, is an important enhancement.

This chapter can hardly satisfy the want of a monographic treatment of a history of Chinese children or childhood. Other than perhaps a multivolume representation looking into the worlds of the very young in its changing physical, social, emotional, and cultural environments, any basic introduction to such a history must unravel the structural elements pertaining to these constructions and consider the analytical perspectives themselves as not beyond question. While documenting historical developments in the conditions of children's health, family bonds, social relations as well as the gender, class, and regional variations lurking behind these forces, the above body of investigation may still be short of a balanced appraisal on this problem not because of some methodological argument of the "correct desciphering," sophisticated reading of source material, but because of the wealth of information left out as insignificant or irrelevant to the nature of the occasion, or to the proper domain of history or knowledge. The Chinese narrative that this attempt at uncovering (in three published monographs, one under production, and a number of articles)[79] is a more concerted effort, yet that too only provides enough information for ambivalent debates and further bewilderment as to the very nature or purpose of historical understanding and of humanistic investigations. If there remain any traces as to whether, or when, children or childhood had even been "discovered" in history, then there is little doubt that very recent developments in modern historiography come indeed shockingly late. They have become the subject of concern and serious interest, as surveyed in the introduction to this book. As a happy rejoinder to this intellectual exercise, this incomplete opening up of chapters in Chinese history looks forward to further deliberation and investigation in historical studies and studies on children and childhood.

Notes

1. The French version of Philippe Ariés book, *L'enfant et la vie familiale sous l'Ancien Régime*, appeared in 1960 in Paris. Its widely circulated English translation, entitled *Centuries of Childhood, A Social History of Family Life*, appeared in 1971.
2. Out of the group, Linda A Pollock's *Forgotten Children: Parent–child Relations from 1500 to 1900* is the earliest full-fledged attempt to confront Ariés' thesis and "re-examine" the existing attitude toward children, adult–children interactions, and early childhood experience in early modern England. Mark Golden's *Children and Childhood in Classical Athens*, Thomas Wiedemann's *Adults and Children in the Roman Empire*, and Shulamith Shahar's *Childhood in the Middle Ages*, though not as critical of Ariés' views as Pollock, all show cultural conditions of childhood in the West, see Linda A. Pollock (1983). *Forgotten Children: Parent–Child Relations from 1500–1900*. New York: Cambridge University Press; Mark Golden (1990). *Children and Childhood in Classical Athens*. Baltimore: Johns Hopkins University Press; Thomas Wiedemann (1989). *Adults and Children in the Roman Empire*. New Haven and London, Yale University Press, 1989; Shulamith Shahar (1990). *Childhood in the Middle Ages*. London and New York: Routledge.
3. See Philip J. Greven, Jr. (1970). "Life and death in a wilderness settlement"; "Independence and dependence in mid-eighteenth-century families". In *Four Generations: Population, Land, and Family in Colonial Andover, Massachusetts*, pp. 21–40; 222–260. Ithaca: Cornell University Press. Greven, like quite a few other scholars, went on to conduct further investigations on childhood experience and children's culture in American history, which shows that family historians paying earlier attention to such perspectives in fact carry a special concern for the "children's question" in history. See Philip Greven (1992). *Spare the Child, The Religious Roots of Punishment and the Psychological Impact of Physical Abuse*. Vintage books; see Greven, *Four Generations*, pp. 21–40, 222–260.
4. Most of John Demo's coverage on Plymouth colony was written with a keen awareness of children's interest in mind. Chapters six ("Parents and Children"), nine ("Infants and Childhood"), and ten ("Coming of Age") in the book *A Little Commonwealth, Family Life in Plymouth Colony*, are of particular concern here.
5. According to Lawrence Stone, the "restricted patriarchal nuclear family (1550–1700)" in England tends to "reinforce" patriarchy by having a combined "permissive" and "repressive" mode in their parent and child relations. Whereas when "the closed domesticated nuclear family (1640–1800)" emerged later on, a "child oriented, affectionate, and permissive mode" of parent-child relations were developed, see Stone, pp. 109–135, 254–302.

6. Two out of four chapters in Steven Ozment's book, *When Fathers Ruled, Family Life in Reformation Europe*, are devoted to conditions of children's existence, Chapter 3, "The Bearing of Children," and Chapter 4, "The Rearing of Children," see Steven Ozment (1983). *When Fathers Ruled, Family Life in Reformation Europe*. Massachusetts: Harvard University Press, pp. 100–177.
7. Chapter 5 in Michael Mitterauer and Reinhard Seider's *The European Family: Patriarchy to Partnership from the Middle Ages to the Present* is entitled "The Young in the Family," see Michael Mitterauer and Reinhard Seider (1984). *The European Family: Patriarchy to Partnership from the Middle Ages to the Present*. Chicago: University of Chicago Press, pp. 93–119.
8. Section III of Beatrice Gottlieb's *The Family in the Western World From the Black Death to the Industrial Age* is a discussion on "procreation and education." Which include Chapter 6, "Conception and Birth"; Chapter 7, "Early Childhood"; and Chapter 8, "Upbringing"; see Beatrice Gottlieb (1994). *The Family in the Western World From the Black Death to the Industrial Age*. New York: Oxford University Press, pp. 111–176.
9. Chapter 6, "Parents and Children: Infancy and Childhood," and Chapter 7, "Parents and Children: Adolescence and Beyond" of Ralph A. Houlbrooke's *The English Family, 1450–1700* give a good documentation of young lives in the English family of the period, see Ralph A. Houlbrooke (1984). *The English Family, 1450–1700*. Essex: Addison-Wesley Longman Ltd, pp. 127–201.
10. Recent studies on women's history bearing some general significance for history of children are too numerous to cite. Those focused on motherhood and domestic conditions can be of particular relevance.
11. In this regard, Randolph Trumbach's coverage in *The Rise of the Egalitarian Family, Aristocratic Kinship and Domestic Relations in Eighteenth-Century England*, for instance, appears to be an early example. Chapters 4, 5, and 6, of the book investigate "Childbearing," "Mothers and Infants," and "Fathers and Children," respectively, see Randolph Trumbach (1978). *The Rise of the Egalitarian Family, Aristocratic Kinship and Domestic Relations in Eighteenth-Century England*. New York: Academic Press, pp. 165–286. By the 1990s, studies on social life in classical times are also giving due attention to children's conditions. Keith R. Bradley's *Discovering the Roman Family, Studies in Roman Social History* has two chapters on the subject in particular, Chapter 3, "Child Care in Rome: The Role of Men", and Chapter 5, "Child Labor in the Roman World," see Keith R Bradley (1991). *Discovering the Roman Family, Studies in Roman Social History*. New York: Oxford University Press, pp. 37–75; 107–124.
12. Margaret L. King's detailed account of *The Death of the Child Valerio Marcello* is a good example, see Margaret L King (1994). *The Death of the Child Valerio Marcello*. Chicago and London: University of Chicago Press.
13. David Hunt's book, though named *Parents and Children in History, the Psychology of Family Life in Modern France*, is primarily a case study of the early childhood of the future Louis XIII as told through his attendant Heroard's Journal, see David Hunt

(1970). *Parents and Children in History, the Psychology of Family Life in Modern France*. New York: Basic Books.

14. Viewing infanticide as a primitive practice associated with the heathen tribes and the backward oriental societies have been an unexamined assumption long in existence in the West. Samuel K. Cohen Jr. began his edifying discussion of infanticide in the lives of Renaissance women with the explanatory observation that in fact recent "essays have suggested that infanticide was not a birth control practice peculiar to Asian populations alone but a normal recourse of families, ... throughout Western civilization," a suggestion that he said still "met with biting criticism," see Samuel K. Cohen, Jr. *Women in the Streets: Essays on Sex and Power in Renaissance Italy*. Baltimore: Johns Hopkins University Press, 1996, p. 149.

15. Peter C. Hoffer and N. E. H. Hull, in their research study on infanticide in early modern England and New England, included children under 8 or 9 years as "infants" in contemporary social and legal practices. Child murders as well as parental neonaticides are equally considered in their investigation. The quantitative evidence in their study is also quite revealing which placed "over 25 percent of all murders heard in the early modern English courts ... (as) infanticides," and "90 percent of all murderous assaults by women were directed at infants," see Peter C. Hoffer, and N.E.H. Hull. *Murdering Mothers: Infanticide in England and New England, 1558-1803*. New York: New York University Press, 1984, pp. xvii-xix.

16. John Boswell's moving book on the abandonment of children in western Europe from late antiquity to the Renaissance, entitled *The Kindness of Strangers*, and David L. Ransel's judicious study on child abandonment in early modern Russia, *Mothers of Misery*, serve as good indications of the historic, as well as geographic range of these recent works, see John Boswell (1988). *The Kindness of Strangers: Child Abandonment in Western Europe from Late Antiquity to the Renaissance*. Chicago: University of Chicago Press; David L Ransel (1990). *Mothers of Misery: Child Abandonment in Russia*. Princeton: Princeton University Press; see also note 17.

17. Joseph Robins' study of "charity children" in 18th and 19th century Ireland, entitled *The Lost Children*, Ruth McClure's study on the London Foundling Hospital in the 18th century, *Coran's Children*, and Rachel Fuchs's study of foundling and child welfare in 19th century France, *Abandoned Children*, though searching and presenting the question from different angles, as their topics suggest, all tell the tales about both the "giving-up" as well as the "taking in" of youth, see Joseph Robins (1980). *The Lost Children: A Study of Charity Children in Ireland, 1700–1900*. Dublin: Institute of Public Administration; Ruth McClure. *Coran's Children*. New Haven: Yale University Press (1981). Rachel Fuch (1994). *Abandoned Children: Foundlings and Child Welfare In Nineteenth-century France*. New York: State University of New York Press.

18. In this regard, changing contemporary concerns are obviously both informing and formulating historical studies. Quite a few studies on family life or childhood history have recently included sections devoted to the questions of child labor or children at work. John Demos and Philip Greven's study on Colonial America and Lawrence

Stone's study on Early Modern England both provide information on children's work. David Herlihy's work on *Medieval Households*, and Peter Laslett's work on England before the Industrial age, titled *The World We Have Lost* also give glimpses of young boys and girls laboring. Thomas Wiedemann, in his account of the lives of adults and children in the Roman Empire detailed quite interestingly the work children performed in the fields and in the vineyards, and the training processes for such skills; see David Herlihy (1985). *Medieval Households*. Harvard University Press; Peter Laslett (1966). *The World We have Lost*. New York: Scribner, pp. 16–17; Thomas Wiedemann. *Adults and Children in the Roman Empire*. New Haven: Yale University Press, (1989), pp. 155–164.

19. Ivy Pinchbeck and Margaret Hewitt's study is a good example that views the problem of child labor together with and in the context of the development of social legislation, see Pinchbeck, Ivy, and Margaret Hewitt. *Children in English Society*, vol. 2, *From the Eighteenth Century to the Children's Act, 1948*. London: Routledge and Kegan Paul 1973.

20. Studies into the pedagogical materials or children's primers can also reveal the world of "children's literature," or the interplay of the literary and the world of children. See, for instance, the number of quite fascinating essays included in *Infant Tongues, the Voice of the Child in Literature* edited by Elizabeth Goodenough, Mark A. Heberle, and Naomi Sokoloff, see E Goodenough, Mark A Heberle and Naomi Sokoloff (eds.) (1994). *Infant Tongues, the Voice of the Child in Literature* Detroit: Wayne State University Press.

21. A number of book-length analysis on the lives of school children and the changing conditions of schooling have been very revealing in highlighting the pedagogical experience of youngsters in historical times. Paul F. Grendler's *Schooling in Renaissance Italy, Literacy and Learning, 1300–1600* is a rich treatment of the subject, covering the education of girls, working class boys as well as vocational and technical training. Raymond Grew and Patrick J. Harrigan's *School, State and Society, The Growth of Elementary Schooling Nineteenth-Century France, a Quantitative Analysis* gives a good structural explanation to the changes in primarily education. The gender and class aspects of schooling are again interestingly illuminated; see Paul F. Grendler (1991). *Schooling in Renaissance Italy, Literacy and Learning, 1300–1600.* Maryland: The Johns Hopkins University Press; Raymond Grew and Patrick J. Harrigan (1992). *School, State and Society, the Growth of Elementary Schooling Nineteenth-Century France, a Quantitative Analysis*. Michigan: University of Michigan Press.

22. The example par excellence are the works produced over the decades by the Cambridge Group for the History of Population and Social Structure, whose very name serves as the best indicator of historical demographers' understanding of their population analysis in relation to the broader and larger process of social change. E. A. Wrigley's *Population and History*, Ronald Demos Lee (ed.), *Population Patterns in the Past* and E. A. Wrigley and R. S. Schofield's *The Population History of England, 1541–1871, A Reconstruction,* are among the best examples showing this connection, see E.A.

Wrigley (1969). *Population and History*. London: Weidenfeld and Nicolson, World University Library; Ronald Demos Lee (1977). *Population Patterns in the Past*. New York: Academic Press; E.A. Wrigley and RS Schofield (1981). *The Population History of England, 1541–1871, A Reconstruction*. London: Harvard University Press.

23. Peter Laslett and R. Wall (eds.), *Household and Family in Past Times*, for instance, gives the mean household size, changing family structures, and residential arrangements, which all bore importantly upon the daily existence of the young. Peter Laslett, in his acclaimed, book, *The World We have Lost*, also estimated that, given the shorter life span and different demographic structure in pre-modern times, children could have made up to 2/5 or more of the total population, see Peter Laslett and R Wall (eds.) (1972). *Household and Family in Past Times*. Cambridge: Cambridge University Press; Laslett, *Op. cit*.

24. Among historical demographers, the works of the family historians and scholars studying the historical ups and downs of local communities are especially keen in making such points. Tamara Hareven's instruction to the edited volume *Family History at the Crossroads*, under the same title as the book, provides a good review and overview on the field's attempt "to connect small-scale life with great structures and transformations," and to consider social change from all three perspectives of "personal time, family time and historical times," see Hareven, "Instruction," in T Hareven and A Plakans (1988). *Family History at the Crossroads*. Princeton: Princeton University Press. pp. vii–ix.

25. In addition to those attempts at deciphering history in entirely psychological terms, such as Lloyd Mause and his associates at the Institute for Psychohistory were interested in producing ("an evolutionary, psychoanalytic theory of human history"), almost all examinations on social life, family history, not the least of all childhood history, are found to be observation and analyses perceived and conducted under a certain Freudian and general psychological terms. Conceptual exercises to look into the "conditions" of children's lives in its "formative" stage filled the pages of such works, often without further questioning of their deeper cultural historical implications. For a typical example of the psychoanalytical application in the study of "successive child-rearing modes" as "a new paradigm for the understanding of historical change," see Davis (1976). "The psychogenic theory of history". In *Childhood and History in America*, pp. 13–36. New York: Psychohistory.

26. Given that the field of psychology in general, and contemporary knowledge in developmental, cognitive, and social psychologies in particular have acted as an important formulating as well as informative force behind historical observation of children and childhood. One wonders whether there should not be times when all these historical discoveries be brought back as materials to reflect upon both the specific cultural stance that modern psychology represents on the one hand, and many peculiarly 19th- and 20th-century Western outlooks it assumes on child-development on the other. A group of scholars drawn to the field of "indigenous psychology (*pen-t'u hsin-li hsueh*)" in Taiwan have been exploring such possibilities with their series of conferences and a bi-annual journal, *Chinese Psychology*.

27. See Jon L. Saari (1990). *Legacies of Childhood: Growing Up Chinese in a Time of Crisis, 1890–1920*. Cambridge, MA: Harvard University Press.
28. See Kinney, AB (ed.) (1995). *Chinese Views of Childhood*. Honolulu: University of Hawaii Press, pp. 1–14.
29. These are all comments made in C. John Sommerville's brief forward to the volume, see Sommerville, "Forward," pp. xi–xiii.
30. Ann Behnke Kinney's essay, the first in the volume, lays out the "Han Notions of the Moral Development of Children" based on the ancient Chinese concern for, "auspicious beginnings and ritual correctness" of humanity. Elegantly entitled "Dyed silk," it provides a useful foundation for the Confucian attitude toward children and early riculcation that was run through history for millenia to come, see Ann Behnke Kinney (1995). "Dyed silk: Han notions of the moral development of children". In *Chinese Views of Childhood*, Ann Behnke Kinney (ed.), pp. 17–56. Honolulu: University of Hawaii Press.
31. Wu Hung's discussion, focusing on the issue of "Private Love" versus "public duty," moves through a host of sociocultural problems implicated in the artistic and hagiographic representations of the image of the child, see Wu Hung's (1995). "Private love and public duty: Images of children in early Chinese art". In *Chinese Views of Childhood*, Ann Behnke Kinney (ed.), pp. 77–110. Honolulu: University of Hawaii Press.
32. Beginning with general remarks based on sketch information revealed by Chinese biographies, autobiographies, and accounts of wet-nurses, Pei-yi Wu's essay entitled "Childhood remembered," moves on to the rewarding and thus far barely noticed materials of parents' writings on children, relating the obvious growth of necrological little of children to what he perceived as an emerging "cult of the child" in late-Ming China, see Wu Hong's (1995). Childhood remembered: Parents and children in China, 800 to 1700. In *Chinese Views of Childhood*, Ann Behnke Kinney (ed.), pp. 129–156. Honolulu: University of Hawaii Press.
33. Charlotte Furth's contribution to the volume builds on her earlier studies on traditional Chinese gynecology and birthing culture to further consider the interrelatedness of biological reproduction with social reproduction. The beginnings and evolution of human life, the birth, and growth of infants and children were understood and managed physically and practically, assisted by China's bio-medical discourse, yet as Furth shows this tradition itself had always been embedded in a particular set of cosmological notions and socio-cultural concerns, see Charlotte Furth (1995). From birth to birth: The growing body in Chinese medicine. In *Chinese Views of Childhood*, Ann Behnke Kinney (ed.), pp. 157–192. Honolulu: University of Hawaii Press.
34. Waltner's article connects the gender-specific character of infanticides with the rising dowries in late imperial China to consider social factors such as the marriage system with the status of children and the treatments they received, see A. Waltner (1995). Infanticide and dowry in Ming and early Ch'ing China. In *Chinese Views of Childhood*, Ann Behnke Kinney (ed.), pp. 192–218. Honolulu: University of Hawaii Press.

35. In her study on the "Relief Institution for Children in Nineteenth-century China," Angela Liang shows the development of such organization as the *bao-yinhui* (Society for the Preservation of Babies) and the changing character of Chinese foundling hospices as activities manifesting a new approach to child destitution as well as a new concept of the child as a complex social being, both at the expense and as a partial result of the declining state leadership, see Angela Liang (1995). Relief institution for children in nineteenth-century China. In *Chinese Views of Childhood*, Ann Behnke Kinney (ed.), pp. 251–278. Honolulu: University of Hawaii Press.
36. Lucien Miller's piece discusses "the adolescent world" in *Honglou Meng*, while Mark Lupher's essay examines the social behavior of "rebel youth" in the 1960s, see Lucien Miller. "Children of the Dream: The Adolescent World in Cao Xueqin's Honglou Meng." In Anne Behnke Kinney, ed., *Chinese Views of Childhood*, Honolulu: University of Hawaii Press, 1995, pp. 219–250; Mark Lupher (1995). Revolutionary little red devils: The social psychology of rebel youth, 1966–1967. In *Chinese Views of Childhood*, Ann Behnke Kinney (ed.), pp. 321–344. Honolulu: University of Hawaii Press.
37. In the introduction to her book on adoption, Waltner gives a thoughtful and broad consideration on the issue from both a cross-cultural and theoretical perspective, which establishes her findings in Ming China in the context of procreation and heredity in historical comparison; see A. Waltner (1990). *Getting An Heir: Adoption and the Construction of Kinship in Late Imperial China*. Honolulu: University of Hawaii Press, pp. 1–81.
38. See H.C. Wang Liu (1959). *The Traditional Chinese Clan Rules*. New York: Published for the Association for Asian Studies by J. J. Augustin; Charlotte Furth (1984). "The patriarch's legacy: Household instructions and the transmission orthodox values". In *Orthodoxy in Late Imperial China*, Kwang-ching Liu (ed.), pp. 187–211. Stanford, CA: Stanford University Press.
39. Angela Ki Che Leung. *Shih-shan yü chiao-hua: Ming-ch'ing tê tz'u-shan tsu-chih* (Philanthropy and inculation: Charity organizations in the Ming-Ch'ing period) Taipei: Lien-ching, 1997, pp. 71–102
40. For instance, see Liu, *Ming-ch'ing Shin-ch'i chia-tsu jên-k'ou yü shê-hui ching-yen pien-ch'ien*; Lee and Campbell.
41. In her analysis on Lu K'un's writing for women, children, and the poor, Handlin explains Lu's work for children. The *Nü-hsiao-êrh yü*, *Hsü hsiao-êrh yü* (*A Sequel to Words for Little Children*), and *Hsiao-êrh yü* (*Words for Little Children*) are efforts embedded in his populist preoccupations and are geared especially for the young audience, see Joanne F. Handlin, *Action in Late Ming Thought: The Reorientation of Lu K'un and Other Scholar Officials*. Berkeley: University of California Press, 1983, pp. 143–147.
42. Much of what I am summarizing here can be found better documented within the systematic treatment in the three monographic studies I have published in Chinese. The two books on infant care and children's health cited in note 44 use centuries of pediatric archive to show the bio-physical and physiological and material conditions of this childhood experience. The title of the third book is *T'ung-nien*

I-Wang: Chung-kuo hai-tzû tê li-shih (*Childhood Tales in the Past: A History of Chinese Children*).

43. Hsiung, *Yu-yu: Ch'uan T'ung chung kuo tê ch'iang pao chih tao*, pp. 5–24.
44. Hsiung, "Chung-kuo chin-shih êrh-t'ung lung-shu tê fu-hsien (The emergence of the discourse on children in Late Imperial China)," pp. 139–170.
45. Chu Hsi's *T'ung-mêng hsü-chih* serves as a good example, see Chu, *T'ung-mêng hsü-chih*, p. 12.
46. Lü, *Hsiao-êrh-yü*, pp. 1–3; Lü, *Hsü hsiao-êrh yü*; Lü, *Nü hsiao-êrh -yü*, pp. 430–432.
47. See Wu Pei-yi. "Childhood Remembered: Parents and Children in China, 800 to 1700." In Anne Behnke Kinney, ed., *Chinese Views of Childhood*, pp. 129–156. Honolulu: University of Hawaii Press, 1995.
48. See Hsiung, *Op. cit.*
49. See Hsiung, "Êrh-t'ung wên-hsüeh", pp. 31–38.
50. See Hsiung, "Shei-jên chih-tzû: chung-kuo chia-t'ing yû li-shih mai-lo chung tê êrh-t'ung ting-i wên-t'i" (Whose children are they: Reflections on the status of children between the family and society in early modern China), pp. 259–294.
51. The category of the National Palace Museum's special exhibition of *Ying-his-t'u* (painting of Children at play), for instance, included the Ming literati Chou Ch'ên's (1450–1535) painting, *Hua Hsien-k'an êrh-t'ung cho liu-hua chü-i*. This work was based on the poetic line: leisurely watching the children willow flowers, in which its young protagonist were reduced to small figures with mere bodily gestures but no visible facial expressions, see *Ying-his-t'u*, p. 32.
52. In an comparative review essay entitled: "Ju-ch'ing ju-li: Ming-ch'ing yu-hsüeh fa-chan yû êrh-t'ung kuan-huai chih liang-mien hsing (To be rational and to be sensible: The contradiction in the early education development and concerns for children in the Ming-ch'ing period)," I have laid out the ambivalent nature in attending to children's interest in the early modern period, see Hsiung, "Ju-ch'ing ju-li: Ming-ch'ing yu-hsüeh fa-chan yû êrh-t'ung kuan-huai chih liang-mien hsing," pp. 313–325.
53. Compare, for example, Ariés's perspective as laid out in the second section of his book, *Centuries of Childhood*, and my own treatment of the sociopolitical implication of elementary education in Ching dynasty China, see Ariés; Hsiung, *T'ung-nien I-Wang*.
54. Hsiung, "Hao-tê-k'ai-shih: Chung-kuo chin-shih shih-jên tzû-ti tê yu-nien chiao-yû (Getting off to a good start — early childhood education of elite families in late imperial China), pp. 201–238.
55. My conclusion for *T'ung-nien I-wang* tries to dwell on this point, see Hsiung, *T'ung-nien I-wang*, pp. 329–338.
56. In the Introduction for an anthology on C*hildhood and Family in Canadian History*, Joy Parr explains how "childhood and family are mostly shaped by historical rather than biological process," which are only minimally founded in nature, see Joy Parr (1982). *Childhood and Family in Canadian History*. California: University of California press, pp. 7–16.
57. For instance see Chêng Hsüan, *Li-chi chu-shu*, chuan 28, p. 243.

58. See Ssû-ma, like the *Li-chi*, drew a plan of the ideal up-bringing for a child from his infancy to his adulthood, only adding still further programs with more specified activities, see Ssû-ma, *Chü-chia tsa-i*; see also Hsiung, *T'ung-nien I-wang*, pp. 80–81.
59. See Ssû-ma, "Chiao-nan-nü (Instructing boys and girls)," *Chü-chia tsa-I* (*A Myriad Rites for the Family*), p. 333; see also Hsiung, *T'ung-nien I-wang*, p. 81.
60. There is thus far no study on family instructions relating to children. For a general analysis on traditional clan rules and family instructions, see Charlotte Furth (1990). The patriarch's legacy: Household instructions and the transmission of orthodox values. In *Orthodoxy in Late Imperial China*, KC Liu (ed.), pp. 187–211. California: California University Press.
61. For a brief introduction to children's primers and other literary productions intended for the young readers in pre-modern China, see Hsiung, *T'ung-nien I-wang*, pp. 16–24.
62. For a brief explanation on the *genre* of *nien-p'u* and its use in understanding personal lives, see Hsiung, "Constructed emotions: The bond between mothers and sons in late imperial China", p. 88.
63. For an introduction to Chinese-pediatrics and the source materials it left behind, see Hsiung, "Treatment of children in traditional China", pp. 73–79; see also Hsiung, *T'ung-nien I-wang*, pp. 16–24.
64. Hsiung Ping-chen's article on "Case histories in Chinese pediatrics and their bio-medical value," discusses about the values pediatric archive enstored for approaching historical epidemiology; in *An-Yang: Chung-kuo ching-shih êrh-t'ung tê chi-ping yü chien-k'ang*, major patterns of health and disease of young children in late imperial China are analyzed, see Hsiung, "Case histories in Chinese pediatrics and their bio-medical value", Paper presented at the conference on *The Case History in Chinese Medicine: History, Science, and Narrative*, January 1998, U.C.L.A.; Hsiung, *An-Yang: Chung-kuo ching-shih êrh-t'ung tê chi-ping yü chien-k'ang*.
65. See Hsiung, "More or less: Cultural and medical factors behind marital fertility in late imperial China", Paper presented at the IUSSP workshop on *Abortion, Infanticide and Neglect in Historical Populations*, October, 1994, Kyoto, Japan.
66. See, e.g., Tu, "Ku-hua chung *tê êrh*-t'ung t'ien-ti" (The world of children as seen in old paintings), pp. 4–15.
67. Hsiung, "Treatment of children in traditional China", pp. 73–79; Hsiung, *T'ung-nien I-wang*, pp. 16–24.
68. Such assumptions are quite common in family history works in European and American studies, see Lawrence Stone (1977). *The Family, Sex, and Marriage in England, 1500–1800*. Harper & Row; C. John Sommerville (1982). *The Rise and Fall of Childhood*. Beverly Hills: Sage.
69. See Wang, "Hsün-mêng ta-I (The principles in child education)", pp. 57–58; Li Chih, "T'ung-hsin shuo (On the heart of the child)", pp. 22–24; see also Hsuing, *T'ung-nien I-wang*, pp. 192–216.
70. Nieh, *Tou K'o Tz'û Hang*.
71. Usually transform as "a compassionate journey."

72. *Tz'ŭ-hang* (lit. *A journey of compassion*) was originally a Buddhist term denoting the human life experience as a passage in the ocean of pains and hardship (*K'u-hai*) in need of constant guidance and compassion from the merciful Bodhisattva. By the late imperial period, the concept was borrowed to represent the special innocent and frail existence of infants and young children, as for instance, expressed in the title *A Tender Voyage*.
73. Hsiung, "The other side of filial piety: Reflections on compassion versus loyalty in late imperial Chinese family relations", pp. 313–359.
74. Elsewhere I have attempted further exploration of the world of children using material evidence.
75. Mark Golden (1990). *Children and Childhood in Classic Athens*. Baltimore: Johns Hopkins University Press; Thomas Wiedemann (1989). *Adults and Children in the Roman Empire*. New Haven, CT: Yale University Press.
76. Lawrence Stone (1977). *The Family, Sex, and Marriage in England, 1500–1800*. Harper & Row.
77. Philippe Ariés (1965). *Centuries of Children: A Social History of Family Life*. Vintage.
78. Hsiung, "Introduction," in *T'ung-nien i-wang: Chung-kuo hai-tzŭ ti li-shih*.
79. See Hsiung Ping-chen's works in works cited.

10

THE WALLS AND WATERS: A COMPARATIVE STUDY OF THE CITY CULTURES IN MODERN CHINA — BEIJING, SHANGHAI, AND HONG KONG*

PHILIP Y.S. LEUNG

Chinese University of Hong Kong

10.1. Introduction

This chapter is a preliminary attempt to analyze and compare the cultural characteristics of three Chinese cities in modern history: Beijing, Shanghai, and Hong Kong. The development and evolution of city culture in these three cities depend very much on the interaction of two environments: the natural and the artificial. The latter refers to a human-built environment which includes architectural forms, city planning, and the transportation–communication system, while the former refers to physical landscape, geographical location, vegetation, and natural resources. The first half of this chapter will examine and analyze the cultural significance of the human-built environment as represented by the city-walls of each city. In the past 200 years, as this chapter attempts to show, the walls built outside or inside the three Chinese cities of Beijing, Shanghai, and Hong Kong had great

---

* This chapter is a reproduction of the Wu Teh Yao memorial lecture given by the author in 2004.

impact on the changing lifestyles and the evolution of political and commercial cultures in these cities. The second half of this chapter will focus on the natural environment especially the waters surrounding the cities — rivers, bays, and harbors, assessing the impact of the "changing waters" on the development of city culture.

10.2. The Walls and City Culture

The city wall was a prominent feature in old Chinese cities. To the Chinese, the walls had both practical values as well as symbolic meanings. The lifestyle and livelihood of the Chinese people in the city were in many ways molded and affected by the design, structure, and functionality of these walls. More important, the evolution and change of city culture was intricately connected to the history of these walls — their design and construction in the early period, their subsequent renovation and reconstruction, and eventually their demolition in the 20th century. From the history of the walls, we could see how the cultural characteristics of the city changed, and how the competition among local elite and the clash of civilizations affected the political and economic development of the city. During the last two centuries when Chinese cities became rapidly industrialized, modernized, and commercialized, the walls' functional values were debated and challenged, and finally the walls were torn down and demolished.

The controversies centering around the preservation and demolition of the walls reflected the cultural tensions between tradition and modernity, and between a land-based political orientation and a open-mindedness toward maritime trade. In the end, the walls in the three cities fell victims to modernization, industrialization, urban renewal, and rapid economic expansion. For comparative purpose and for better understanding of the relationship between walls and cultural development, we shall include the city-walls of Beijing in this part of the chapter, but only concentrate on Shanghai and Hong Kong when we examine the element of water.

10.3. Beijing — The Walls Stood Tall

Beijing was a city of prominent and visible walls. Walls of different heights and sizes, and walls of stone and walls of mud were aplenty: the walls of the

Forbidden City or Palace City, the walls of the Imperial City, the walls of the Inner City, the walls of the Outer City, and walls around the sacred temples, and walls surrounding noble houses and imperial gardens, and of course, sections of the Great Wall in the outskirts of the city. The walls were constructed in the pre-modern period and they were meant to protect the imperial palaces and the royal families; they were built around the old capital to guard the capital from outside attacks by rebels and invaders. They were erected around the sacred grounds of the Temple of Heaven and other holy places to prevent ordinary intruders. In other words, one of the primary and most important reasons for the construction of the walls in Beijing was for the protection and defense of the city and the noble people and sacred altars therein.

The old city-walls were built more than 2000 years ago in the ancient city of Jizhou (薊州) and Yanjing (燕京). Subsequently more walls were built when a new dynasty appeared and when new rulers came in. Over the last 600 years, Beijing has been the national capital of China, and because of that, more buildings, palaces, pagodas and towers, and walls were built in and around the city.

Beijing was, and still is, a city of prominent walls.

10.3.1. *History of the walls*

For centuries Beijing had been a city with many walls. First, there were the walls of the old city of Jicheng (薊城), later changed to the city of Youzhou (幽州), and then to the city of Yanjing (燕京). The ancient city of Jicheng was established, according to Chinese legends, some 2400 years ago during the reign of Sage-king Shun (舜).[1] The walls were renovated by the state of Yan when the city was made capital of this small state in the north during the Warring States period. A new walled city was constructed in the south around 70 AD in the Eastern Han and it was named Youzhou in the period of the Three Kingdoms.[2] After that the city came to be known as Yanjing, and it was made capital by the Khitan Liao (遼) and by the Jurchen Jin (金) dynasties. The city walls of Yanjing formed the shape of a square, with 36 *li* (里) on each side. The height of the city wall was three *zhang* (丈) and the width at the base was about one-and-a-half *zhang*. The Khitan Liao added an inner wall for better protection and defense. The Jin also expanded and renovated sections of the wall (using mud bricks) to make it the "Central Capital" (zhongdu, 中都) of the state. According to one source, the circumference of the city wall of the "Central Capital" was about 54 *li*.³ The city was conquered by Mongols under Genghis Khan in the beginning of the 13th century, and later the Mongol (or Yuan, 元) ruler Kublai Khan adopted the city as the "central capital" in 1267 AD. In 1272, its name was officially changed to "Great Capital" (dadu, 大都), and from then onward to the end of the Qing (清) or Manchu dynasty, Beijing had remained the capital of China for about 600 years.⁴ Most of the city-walls constructed by Kublai Khan were preserved into the Ming (明). This old walled-city was called the "Inner City" (neicheng, 內城) when a new wall was constructed during the Yongle (永樂) period (completed around 1421) of the Ming dynasty to include a vast piece of territory outside the main gate of the old walled city to form the "Outer City" (waicheng. 外城).

The walls of the "Outer City," constructed in the 14th century under the Ming, represented the outermost layer of city-walls of Beijing, the imperial capital. Sections of the walls were demolished in the mid-20th century but certain parts of the walls have been maintained in the present-day Beijing. Besides the walls of the "Outer City," there were more walls in Beijing: First, walls of the "Inner City" (neicheng) which were built in the Yuan dynasty when the Mongol ruler made the city the capital of their vast empire. Within the walls of "Outer City" and "Inner City" there were more walls: First, the walls of the "Imperial City" (huangcheng, 皇城) in which the government offices, imperial palaces and houses and courts of the nobilities were located; and in addition, the walls of the "Forbidden City" (zijingcheng, 紫禁城) or the "Palace City." These cities were all surrounded by walls that protected the palaces and people within, and prevented common people from intrusion. The walls of the Imperial City and the walls of the Forbidden City were decorated with elaborated gates, guard towers, and other architectural structures and sculptures for a variety of purposes including *feng shui* (風水) or geomancy. In fact, the design and construction of the entire capital was in line with astrological and *feng shui* alignments with the Palace City at the center.⁵ Designed by Liu Bingzhong (劉秉忠), an expert architect familiar with the layout and characteristics of ancient Chinese capitals such as Changan (長安) and Luoyang (洛陽), the new capital of the Mongol empire embraced all essential elements of Chinese geomancy that justified its political significance and locational centrality. The construction work was completed in 1283, a few years after Kublai Khan elevated the city from the status of "central capital" (zhongdu) to that of "great capital" (dadu) in 1272. It became a great city in the 13th and 14th centuries with about half a million population consisting of Mongols, Jurchens, Tibetans, Chinese, and dozens of racial groups from Central and Northern Asia. It was ransacked during the rebellion of the 1360s. After the fall of the Mongol dynasty, the Ming Emperor Yongle decided to rebuild the city as his "Northern Capital" (Beijing, 北京) although the official capital of the Ming was located in Nanjing (南京). The rebuilding of Beijing proved to be a major construction project that lasted more than 15 years. More palaces and temples were built within the city, and sections of the city-wall were renovated throughout the early Qing dynasty, but the layout and the main structures remained unchanged. In the early 20th century, advocates of modern city planning and city reconstruction called for the demolition of the old walls to pave way for new buildings and infrastructures. The new government of the People's Republic generally sided with these city reformers, and as a result, most of the city walls were torn down for road expansion and for new construction projects in the 1950s despite the objection of a few cultural scholars and professional architects such as Liang Sicheng (梁思成) and Hou Renzhi (侯仁之).[6] However, certain sections of the walls have been preserved, together with most of the imperial palaces and sacred temples.

10.3.2. *The walls and development of imperial Beijing*

The walls of Beijing, in more ways than one, shaped and defined the city. As mentioned earlier, the most common function of the walls was for protection. The city walls of Beijing protected the royal family, the government officials, and the people living in the imperial capital. Since these people were of great significance, the walls were high and sturdily built, usually with stones and hard bricks. The walls were thick, double-layered and surrounded with moats that helped in defense. If the invaders or rebels broke through the walls of the "Outer City" there were more walls to protect the "Inner City" and more walls to protect the "Imperial City" and the "Forbidden City" (see Figure 1). The concentricity of the walls of the imperial capital was not only for better protection of the royal family, but it also revealed the growing status and significance of the people from

226　　　　　　　　　　*Philip Y. S. Leung*

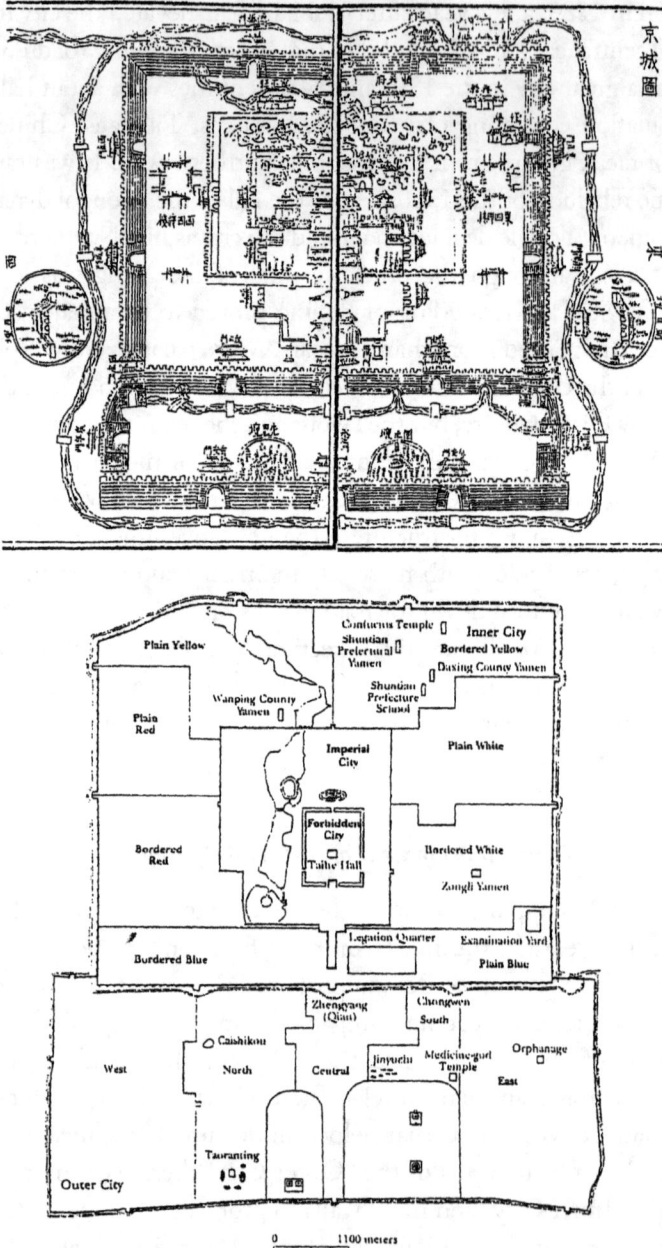

Figure 10.1　The Walled City of Beijing, circa 1684
Source: Adapted from Susan Naquin, *Peking: Temples and City Life, 1400–1900*. Berkeley: University of California Press, 2000, pp. 356, 426.

outer to inner, and from periphery to the center. The walls of Beijing, in other words, not only protected the people within from outside attacks, it also divided the people living within. The walls of each city were also lines of demarcation preventing people from free intermingling. The Manchu or Qing dynasty basically maintained the design and structure of the city with only minor changes, primarily adding more palaces and building structures throughout the first 100 years. However, one important policy of segregation was initiated by the early Manchu government using the walls of the "Inner City" (hence also known as Tartar City) as boundaries. The Han Chinese were not permitted to reside in areas within the "Inner City," including that of the Imperial City and Forbidden City. They had to move out of the walls of the "Inner City" into a newly developed area within the walls of the "Outer City" (waicheng, 外城).[7] In other words, the walls of the "Inner City" served the purpose of segregation in addition to that of protection.

As each city-wall had its gates and guard towers, it was not easy for the people of Beijing to move around the city without documentation because the gates and walls prevented free movement of the passengers in and out the cities. The walls stood tall and were usually decorated with guard towers and the gates were given names such as "Shen Wu Men, 神武門" (Martial Gate), "Tai He Men, 太和門" (Ultimate Peace Gate), "Tian An Men, 天安門" (Heavenly Peace Gate), and "Wu Men, 午門" (Noon Gate), and so on. The towers and the high walls were imposing and sometimes quite threatening. The gates with names written in huge characters at the top looking down at the passengers were constantly guarded by soldiers. On top of the wall there were watch-towers and archery stands. This instilled in the ordinary passengers both a sense of fear and awe. The restriction in movements and regular checking of documentation and identity reminded constantly the residents of Beijing their ethnic and class identities, giving rise to a general acceptance of hierarchy and a high level of status consciousness. Words such as "No entry" or "No trespassing" were written all over the walls, so to speak. There were so many boundaries for the privileged and excluded few, ordinary people in Beijing had to settle with a hierarchical structure and a submissive attitude. In such a place, ideas of equality and liberalism could find little or no breeding grounds.

However, on the other hand, the residents of Beijing were proud of their status as inhabitants of the center of the "Middle Kingdom" literally living under the feet of the "son of heaven." The walls of Beijing were not only a physical boundary that separates "inner" and "outer," but a cultural boundary that denotes center and periphery. The sense of centrality of the capital in the nation as well as in the universe gave rise to a widespread feeling of superiority and cultural vigor that was often prevalent among the Beijing city dwellers in the past especially among the scholar-officials. This cultural pride and sense of leadership remain quite apparent among the contemporary elite of Beijing despite the demolition of most of the old city-walls.

10.4. Shanghai — The Walls were Crumbling

Shanghai was not a capital or a mega-city five centuries ago when Beijing had already established its prominence. Shanghai was a commercial town and trading center before its walls were erected in the Ming dynasty. The city walls were built primarily for defense against the frequent raids and harassment of the pirates who came from the sea. The walls, however, were built with mud bricks and not as sturdy and permanent as the Beijing walls. In addition, the walls were relatively low and the enclosed area was limited to what was known as the "Chinese City" or "Southern City" (nanshi, 南市) in the 19th century. The walled city of Shanghai, therefore, constituted only a small section of the new city of Shanghai in the modern period beginning with the opening of the city to foreign trade in 1843. The walled-city was only one of the tri-cities in Shanghai, together with the twin cities, namely the International Settlements and the French Concession (see Figure 2). The erection and demolition of the walls of the "Chinese City" in Shanghai tells a fascinating story of cultural adjustment and power struggle among the local elite.

10.4.1. *History of the walls*

Shanghai's city-walls were built in the 17th century in the Ming dynasty. Before that Shanghai was a small market-town located in an open plain adjacent to the Huangpu River. Its increasing significance as a regional

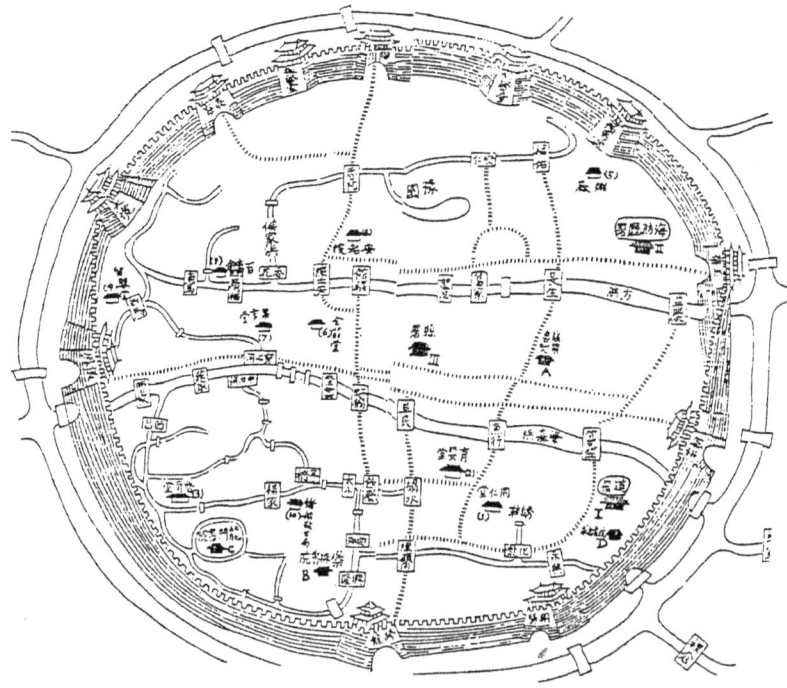

Figure 10.2 The Walled City of Shanghai, circa 1872
Source: Leung Yuen Sang, *The Shanghai Taotai: Linkage Man in a Changing Society, 1843-90*. Singapore: University of Singapore Press, 1990, p. 140.

trade center made it the choice of the Yuan government as the seat of a district *yamen* (衙門) (xian, 縣) in 1292. A Yuan map shows a sprawling town, without walls, as Linda Cooke Johnson, a specialist of early Shanghai history, notes, "but having important county offices, a Yuan naval garrison and the headquarters for the grain tribute."[8] The city walls were not built until the Jiajing (嘉靖) period of the Ming dynasty. During the mid-15th century, the Lower Yangzi was repeatedly invaded by Japanese pirates and the threat led to a communal decision to build a wall for better defense of the city.

The city wall had a circumference of nine *li* with a height of two *zhang* and four Chinese feet. There were seven gates and three of which were connected to the waters of River Huangpu (黃浦) running by the city. In 1598, another five feet of bricks were added to the height of the old wall for better defense purpose, and one more gate was constructed for water traffic.[9]

Within the walled "Chinese City," there were all the government offices or *yamen*, from the *Taotai*'s (dao-shu, 道署) to that of the magistrate's (xian-ya, 縣衙). The walls were interpolated with watch-towers and the gates were also regularly guarded by soldiers. The city wall of Shanghai, like any other walled-city in China, was supposedly built for protection to provide security for government offices and their occupants from local rebels or from foreign invaders. However, in the city of Shanghai, the walls performed a reverse function in the 1850s when a rebel group called Xiao Dao Hui (小刀會) (Small Sword Society) took over the walled-city and drove the Qing officials outside, taking refuge in the foreign settlements. With the assistance of foreigners, the Qing government eventually recaptured the walled-city and re-established peace and order in Shanghai. During the fighting several sections of the city-wall were destroyed by modern firepower and explosives, and due to these new gaps and holes, more gates were installed between the walled-city and the settlements. As a result, there were better transportation, communication, and more freedom in people's movements between the walled city and other two "cities" in Shanghai. Further economic development of the settlements attracted more Chinese immigrants into the International Settlements and the French Concession from the "Chinese City" as well as from other parts of China. Even though the Qing officials maintained that the "Chinese City" was the political administrative headquarters and power center in Shanghai, more and more Chinese established their business and social respectability outside the walled-city in the post-Taiping era. An increasing number of Chinese officials also preferred to work and live inside the settlements especially after retirement. For example, Shao Youlian (邵友濂) and Nie Jigui (聶楫槼), both served as Shanghai's highest-ranked official for the Qing government as Circuit Intendant of Su-Song-Tai (Su-Song-Tai Dao, 蘇松太道 or Shanghai Daotai, 上海道台) as it was generally known, stayed on and lived in Shanghai after their retirement from office. Many of the ex-officials in Shanghai turned business adventurers or industrialists in the twin settlements. These well-connected elite saw the diminishing role of the walls that separated their old power hub and their new business ventures and social activities. Many of them joined with the new local elite who were commercial leaders, calling for demolition of the walls, hence the so-called "Demolish City Movement" (*chai-cheng (qiang) yundong* 拆城 (牆) 運動) at the turn of the century.[10]

The walls were officially torn down in January 1912, after the collapse of the Qing dynasty. The *Taotai yamen* and the eastern and southern sections of the wall were the first to be demolished. The principal reason cited by the local advocates was: "For the convenience of transportation."[11] The western and northern sections were also torn down and the moats were filled and transformed into new roads or "roads for horse-carriages, *ma-lu*, 馬路") which when completed in 1914 became the first-generation of the circular road around the city with the names of Fahua Minguo Road (法華民國路) and Zhonghua Road (中華路).

10.4.2. *The walls and development of modern Shanghai*

The story of the walled-city of Shanghai and the decline of its significance in the modern period represents a clash of two cultures, East and West, and a transition from traditional political culture to new politics dominated by elite from new economic and cultural backgrounds. Within the walls of the old city, traditional power structure with the *yamen* as center remained strong until the Taiping era. After mid-19th century, however, new sources of wealth and power came not from within the walls, but from out — from the open seas, i.e., foreign trade and westernized ideas and programs. Even the Chinese government moved outside the walled-city when it decided to participate in modernization and open new economic and industrial ventures such as the China Merchant Steamship Company, the Telegraph Bureau, and the Kiangnan Arsenal. Even the Shanghai Taotai, the official ruler of Shanghai, had established a branch office, the *Yang-wu Ju* (洋務局) in the settlements for dealing with foreigners and related matters such as modernization projects.[12] These reform-minded officials and modernization advocates needed to function in an open space within which transportation–communication was more convenient, and supply-demand market forces were readily at work. The walls of the Chinese City thus became a controlled space not conducive for new political experiments, new educational programs, and new business ventures. The walled city represented not only the bastion of traditional bureaucratic power but also was a place where traditional education (the *shu-yuan*, 書院) and local gentry concentrated. To a certain extent, the wall-city with its Suzhou landscaped gardens like Yu Yuan (豫園) and Chenghuan Temple (城隍廟) was also an area of cultural preservation. The cityscape within the walled city and that of the foreign settlements were strikingly different. Traditional Chinese housing and architecture were the norm within the walled city. The means of transportation were also traditional: the single-wheeled carts, the ox-drawn carriages, the human-carried sedans, etc. The streets and alleys were narrow and muddy. Whereas the streets and roads in the settlements were relatively wider and well-paved, with high buildings along the two sides, usually in European style. Some streets near the Bund (wai-tan, 外灘) such as Nanking Road (Nan-jing lu, 南京路) were decorated with well-crafted stony structures: cathedrals, churches, club houses, and banks. There were horse-drawn carriages, ricksaws or *Jinricksha*, and in the early 20th century, trams and imported motor cars. The striking difference left deep impression on the minds of the visitors from the Chinese City and from other parts of China. Many felt that "they were in a foreign country."[13] During the late 19th century, more and more local elite in Shanghai, including those who lived within the walled city, were interested in the new culture, new fashions, and new lifestyles in the neighboring areas beyond the walls. The drive to be an integral part of the new economy and new culture of the larger city of Shanghai as defined by the characteristics of the settlements was the principal force to break through the walls and to tear them down. In fact, once the walls were demolished, the area within the "Chinese City" adjacent to the foreign settlements, for example, the East Gate (Dong Men, 東門) district, transformed itself rapidly into a busy area with paved roads with horse-drawn carriages, and lined with electric lightposts, westernized shops, and buildings.[14] The Shanghai people of the new century had chosen an open environment without walls for modernization and development. Thus the walls that were seen previously as inhibiting traffic and communication between the walled city and the foreign settlements were now considered obstacles of modernization. A few reformers of the 1890s suggested that the demolition of the walls would be beneficial to both societies, inside and outside. The suggestion was considered by authorities to be too radical in the late 19th century, but the "demolition" movement picked up momentum in the early 20th century and was finally translated into action in 1912. Without the walls, came better economic and cultural integration between the old city and the settlements. But to some Chinese who clung to tradition and the radicals who called for "total westernization," the boundary remained there even though the walls were invisible.

10.5. Hong Kong — The Walls Went Underground

For centuries Hong Kong had no palaces, no great architectural structures and no walls. It was a small fishing town before the Opium War and there was no official *yamen* in the area. After its cessation from China to the British in 1842, it became a British colony and port of free trade, and from this modest beginning, it developed rapidly over the course of 100 years from a fishing town into a metropolis and commercial city of international fame in the mid-20th century. On the surface, Hong Kong was, and is, a city without any walls. But there was a walled city in Hong Kong, in Kowloon rather, a small walled area known as the "Kowloon Walled City" (Jiu long zhaicheng, 九龍寨城) (see Figure 3). The walls were built a century ago and the walled area stood as a symbol of preservation and contradiction in the course of modernization and colonization. Much of the activities within the walled city had been conducted underground literally as well as figuratively before the walls were demolished. The area was finally cleared up and designed for resettlement by the government in the 1980s.

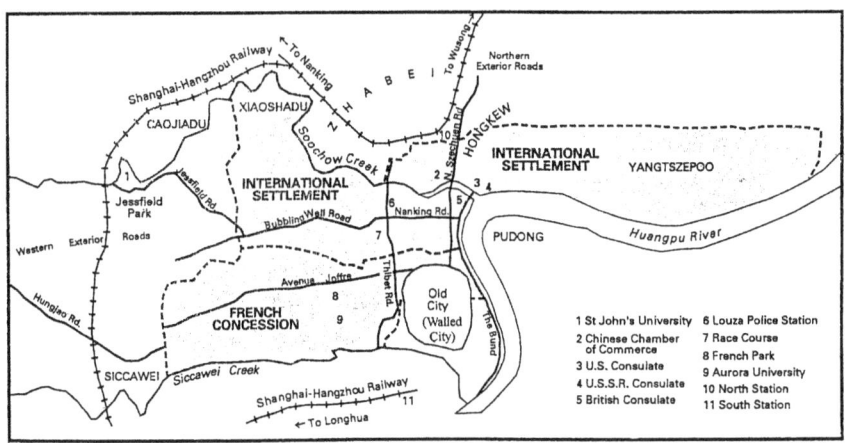

Figure 10.3 City Map of Shanghai, circa 1900
Source: Nicholas R. Clifford, Spoilt Children of Empire: Westerners in Shanghai and the Chinese Revolution of the 1920s. Middlebury College Press, 1991, pp. xviii.

10.5.1. *History of the walls*

When the British took over Hong Kong island in 1843, the Chinese government ordered the construction of a wall on the Kowloon peninsula for the military defense of the coast. The wall, completed in 1847, consisted of four gates and six watch-towers, was well installed with iron cannons along the parapet.[15] Before the construction of the wall, on the same site stood an old fort built in the 17th century for the defense of the coast from pirate raids. Since 1843, the fort and subsequently the walled city had been placed under the administrative responsibilities of the Assistant Magistrate of the Xinan (新安) County.[16] How large was the walled city? According to the report of a Hong Kong historian, "it formed a rough parallelogram measuring 700 feet by 400 feet, enclosing an area of 6.5 acres. It (the wall) was built of granite ashlar facing, 15 feet in width at the top, and averaged 13 feet in height. There were six watch towers and four gateways, with doors of wood lined with iron sheeting."[17] After the Beijing Convention, the British acquired more territories from China, but the Chinese government kept the Kowloon Walled City (jiu long zhaicheng, 九龍寨城), which was barricaded by walls and hence the name, under Chinese control and military garrison. At a later date, the wall was extended up the hill, rising to about 150 feet above the plain where the walled city was located.[18] A controversy developed in 1898 when the British further acquired the New Territories north of Kowloon from China in a lease of 99 years. The original agreement stated that "It is …. agreed that within the city of Kowloon the Chinese officials now stationed there shall continue to exercise jurisdiction except so far as may be inconsistent with the military requirements for the defense of Hong Kong."[19] The cause was vague and soon it led to argument between the British and the Chinese officials concerning the power of jurisdiction within those walls. The British in Hong Kong, in December 1899, stated in an Order in Council, that "the exercise of jurisdiction by the Chinese officials in the City of Kowloon having been found to be inconsistent with the military requirements for the defense of Hong Kong, it is expedient that … the Chinese officials within the City of Kowloon should cease to exercise jurisdiction therein, and that the said City of Kowloon should become part and parcel of her Majesty's Colony of Hong Kong."[20]

However, the Chinese government never recognized this unilateral act and continued to claim sovereignty over the walled city area. The walls had remained there for the decades and the British never followed up with their claim of jurisdiction in the next half century or so. Thus the walled city area had become a land of lawlessness and a city of darkness run by the Triads. Without maintenance, the walls became dilapidated and sections were demolished in the early 20th century. But they were still clearly visible as shown in the old photos of the 1920s and 1930s. It was the Japanese air raids and the bombardment that finally brought down most, if not all, of the old city walls. And after the war, the area became a city of squatters and refugees who flooded Hong Kong from the Chinese mainland trying to escape the civil war. The walls were gone, but the area remained a controversial territory where British colonial rule found it difficult, if not impossible, to establish its authority. The police and ordinary citizens of Hong Kong were reluctant to go into the area. The thugs and gangs ruled the city and in order to avoid outright embarrassment to the police they operated their criminal activities literally in an underground city of alleys and tunnels infested with insects, rats, and diseases.

10.5.2. *The walls and development of colonial Hong Kong*

The impact of the Kowloon walled city in the development of city culture of Hong Kong, by any standard, has been insignificant. The original purpose for constructing those walls in the mid-1840s was for coastal defense of the peninsula and surveillance of the British on the Hong Kong Island. The expansion of British colonial in the second half of the 20th century into the Kowloon peninsula and the New Territories through the 1860 Treaty and 1898 Lease, respectively, had rendered the original purpose of the wall impracticable and useless. The walls, in the post-1860 period and especially in the 20th century, had more symbolic meanings than practical functions in the British colony of Hong Kong. In the first place, the walled area had no official *yamen* and therefore was not directly under Qing governmental control. Second, the enclosed area was small and isolated. There were only a few hundred residents within the walled city and many of them had to venture out into the neighborhood areas of Kowloon or the New Territories which were under British rule. But the fact that the Chinese government never recognized the British claim of jurisdiction over the area meant that this walled area was officially under Chinese imperial sovereignty as a lot of patriotic Chinese would like to argue. So, the walled-city has long been considered an islet of China in a British colonial environment. Since the Hong Kong government was reluctant to occupy the area, and the Qing government and also the subsequent governments in China never sent in troops or dispatched officials into the area to reclaim its sovereignty, the walled city had been left pretty much on its own, leaving the power of control in the hands of drug lords and Triad gangs. After the walls were destroyed, the area remained a lawless slum-city crowded with poor squatters, refugees from the mainland, drug addicts and prostitutes, and thugs and gangsters. Ordinary citizens of Hong Kong for a long time had kept themselves away from this area. A visitor to the old walled city before its demolition in the 1960s commented, "(its) a dismal and forbidding place which lies just west of Kai Tak Airport in Kowloon. For generations it had been the hideout of robbers and murderers. ... (it) was not part of the crown colony, but an eight-acre patch of stateless ground. ... Britain and China wrangled inconclusively over it while the dingy little enclave-within-an-enclave went its own way, harbouring killers and thugs who fled into its narrow alleys to escape the police of both countries. Until 1960 it was worth your life to venture into those alleys."

In other words, the Kowloon walled-city of Hong Kong neither protected the Chinese elite nor the common people. It was not a place for princes, priests, and the police, or a place regulated by laws and rituals. In post-war Hong Kong, it had become a symbol of the contrary — lawlessness, protection for criminals and thugs, and cancerous to community development. The walled city's negative image and all the symbolic meanings associated with it had lasted for many years in the mind of the Hong Kong public until the 1970s and 1980s when the Hong Kong government made decisive steps to clear up the city and find resettlement for its residents. After that the walls were gone, but one may assume in many parts of modern Hong Kong the old city walls are still there, only these walls which create boundaries and signify power and hierarchy have become invisible in the society.

10.6. The Waters and Cultural Space

The "feng-shui" (wind and water) elements were extremely important in the building of Beijing. Its palaces, city-walls, towers, and streets were all aligned with geomancy. But the water element in "feng-shui" did not refer to the water levels of the bay or the location of the rivers and harbors in the Beijing context. In essence, Beijing was and still is, a continental city and "imperial" capital.[21] Unlike Shanghai and Hong Kong, it is not a port-city or built for commercial convenience. In that sense, the waterfronts and waterways played relatively insignificant role in the development of the city, especially in the area of business and commerce. The waters of Beijing in the history of the construction of the city, always presented as ingredients of a human-built environment in the forms of moats, canals, ponds, and lakes, serving to protect the city and to decorate the palaces and other architectural structures within the city rather than to provide transport or to facilitate commerce (Figure 4). In the case of

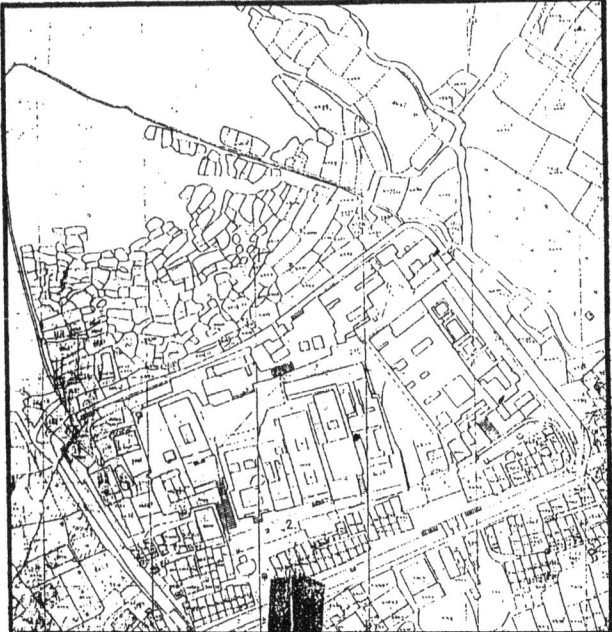

Figure 10.4 The Kowloon Walled City, 1900
Source: Lui, Adam Yuen-chung, *Forts and Pirates — A History of Hong Kong*. Hong Kong History Society, 1990, p. 101.

Shanghai and Hong Kong, however, the rivers, harbors, and bays have been important elements affecting the development of economic and community life. In the period before the opening of Shanghai to foreign trade, the riverways and the canals provided vitality and business to the local people — fishermen, boatmen, merchants, and peddlers on the two sides of the canal and the rivers, and canal irrigation was extremely important to cotton cultivation, the principal agric-economy of the entire Jiangnan or Lower Yangzi area. In Shanghai, the Suzhou River, the Wusong River, and the Huangpu River were main waterways upon which regional transport and daily local commute were depended. Because of the natural environment of well-connected waterways, Shanghai had become a regional trading center in the Lower Yangzi delta as early as the Song and Yuan dynasties. The Grand Canal, a human-built waterway, was also important to Shanghai's development as a center for collecting tribute grains and transportation of salt and other commodities to the north. Because of the regular nature of the tributary operations, the Canal had helped the economic growth and social development of the cities along the Canal between Shanghai and the imperial capital of Beijing, notably Tianjin, Jinan, and Yangzhou. A tribute grain mission usually comprised dozens of boats and hundreds of soldiers and labourers, and in certain sections of the Canal, hundreds and thousands of boat pullers. There were other boats and commodities allowed to travel by the Canal on which much of the business of the Canal cities depended. Since the transportation of tribute grain and salt was an important political assignment involving frequent correspondences and communications back and forth between the central government and provincial officials, the local officials and the gentry-elites in the region therefore looked upon the Grand Canal and its functions more in political than economic terms. But beginning from the mid-19th century, the transportation of tribute grains had found another route — through sea transportation (haiyun), first by Chinese junks and later by steamships, thus leading to the economic decline of the inland Canal cities with the exception of Tianjin which had access to the sea via the river leading to Taku Bay and the Bohai Gulf. At any rate, in Shanghai the waterways — rivers and canals — represented an integration of the natural and the human-built environments. Together they shaped the economic and political culture of the city for a long time. But in Hong Kong there was absence of a complicated network of riverways and canals, and what was prominent were the deep water harbors and bays and the open sea, an important factor in commercial development in the steamship age. Let us first turn to Shanghai's waters.

10.6.1. *Shanghai — waterways and waterfronts*

Shanghai's economic progress since the Song-Yuan period, as aptly pointed out by Mark Elvin, had been closely connected with the intricate network of waterways that covered the city and its vicinity.[22] The waterways supplied irrigation water for a high-yield agriculture (cotton and silk) and served as the means of communication for a flourishing water-borne commerce (see Figure 5). He said, "Carts and even wheelbarrows hardly existed, and for any journey beyond an easy walk the universal form of transport was the boat."[23] Shanghai merchants who "went to other places in search of a sale" were called "water-borne traders" (shuike).[24]

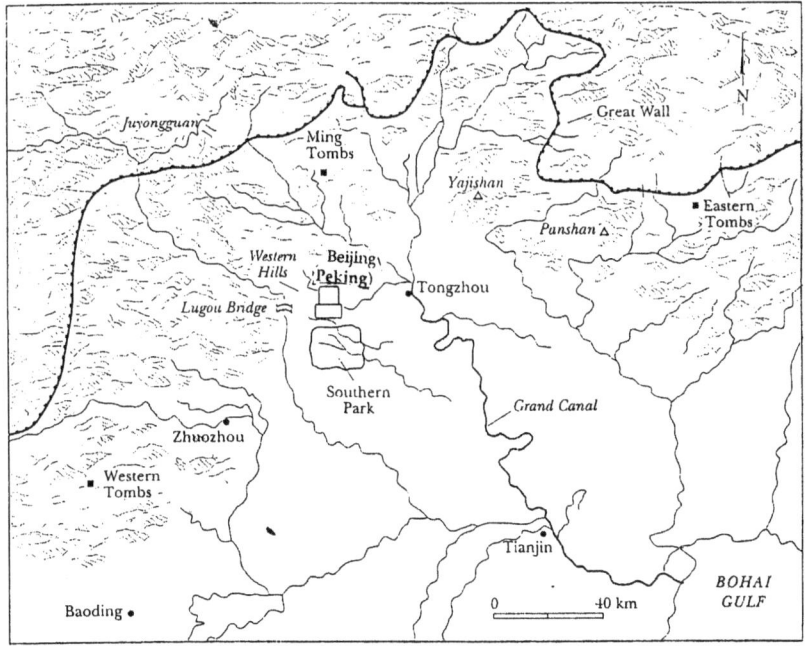

Figure 10.5   The Waterways of Beijing
Source: Susan Naquin, *Peking: Temples and City Life, 1400–1900*. Berkeley: University of California Press, 2000, p. 12.

The Shanghai Rivers not only provided transport and business for the local residents, they also connected the city with other market-towns and cities in the larger Jiangnan area — cities in the south like Jiaxing, Songjiang, and Huzhou and Hangzhou in Zhejiang province; northern cities such as Nanjing, Changshu, Taicang, and Jiading; and cities in the west of Shanghai like Qingpu, Wujiang, Suzhou, and Wuxi. The mulberry and cotton farmers depended on irrigation water from the canals and rivers, the silk weaving industry and other local handicraft industries depended on the water transport; and other locals made their living on fishing, peddling on boats, and business related to leisure rides. At any rate, the waterways were a significant part of the local economy and city life in Shanghai (Figure 6).

The most important change in the 19th century Shanghai, however, took place on the waterfront, and not the river network. The rapid development along one section of the Huangpu River near the Wusong River that leads to the coast and open sea, the Bund (*wai-tan*

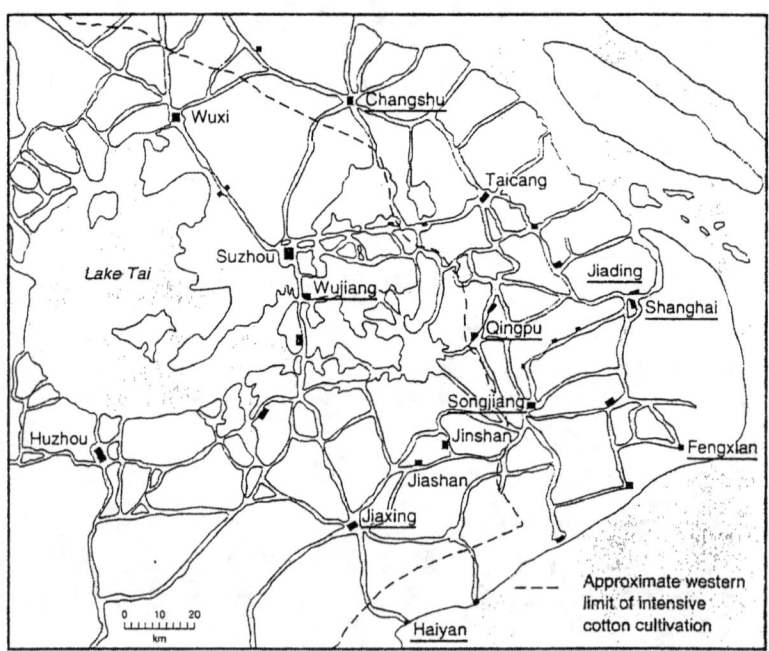

Figure 10.6 The Waterways around Shanghai, circa 1600
Source: Mark Elvin, *Another History: Essays on China from a European Perspective*. Broadway, Australia: Wild Peony, 1996, p. 108.

in Chinese) as this waterfront was called by Westerners is the most remarkable story of modern Shanghai. This section of the Huangpu waterfront was transformed by the arrival of the new ships from the West, the steamships. Long before the advent of the steamship age, Chinese junks had been prying through the Wusong and Huangpu in different sizes and shapes, linking the city to inner Chinese cities along the Yangzi and to other coastal cities of China. In other words, the sea route was not new. But the oceanic ships were unlike the traditional Chinese junks. Many of them were huge and heavy (more than 1000 to 2000 tons), they were driven by steam engines, and they were fast and sturdy. But most importantly, they came from distant countries such as Britain and the United States and carried new cargoes and commodities such as machinery, textile, glass, and other industrial goods. The "Bund" and its adjacent "foreign settlement" soon became a new Western city standing along the old Chinese walled-city on the south. Along the

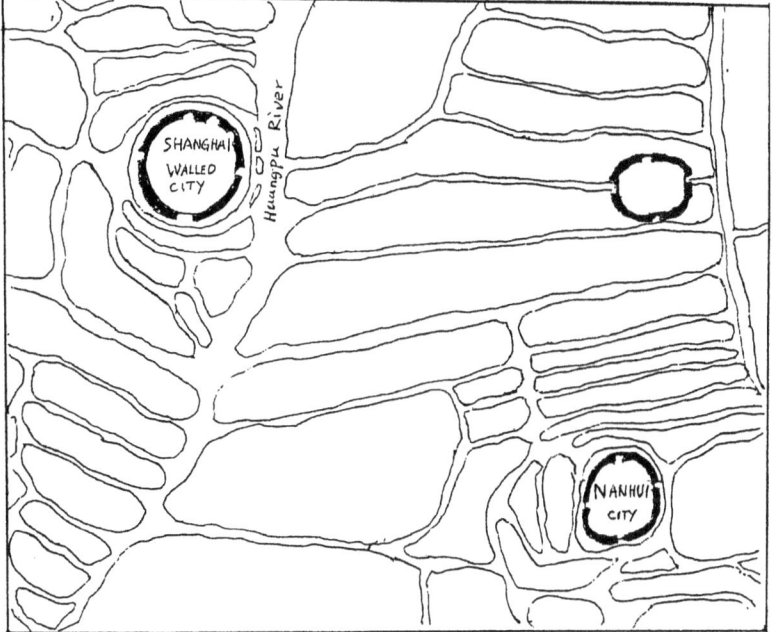

Figure 10.7 Shanghai Waterways, circa 1600
Source: Mark Elvin, *Another History: Essays on China from a European Perspective*. Broadway, Australia: Wild Peony, 1996, p. 103

waterfront, Western banks, go-downs, cathedrals, and other buildings were constructed, with wharves, piers, and "jetties" stretching out into the Huangpu River from the bank of the river. The new settlement and its new constructions signaled a new age of sea transport and an increased commercial relations with the Western world. The new business brought on by the steamship age and the rapid growth of import–export trade are familiar stories well documented in Kwang-ching Liu's *Anglo-American Steamship Rivalry in China. 1862–1874*, Linda Cooke Johnson's *Shanghai From Market Town to Treaty Port, 1074–1858*, and other books on Shanghai. It is suffice to say, the waterfront of Shanghai, the Bund, was a symbol of this new commercial development and increased maritime trade.

The activities on the Bund, however, were not confined to commerce and business. The waters, to the amazement of many Chinese, meant much more than navigation and transport. The Huangpu River represented a changing culture. Water sports of all kinds such as rowing, yachting, swimming, and skiing became part of social life in this section of Shanghai, although most participants were foreigners before the turn of the century. For example, the Shanghai Rowing Club was established in 1864 by foreigners living in the International Settlement. The Club had its own club house, harbor and boat shelter, occupying over 1000 square meters of land near the mouth of the Suchou River where it joined the Huangpu River. The Club had its swimming pool, game room, and bar, a symbol of Western culture in the eyes of the local Chinese.[25] The first rowing contest was held in 1863, and the annual contest had become a regular event celebrated by both Westerners and Chinese alike.[26] In 1865, a rowing contest was held near the Suzhou Creek with teams from the British 67th Regiment, and Hong Kong merchant houses such as Tung-foo and E-ho. Eventually the Tung-foo team became the winner of the contest.[27] In the rowing contest held next year, it was the American team who won the "Holland Cup," but the British won it back in the following year (Da Guan). It was reported that the 1906 event had attracted more than tens of thousands of spectators and alarmed the Municipal Council because of the over-crowdedness and traffic congestion it caused.

10.6.2. *Hong Kong — centrality of the victoria harbour*

Shanghai in the 19th century was going through a transitional process from a river port to an international seaport. In the process the waterways — the Huangpu River, the Suzhou River, the Songjiang River, and other rivers and canals that made up the local waterway network still retained much of their traditional outlook and economic functions. The rapid transformation occurred only in certain sections of the Huangpu, notably the Bund, which showed clearly the impact of foreign trade and maritime culture. But Shanghai was still primarily a riverport just like Canton although in the late 19th century and the early years of the 20th century, the seaport characteristics had gradually become more prominent in Shanghai. On the other hand, Canton never became an international city in the modern century. Once the only port in China designated for foreign trade, the city never welcomed foreigners and Western culture with the openness of Shanghai. With the exception of the Hong merchants and the compradors who made great profits out of external trade, most officials and commoners in Canton were not particularly enthusiastic about foreign intruders and their culture. In fact, most people were hostile toward Westerners, and this attitude was reflected in a series of anti-foreign riots such as the San-yuan-li incident and the city-entry dispute.[28] British Hong Kong, as a new city by the sea after the Opium War, did not have the traditional baggage of riverine culture as did Shanghai and Canton. The local rivers had almost no bearing on the economic and cultural development of the city. From the beginning of its cession to the British in 1842, the development of the island city had been based primarily on maritime trade. The most significant factor affecting trade development, in the age of the steamship, was a deep-water harbor and good port facilities. Hong Kong's Victoria Harbour, in this regard, was ideal for anchorage of heavy-tonnaged ships. Moreover, the British colonial government with its free trade policy also contributed to the rapid growth of the city of Victoria (now the area of Central and Sheung Wan). Based on their experience in India and British Southeast Asia, especially in Penang and Singapore, the British knew very well the importance of foreign trade and the function of the port. Along the bund in the City of Victoria, office buildings of various agency houses and banks, warehouses, and go-downs were constructed, and on the waters of the Victoria Harbour were ships and boats of various types, steamships, lighters, cargo boats, Chinese junks, etc., all for trading purposes. Unlike the ports of Canton and Shanghai where interaction of the sea and the river was regularly present, mounting to what we could describe as the meeting of two economies/cultures (riverine and oceanic) or the "fusion of two horizons" to borrow Gadamar's phrase, Hong Kong's city development in the 19th century clearly shows a preponderance of maritime commercial culture, the characteristics of an entrepot port. In other words, it is no exaggeration to say that the dominant "waters" in Hong Kong was the sea or the ocean.

In the early history of Hong Kong, the open sea or ocean had been commonly equated with pirate activities such as Zhang Baozai's. Some places in Hong Kong like Stanley were associated with fisheries and not foreign trade. The Victoria Harbour, however, had projected a new and different image of a busy commercial mart frequented by steamers from all nations, the British P & O liners, the Russells & Co. ships from New York, the iron-clad ships of Butterfield & Swire, and later the China Merchant Steam Navigation Co., ships (zhaoshang ju). In the early 20th century, Hong Kong had become one of the busiest international trading ports. In 1907, the vessels entered and cleared in Hong Kong amounted to 507,634 with a total tonnage of 36,028,310. These ships for foreign trade were listed as follows[29]:

	Number of vessels	Tonnage
British ocean-going ships	3,756	7,216,169
Foreign ocean-going ships	4,621	7,720,875
British river steamers	6,828	4,630,364
Foreign river steamers	1,310	743,992
Steamship under 60 tons	1,581	70,021
Junks	29,564	2,651,470
Total foreign trade	47,660	23,032,891

According to Tsai's calculation, "during the year 1907 everyday an average of 1,390 large and small vessels of 98,707 tons entered and cleared the Hong Kong port, discounting large number of lighters, cargo boats, passenger boats, water boats, and fishing crafts of all kinds. This record exceeded that of any port in the world at the time."[30]

In addition to international trade, the steamship also represented technological change and modernization which in the Chinese eye was also associated with Western culture. The steamship was produced and maintained by a shipyard which in the West was a symbol of advanced technology and modern enterprise, like the dockyards of Liverpool in mid-19th century Britain. In post-Taiping China during the period of self-strengthening from the 1860s to the 1890s, the Jiangnan Shipyard (jiangnan zaoquan ju) in Shanghai and the Mamei Dockyard in Fuzhou were also looked upon as symbols of modernity and advanced technology. The steamship and modern dockyard were twins in modern port-cities such as Hong Kong. Then around the docks were other related industries like machine shops, appliances and tools stores, engine repairing shops, and eateries and lodging places for the large number of coolies involved in loading/unloading and carrying of cargoes to or from the steamers. A two-tier seaside community consisting of house merchants and Chinese compradors on the top and a class of shipping-related laborers and coolies at the bottom emerged with the development and expansion of the wharves, the offices and warehouses on the bund and the improvement of port facilities at the harbor. But everything was directly or indirectly related to shipping and the sea. Thus we may say the Victoria Harbour and its waters held a central role in the development of the city of Hong Kong.

Notes

1. Osvald Siren (1924). *The Walls and Gates of Peking*. London: John Lane Ltd, translated into Chinese by Xu Yongquan (許永全) (1985). Beijing: Yanshan chubanshe, p. 13.
2. *Ibid.*, pp. 13–14.
3. *Ibid.*, p. 16.
4. Jeffrey F. Meyer (1976). *Peking as a Sacred City*. Taipei: Chinese Association for Folklore, pp. 28–29.
5. Chen Xuelin (Chan Hok Lam) (陳學霖) (1996). *Liu Bowen yu Nazha cheng* 劉伯溫與哪吒城. Taipei: Dong Da Tushu Gongsi p. 38.
6. For a brief account of the demolition of the old city-wall in Beijing, see Hou Renzhi's 1988 essay in *Liu Bingsen lishu Ming Beijing cheng chengqiang yiji weixiu ji* (劉炳森隸書明北京城城牆遺蹟維修記). Beijing: Zijincheng chubenshe, 1996, appendix.

7. Chen Xuelin (陳學霖). *Liu Bowen yu Nazha chen*, p. 48.
8. Linda Cooke Johnson (1993). *Cities of Jiangnan in Late Imperial China*. Albany: State University of New York Press, p. 155.
9. Zheng Zu'an (鄭祖安) (1999). *Bainian Shanghai cheng* (百年上海城). Shanghai: Xuelin chubanshe, p. 5.
10. *Ibid.*, pp. 6–8.
11. *Ibid.*, p. 7.
12. See Yao Gonghe (姚公鶴) (1967). *Hushang xianhua* (滬上閒話). Taipei. Rpt.
13. Chen Qi Yuan (陳其元) (1873). *Yongxianzhai biji* (庸閒齋筆記). Shanghai: Shenbaoguan (申報館), preface, juan 卷 7, 4b.
14. Tang Zhenchang (唐振常) (ed.) (1999), *Shanghai: Road to Prosperity*. Shanghai, 1842–1949 Hong Kong: Commercial Press.
15. Jackie Pullinger (1989). *Crack in the Wall: The Life and Death of Kowloon Walled City*. London: Hodder & Stoughton, pp. 18–19.
16. See Elizabeth Sinn (1987). "Kowloon walled city: Its origin and early history". In *Journal of the Hong Kong British Royal Society*, 27, pp. 30–31.
17. *Ibid.*, p. 31.
18. For a description of the wall up the hill, see Walter Schofield's note "Defence Wall at Pass Between Kowloon City and Kowloon Tsai," in *Journal of the Hong Kong British Royal Society*, 9 (1969), 155–156. For a recent study of the history of the walled-city, see Gao Tianqiang (2001). "Ershi shiji qian jiulongcheng diqu shilue" (A brief history of the Kowloon Walled-city before the twentieth century). In *Jiulongcheng* (Kowloon City), Zhao Yule and Zhong Baoxian (eds.), 45–94. Hong Kong: Sanlian shudian.
19. Jackie Pullinger. *Crack in the Wall*, p. 13.
20. *Ibid.*
21. Susan Naquin's (2000) new book *Peking: Temples and City Life, 1400–1900* from the UC Press, stresses this point, p. 12.
22. Mark Elvin (1997). *Another History: Essays on China from a European Perspective*. Washington, D.C.: Empress Publishing, p. 101.
23. *Ibid.*, 102.
24. *Ibid.*, 109–110.
25. Xiong Yuezhi (熊月之) *et al.* (eds.) (1997) *Lao Shanghai Mingren Mingshi Mingwu Daguan* (老上海名人名事名物大观). Shanghai: Shanghai Renmin chubanshe, p. 376
26. *Ibid.*, p. 200.
27. *The Chinese and Japanese Repository*, XII, May, 91 (1865).
28. Frederic Wakeman (1997). *Strangers at the Gate: Social Disorder in South China, 1839–1861*. California: University of California Press.
29. Tsai Jung-fang (1995). *Hong Kong in Chinese History: Community and Social Unrest in the British Colony, 1842–1913*. New York: Columbia University Press, p. 34.
30. *Ibid.*, p. 35.

INDEX

Ah Cheng 93
Alexis de Tocqueville 4
Alfred Rosenberg 147
Angela Liang 179, 217
Ann Behnke Kinney 177, 216–218
Ann Waltner 179, 180
Anwar Ibrahim 16, 21
Armando Gnisci 136
Asian values 5, 6, 17, 19, 129

Beijing 2, 6, 22, 37, 43–46, 48, 68, 78–80, 88, 100, 102, 103, 105, 109, 221–227, 228, 234, 237–239, 245
Bertrand Russell 128
bilingual 97, 104
Boutros-Ghali 2, 3, 20
Britain 82, 84, 236, 241, 245
Buddhism 8, 9, 32, 73, 88, 128, 132, 133, 198
Buddhist 3, 9, 69, 73, 78, 111, 112, 129, 132, 220
Butterfly School 92

Cai Yuanpei 33, 42
Canton 99, 243, 244
Cantonese 89–91, 98–101
Carl Hempel 163
Catherine Lim 96, 97, 109
Charles Dickens 91

Ch'êng-Chu school 181, 183
Chenghuan Temple 232
Chen Yinke 132
Chen Zuyi 118, 125
Chinese-American 17, 96
Chinese-ness 33, 96, 180
Chinese civilization 25, 31, 41, 142
Chinese Communist Party 34, 36
Chinese culture 83, 90, 94, 97, 99, 107, 108, 128, 129, 141, 142
Christianity 8, 32, 69, 80, 81
Christians 68, 79, 80
Communist 4, 31, 45
Confucian conceptions 6
Confucian Humanism 1
Confucianism 6, 8, 21, 23–42, 44, 46, 49, 57, 59, 61–63
Confucian principle 148
Confucian thoughts 142
Confucian tradition 1, 2, 18, 21, 28
Confucius 15, 20, 22, 25–27, 30–34, 37, 50–57, 59, 62, 68, 71, 72, 80, 86, 87, 142, 148
Confucius Foundation 6, 22
cultural assimilation 134
cultural hegemony 136, 137
cultural isolationism 134–136, 138
cultural plurality 127, 129
cultural relativism 134, 135

Cultural Revolution   26, 27, 36, 47, 48, 50, 85

Darwinian evolution   162
Darwinian theory   161
David Hall   142
Deng Xiaoping   27, 36, 43
Donald O. Hebb   162, 170
Dong Zhongshu   59

Earl Miner   138
East Asian   6, 18–21, 23, 42, 51, 58, 136
Edward Shils   15
Eleanor Roosevelt   1
Emperor Chengzu   115
Emperor Jianwen   116
Emperor Xuan Zong   119
Emperor Yongle   116, 119, 225
England   69, 82, 152, 173, 174, 211–215, 219, 220
Enlightenment   2, 6–12, 18, 19, 28, 41, 44, 46, 177, 201
Erwin Schrodinger   153
European culture   133, 142
Ewert Cousins   11, 21

Fei Xin   121
Felix Guattari   97, 109
feng shui (geomancy)   224, 237
Forbidden City   223–225, 227
Four Mini-Dragons   9, 21
Francois Jullien   130, 142
Franz Kafka   97
French Concession   228, 230
Fukienese   89, 90, 98

Genghis Khan   69, 224
Genome Project   148, 162, 168

George Sarton   59
Germany   25, 84, 85, 88
Gilles Deleuze   89, 97, 109
Globalization   11, 129–133
Gong Zhen   119, 122
Grand Canal   238
Great Leap Forward   36
Great Tradition   32
Great Wall   223
Guangdong   71, 77, 89, 91, 98, 112–115
Guomindang   31, 33, 100, 107

Han Shaogong   93, 94, 109
Hong Kong   2, 9, 19, 21, 30, 37, 38, 43–48, 63, 65, 82, 83, 88, 97–102, 105, 123, 124, 152, 153, 170, 221, 222, 233–238, 242–246
Hou Hsiao-hsien   100
Hou Renzhi   225
Houston Stewart Chamberlain   147
Huangpu River   228, 238, 240, 242, 243
Hua Yan   129, 133
Hu Hanmin   33, 45
human rights   1–7, 12, 16–20
Hu Shi   91, 92, 94, 95, 109, 141

India   25, 58, 70, 71, 77, 82, 89, 101, 107, 108, 111, 112, 120, 123, 128, 132, 243
individualism   2, 6, 7, 19
Industrial Revolution   3
International Settlements   228, 230
Islam   8, 9, 16, 21, 32, 68–70

Jacobinism   138
James Lee   180

James Legge   50, 52, 54, 63, 81, 82, 85, 86, 123
Japan   9, 21, 24, 27, 28, 30, 33, 35, 37, 44, 60, 64, 77, 84, 112–116, 129, 219
Jiangnan   238, 240, 246
Jinan   88, 238
Joanna Handlin   180
John Sommervill   178, 216, 219
Jon Saari   177
Joseph Needham   52, 55, 56, 64, 73
Judaism   8
Jurchen Jin   223

Kang Youwei   30–32
Kawabata Yasunari   140, 143
Khitan Liao   223
Kiangnan Arsenal   231
Kim Yung-Sik   58, 60, 64, 65
Kong Qiu   49
Kowloon   233–236, 246
Kublai Khan   68, 69, 224, 225
Kwang-ching Liu   217, 242

Lao She   89–91, 109
Liang Qichao   30, 31, 46, 123
Liang Sicheng   225
Liang Souming   26, 32, 38, 45
Linda Cooke Johnson   229, 246
Lin Yutang   107
Li Po   139–141
Literary Revolution   91, 109
Liu Bingzhong   224
Liu Ts'ui-jung   180
Li Zhizao   75–77, 79, 87, 88
London Missionary Society   81
Lu Gwei-Djen   55
Luo Guanzhong   61
Luo Maodeng   117, 121

Lu Xun   53, 64, 91, 93, 141

Macau   71, 79, 82
Ma Huan   121, 125, 126
Malacca   71, 82, 84, 117–121, 124, 125
Malaysia   9, 10, 16, 18, 95, 97, 99, 109, 129
Mandarin   71, 90–93, 95, 96, 98–101, 106
Mandate of Heaven   13, 34
Mao Dun   141
Mao Zedong   27, 36, 45, 102
Marco Polo   68–70, 76, 81, 87
Mark Elvin   239–241, 246
Marxism   46, 161
Matteo Ricci   70–73, 77, 80–82, 84, 86, 87
May Fourth Movement   26, 31, 33, 34, 43, 46, 50, 53, 57
Mencius   12, 27, 56–58, 63, 64, 83
Michael Clyne   151
Michael Mitteraner   173
Michael Scriven   161, 170
Middle Kingdom   228
Mou Zongsan   26, 38
Myoe Shonin   139, 140

Nakayama Shigeru   58
Nanjing   33–35, 71, 77, 79, 117, 119, 120, 225, 240
nationalism   16, 17, 23–33, 35–48, 92
Nationalist Party   31, 34
Neo-Confucian   20, 60, 61, 181, 182, 189, 202
Neo-Confucianism   20, 129, 133, 184
New Life Movement   33

New Literature   91, 92
New Territories   234–236
Nie Jigui   230

Opium War   81, 82, 84, 233, 243

Paul Dirac   153
Philip Greven Jr.   172
Phillip Ariés   209
Pit Corder   151, 169
Plato   50, 53, 58, 148

Qian Mu   26, 38
Quanzhou   70, 112, 113

Reinhard Sieder   173
Robert Bums   130
Roger Ames   142

Salman Rushdie   103, 106, 107, 110
Samuel Huntington   7
Shamanism   9
Shanghai   221
Shao Youlian   230
Shen Congwen   93
Shintoism   9
Shu Shi   130
Siam   113–115, 117–119, 124, 125
Singapore   2, 9, 17–19, 37, 47, 65, 67, 70, 89, 90, 95–101, 109, 229, 243
Society of Jesus   71, 77
Socrates   50, 53, 58
Soviet Union   4, 24, 25, 161
Sun Simiao   62
Sun Yat-sen   27, 30, 31, 33, 34, 46
Suzhou   70, 83, 232, 240, 242

Taiwan   9, 10, 21, 33, 35, 37, 38, 44, 84, 93–95, 98–101, 104, 105, 215
Tang Junyi   26, 38, 41
Taoism   8, 9
Taotai   229–231
Theodore de Bary   6, 88
Tiananmen   26
Tianjin   238
Tiantai   129, 133
Triads   235
Tu Wei-Ming   20, 21, 26, 38, 47

United Nations   2, 20, 25
United States   3, 4, 18, 98, 168, 241

Vienna Declaration   4, 20

Walter Whitman   141
Wang Anyi   94
Wang Jinghong   116, 117, 119, 121
Wang Tao   83, 84
Wang Yangming   75, 131
Wang Zhenhe   93, 94
Warring States   58, 223
Western culture   71, 128, 142, 242, 243, 245
Wong Yoon Wah   90
Wu Hung   178, 216
Wu Pei-yi   178, 218
Wu Teh Yao   1, 2, 19, 20, 23, 87
Wu Zhihui   33, 48

Xiao Dao Hui   230
Xiong Shiyi   26
Xi Zezong   52, 56, 64
Xu Guangqi   75–77

Yangzhou   112, 238
Yan Hui   53

Yuan Shikai   31
Yu Hua   94, 109
Yu Ying-shih   26, 38, 46, 48
Yu Youren   33, 48
Yu Yuan   232

Zen   129, 133
Zhang Baozai   244
Zhang Binglin   31, 32, 45, 48
Zhao Kuangyin   112

Zheng He   116–122, 124–126
Zheng Wanlong   93
Zhu Di   115
Zhuge Liang   61
Zhu Xi   60, 61
Zhu Yuanzhang   112, 114, 115
Zhu Yunming   119, 120
Zi Gong   51, 55

ABOUT THE EDITOR

WONG Sin Kiong (黄贤强), Ph.D., is Associate Professor of Chinese Studies at National University of Singapore. He was Head of the Department of Chinese Studies and concurrently Chairman of the Wu Teh Yao Memorial Fund from 2007 to 2011. His publications include *China's Anti-American Boycott Movement in 1905: A Study in Urban Protest* (2002), *Singapore Chinese Society in Transition: Business, Politics, & Socio-Economic Change: 1945–1965* (co-authored, 2004), *Trans-regional and Cross-disciplinary History: New Perspectives on Modern China and Nanyang Chinese Studies* (in Chinese, 2008), and *Ethnicity, History and Culture: Trans-regional and Cross-disciplinary Studies on Southeast Asia and East Asia — In Honor of Wang Gungwu on His 81st Birthday*. 2 vols (in Chinese, editor, 2011).